RESEARCH HIGHLIGHTS IN SOCIAL WORK 23

# Social Work and the European Community

## The Social Policy and Practice Contexts

*Edited by Malcolm Hill*

Jessica Kingsley Publishers
London

First published in the United Kingdom in 1991 by
Jessica Kingsley Publishers Ltd
118 Pentonville Road
London N1 9JN

Copyright © 1991, University of Aberdeen, Research Highlights Advisory Group, Department of Social Work

**British Library Cataloguing in Publication Data**
Social work and the European Community. - (Research
  highlights in social work v.23).
  1. European Community. Social services
  I. Hill, Malcolm II. Series
  361.94

ISBN 1-85302-091-5
ISSN 0955-7970

Printed in Great Britain by
Billing & Sons Ltd, Worcester

# Contents

# The Contributors

Malcolm Hill

Malcolm Hill has an MA in Geography from the University of Oxford. He worked as a social worker in inner London for eleven years. In 1979, he moved to Edinburgh where he obtained a PhD in Social Science based on research leading to the publication *Sharing Child Care in Early Parenthood* (RKP, 1987). Subsequently, he has been involved in several research projects concerning adoption and is currently Lecturer in Social Work at the University of Glasgow.

Richard Parry

Richard Parry is a Lecturer in Social Policy at the University of Edinburgh. He contributed the United Kingdom sections of *Public Employment in Western Nations* (Ed. Richard Rose, 1985) and *Growth to Limits* (Ed. Peter Flora, 1986-88). Recent publications include editing *Privatisation* in this Research Highlights series; and articles about the Welfare State, needs and services in *Politics in Western Europe Today* (eds. D.W. Urwin and W.E. Paterson) and *Needs and Welfare* (Eds. Alan Ware and Robert E. Goodin).

Walter Lorenz

Walter Lorenz was born in Stuttgart, and obtained his first degree at the University of Tübingen. He undertook professional training in social work at the LSE, after which he practised for several years in inner London. Since 1978, he has been Lecturer in Social Work at University College, Cork, in the Republic of Ireland. There he has initiated and developed a number of European exchange programmes. Amongst his research interests and publications in Germany, Ireland and the UK are issues arising from different European traditions of social work.

**Hans-Jochen Brauns**

Hans-Jochen Brauns studied law at the Freie Universität, Berlin and the Universität Hamburg. He obtained a doctorate in jurisprudence in 1969 from the Ruhr-Universität, Bochum. After a period of teaching public and constitutional law, he became Professor of Public Administration at the Fachhochschule für Sozialarbeit und Sozialpädagogik in 1974. Since 1986, he has been the Director of the Deutscher Paritätischer Wohlfahrtsverband, Berlin. The topics of his publications include constitutional law and political history, law and social work education, information technology and social work.

**David Kramer**

David Kramer studied history and political science at the University of Redlands, the Freie Universität Berlin and Tulane University, where he obtained a PhD in 1973. After thirteen years as Professor of Social Policy at the Fachhochschule für Sozialarbeit und Sozialpädagogik, he has since then represented the German Marshall Fund of the United States in Europe.

His publications have been about social work history, social policy, social work education, information technology and contemporary studies.

Charlie McConnell

Charlie McConnell is a Director with the UK based Community Development Foundation. He is also a member of the Committee of the European Social Action Network and currently a Consultant to the Council of Europe and Standing Conference of Local and Regional Authorities on Community Development. Publications include *Deprivation, Participation and Community Action* (Routledge, 1981) and *Community Work in the 80s* (NISW, 1984). He has edited special issues of the *Community Development Journal.*

Peter Stathopoulos

Peter Stathopoulos received his BA at Concordia University (Montreal) and an MSW in Community Organisation and Planning at McGill University. He completed doctoral studies in social policy at the Heller Graduate School for Advanced Studies in Social Welfare at Brandeis University (Massachusetts). He has worked as a community organiser and social planner in both rural and urban parts of Greece, Canada and the United States. He has collaborated in research projects at Columbia, Brandeis and Athens Universities. Currently he is Professor of Social Policy and Planning in the Department of Social Work at the Technological Educational Institute in Athens. Recently he has published an English-Greek and Greek-English *Dictionary of Social Science Terms and Abbreviations* (Kardamitsa, Athens, 1989) and a book on 'Community Work' (Athens, 1990).

Jacob Vedel-Petersen

Jacob Vedel-Petersen graduated in psychology at the University of Copenhagen in 1958 and has trained as a child and family psycho-therapist. He worked as a child psychologist, research associate and lecturer in child psychology, before becoming Director of the Danish National Institute of Social Research from 1979 to 1989. He has been responsible for research concerning family life, delinquency, housing and health. In collaboration with others, he has published a number of books in Danish.

Helen Armstrong

Helen Armstrong is Senior Development Officer in the Child Abuse Training Unit at the National Children's Bureau, London. Previously, she worked in industry, and in further education as trainer and consultant. Amongst her publications are *Community Care in Rural Areas* (with Catherine Thompson, NCVO, 1986); *A Positive Model* and *Working with Sexually Abused Boys* (both with Anne Hollows, NCB, 1989).

Anne Hollows

Anne Hollows is Senior Development Officer in the Child Abuse Training Unit at the National Children's Bureau, London.

She has worked in both England and Scotland in probation and social work, as practitioner, researcher and manager. She is involved in training about child protection under the Children Act, 1989. Her publications include *A Positive Model* and *Working with Sexually Abused Boys* (both with Helen Armstrong; NCB, 1989). She has also written about social work in prisons and the use of computers in relation to welfare benefits.

Hans-Joachim Trapp

Hans-Joachim Trapp worked for about fifteen years as Training Officer for the Paritätsiches Bildungswerk (which is part of the Deutscher Paritätischer Wohlfahrtsverband). He was responsible for training and advice in relation to prison social work, juvenile justice and youth work. He is now Head of Department in the Saarland Ministry of Social Affairs in Saarbrücken, Germany.

Christian von Wolffersdorff

Christian von Wolffersdorff is Head of Department for youth services research at the Deutsches Jugendinstitut (German Youth Institute) in Munich. He also teaches social work students about delinquency and institutional care. He has published a number of works concerning drug problems, juvenile prisons, institutional care and intermediate treatment. His latest book is about closed institutions in West Germany (*Geschlossene Unterbringung in Heimen*, DJI, Munich, 1990: Co-authored with Vera Sprau-Kuhlen, in collaboration with Joachim Kersten).

| | |
|---|---|
| Robert Leaper | Robert Leaper obtained an MA at Cambridge and a Diploma in Public and Social Administration at Oxford. In 1986 he was awarded the Doctorat (Honoris Causa) at the Université de Rennes. From 1970 to 1986, he was Professor of Social Administration at the University of Exeter. He has published widely, particularly on issues to do with comparative social policy and community care. He was joint editor (with A. Yoder) of *Community Care - Myths and Realities* (Martinus Nijhoff, 1985). Since 1973 he has edited the journal *Social Policy and Administration*. |
| Jennifer Speirs | Jennifer Speirs qualified as a medical social worker in Edinburgh and worked in a number of hospitals in London before returning to Scotland to work as a generic social worker in Lothian Social Work Department. She spent eleven years as an area team senior social worker with particular responsibility for services for the elderly. For three years she was Convenor of the Scottish Committee of BASW. She is currently Director of Family Care, a voluntary social work agency which holds the adoption contact register for Scotland. She has a particular interest in services for people with fertility problems and is secretary of BASW's Project Group on Assisted Reproduction. |
| Franz Hamburger | Franz Hamburger studied sociology, philosophy and educational sciences at the Universities of Heidelberg and Cologne. |

He was awarded an MA and D Phil at Heidelberg. Since 1978 he has been Professor of Social Pedagogy at the Pädgogisches Institut at the University of Mainz.

Astrid Sänger

Astrid Sänger studied educational sciences at the University of Mainz, where she obtained a Diploma in 1976. She is currently a Research Fellow at the Pädagogisches Institut in Mainz.

## Editor's Note

The chapters for the book were prepared shortly prior to German reunification. Therefore, several chapters refer to West Germany and were unable to take account of the implications of the reunion, except prospectively.

## Acknowledgements

I would like to thank the contributors for all their hard work and generous responses to my editorial requests and comments. The suggestions and support of Gerard Rochford, Joyce Lishman and other members of the Research Highlights Advisory Group have been much appreciated. I am very grateful to Anne Forbes for her promptness and patience in typing and revising draft chapters.

# Chapter 1

# Approaching with Caution:
# Social Work and the European Community
# from a British Perspective

## Malcolm Hill

### Introduction

During its long history as a trading nation, Britain has established world-wide political, economic and social relationships. In the 20th century, there have been perhaps three principal orientations - to the Commonwealth for historical-political reasons; to the United States for cultural and language reasons; and to Europe on account of physical proximity and extended historical involvement. Social work in the United Kingdom has mostly been associated with the United States and to a smaller extent the Commonwealth, with most of the theoretical and practice importations coming from the former. Europe has had comparatively limited direct influence, with perhaps Freud and the neo-Freudians, Marx and the post-Marxists being the main exceptions. These however were influences from outside social work practice and probably most people involved in the social services in the UK have been quite ignorant of how their equivalents on the continent went about their work.

Recently, changes have occurred which have brought social work more into the sphere of consideration of the EC and, conversely, have led social workers in the UK to take more cognisance of the EC. The roots of the EC lie in the European Coal and Steel Community established by the Treaty of Paris in 1951. The six founder members of the ECSC (Belgium, France, Germany, Italy, Luxembourg and the Netherlands) went on to sign the Treaty of Rome in 1957 which created the European Economic Community. This had wider aspirations but again was primarily an economic association:

**Table 1: Significant dates in the evolution of the European Communities**

1951    Treaty of Paris created the European Coal and Steel Community

1957    Treaties of Rome established the European Economic Community
        and the European Atomic Energy Community

1966    Common Agricultural Policy agreed

1974    Decision to set up the European Council

1975    European Regional Development Fund established

1979    1) European Monetary System created
        2) European Currency Unit set up
        3) First directly elected European Parliament

1986    Signing of the Single European Act

The EEC, ECSC and Euratom were merged in the 1960s.[1] By the time the United Kingdom joined in 1973 alongside Denmark and Ireland, both the size of the association was expanding and its sphere of interest was growing. The subsequent accession of Greece (1981), Spain and Portugal (1986) resulted in a Community of twelve member states with nine official languages:

**Table 2: Member states of the European Community (1990)**

| Country | Year of Entry |
| --- | --- |
| Belgium | 1959 |
| France | 1959 |
| Italy | 1959 |
| Luxembourg | 1959 |
| Netherlands | 1959 |
| West Germany (Federal Republic) | 1959 |
| Denmark | 1973 |
| Ireland | 1973 |
| United Kingdom | 1973 |
| Greece | 1981 |
| Portugal | 1986 |
| Spain | 1986 |

A few other countries have association agreements (eg Turkey, Malta, Cyprus) and Austria has applied for membership. Since 1989 the dramatic thawing of the frozen post-War geopolitical divides in Europe have opened up possibilities of marked geographical extension eastwards of the EC in future, presumably with some modification of its nature and purpose. The re-unification of Germany will provide a pointer to such developments and may act as a prototype for merging markedly different economic and welfare systems.

In the 1980s there was an accelerating trend in the enlarged Community towards greater political and social co-operation, symbolised by the omission of 'Economic' from its name to make it simply the European Community in general parlance. These developments were by no means straightforward or uncontested, but there has been a gradual extension of European legislation and regulation to cover more social issues. Moves to create a Single Market by 1992 were accompanied by greater attention to issues of particular interest to social workers, such as poverty, gender equality, migration and the recognition of professional qualifications.

Hence the time seemed right for a book in the *Research Highlights* series reviewing the position of social work in relation to the EC and its member countries. It is hoped that this volume will be of interest to social work practitioners, academics, policy makers, managers and others, throughout Europe and elsewhere. We have not included material which relates primarily to the UK in this volume, although several chapters (like this one) are written from a UK perspective and make comparisons and contrasts with the British situation. The aim has been to include contributors of several nationalities; chapters which include cross-national comparisons as well as some related to just one country; and contributions which are of a general nature followed by others which deal with specific themes or client groups.

There are inevitable problems in comparative enterprises such as this. Systematic cross-national studies in the welfare field have been rare. Many texts which include comparative material tend simply to juxtapose non-standard information from a selection of countries or use global statistics based on differing definitions. A coherent theoretical basis for comparison is often lacking, whilst it is often forgotten that differences within countries may be as significant as those between them.[2] In this book emphasis is placed on the interplay of social policy, socio-economic trends and social work. Where possible we have tried to adhere to the empirical emphasis of the overall series, but in some instances use has been made of close personal acquaintance with key developments and innovations.

This introductory chapter will outline:

1. The social policy contexts within the countries of the European Community

2. The structures of the EC and its influence on social issues and social work

3. Social work developments in the EC.

In passing, references will be made to a longer than usual bibliography, as it was thought useful to bring together a list of many of the key texts available in English.

## Welfare and Social Policy in the European Community

With their historical interconnectedness and shared cultural heritage, West European countries have many common characteristics and trends, although these are not, of course, confined to EC members. Demographic changes over the last 100 years have shown many similarities, Ireland being a notable exception with its long period of declining population and late marriage. More recently, patterns have been broadly comparable, though with differences in timing and degree.[3] These include the decrease in birth rates after the surge of the 1950s and 1960s, delayed marriage, increased divorce and cohabitation, an ageing population and expanded female employment.[4] All EC countries now have low fertility rates, often below replacement level, though that of Ireland remains considerably higher than the rest.[5] Whilst detailed attitudes vary and there remain considerable differences in political emphasis and religious influence, 'values are often similarly conceptualised across Europe'.[6]

All EC countries have developed some kind of welfare state which experienced substantial expansion in size and scope during the post-War decades (see Chapter 2). By and large, European countries have developed more generous and comprehensive public services and social security systems than has been the case in North America.[7] Within the EC the British Isles and the Mediterranean members have traditionally spent a lower percentage of GDP on social security than the others, as a result of historical tradition and relative prosperity. Many factors have been shown to influence the particular forms taken by welfare states, including the needs of capitalism; democratic ideals; religious beliefs and the relative importance of the Church; employer and trade union lobbying; and women's movements (Chapters 2, 3, 4).[8] There are two principal and differing traditions in social assistance,[9] although over the years each has acquired some features of the other to become more hybrid:

a) the Bismarkian approach popular in continental Europe focuses on generous employment-based rights and social insurance, but with weaker rights for those outside the labour market. Benefit entitlements are based on occupational groupings, whilst rates of payment are usually in proportion to earnings for periods of economic inactivity including retirement.[10]

b) the Beveridge or Anglo-Scandinavian model concentrates on universal benefits financed largely from taxation. This system relies more on flat-rate payments.[11]

Correspondingly social assistance is administered by Central Government in the UK and Ireland, but elsewhere it is the responsibility of local authorities (eg Belgium, France) or a range of autonomous funds (eg West Germany).[12] Hence in some countries, such as France, there is no integrated system of income maintenance to act as a safety net for those who are inadequately covered by social insurance or mutual aid arrangements.[13]

From the mid-1970s onwards economic concerns and ideological critiques have been associated with cutbacks and a 'crisis' in governmental commitment to the welfare state, although the evidence is that many particular services retain widespread popular support.[14] Greece, Spain and Portugal are partial exceptions to this pattern, since their recent returns to democracy were followed by a period when their less developed social service provision continued to expand longer (Chapter 5).[15] Long-standing free-market opposition to public welfare has been joined by a newer disenchantment with bureaucratisation (Chapter 7).[16]

Many European countries have an explicit family policy (eg West Germany) and/or a Ministry responsible for co-ordinating family affairs, which contrasts with the implicit and fragmented nature of family policy in Britain.[17] France, Luxembourg, Portugal, West Germany and the three Belgian communities all have a Minister for the Family. Sometimes, as in the Netherlands, there is a minister responsible for ensuring that policy changes take account of the potential implications for children and youth.

France pioneered the introduction of family allowances which are co-ordinated at local level and integrated with composite family services. A tradition of generous allowances was established partly in response to long-standing concerns about the French birth rate.[18] Elsewhere state contributions towards the costs of childrearing are largely separate from service provision. Universal family allowances exist in most EC countries (unlike the US) in order to increase the resources of households with children to compensate for their greater costs. Sometimes the rate paid per child is uniform (as in the UK), but elsewhere the amount varies according to birth order and age.[19] Most are paid to all families, but some are means-tested (eg Italy).[20] In Germany, foster parents may claim family allowance.[21] The amounts paid (as a percentage of average earnings) have traditionally been much higher in the centre of the EC (especially France, Belgium and Luxembourg) than in outer countries like Ireland, Italy and Denmark.[22]

A common principle affecting welfare provision in continental Europe is that of *subsidiarity* (Chapter 3). This means that government and large-scale organisations should normally only take on functions that cannot be fulfilled by social institutions at a 'lower' level or of a less formal nature.[23] For example, central government should only intercede when it is inappropriate for local government, which in turn should only shoulder responsibilities where voluntary or religious bodies are unable to do so. In Italy, for example, the Catholic church has had a strong position in the provision of social services, so that state initiatives have mostly consisted of individual programmes targeted at specific needs.[24] This is a somewhat different perspective from that prevailing in British social work circles where the state is seen to provide the basic services, with the voluntary and informal sectors having innovatory or specialist functions, although that view has been challenged over the last decade by a strong central government committed to privatisation and reduction of local authority powers.[25]

Also important are the linked concepts of social marginality and cohesion. Social policy makers are concerned with those groups who are marginal in the labour force and/or socially isolated or stigmatised. Thus strategies for dealing with poverty, crime or disability may be directed at what the French call *insertion*, ie the social and economic integration of people who for whatever reason are outside mainstream society. Insertion tends to place greater emphasis on training for employment than the English concept of normalisation, although it does embrace social and cultural aspects too.

This brief overview of significant features of social policy in individual states will now be followed by a summary of the supranational institutions of the EC and their influence on social affairs.

## The European Community - Institutions and Legislative Framework

The EC has four main seats of power, influence and policy-making, each with a distinctive role and composition.[26]

- *The European Commission* - drafts and monitors legislation and is responsible for the administration of EC finances and policies. Consists of seventeen political appointees (according to national quotas).

- *The Council of Ministers* - does not initiate legislation, but makes decisions, agrees statutes and policies. In theory it is a single body, but in practice has different compositions for different purposes, consisting of Ministers and non-voting civil servants from the governments of the Member states. High level policy matters are decided by Heads of Government. Presidency rotates amongst the twelve countries every six months.

- *The European Parliament* - has powers to scrutinise and delay proposals and draft legislation, but little formal authority. It can amend or even reject budgets, which are drafted by the Commission and forwarded with modifications by the Council. Members of the Parliament are now directly elected by the general population.

- *The European Court of Justice* - safeguards the competence and validity of Community Law; handles disputes and complaints of non-compliance. Consists of one judge from each member state plus a President.

There are also many other specialised agencies (eg the European Investment Bank; Court of Auditors) and support committees. The Commission is supported by a secretariat organised into Directorate-Generals, of which DG V deals with Social Affairs.[27] Since the Council is not a permanent body, much of its day to day work is delegated to a full-time Committee of Permanent Representatives (COREPER).

Policy-making by the EC has always resulted from a complex process of negotiation amongst its own supra-national institutions (each with its own functions and interests) and individual national governments. The main participants are political and professional elites. Lobbying is often difficult to co-ordinate and ineffective, especially for 'grass-roots' organisations. However, some influential lobbies have been built up, such as voluntary organisations concerned with poverty; women's groups; Eurolink Age and Coface (a network of family organisations). The Commission has a pro-active role, often prompting moves towards radical change, whilst national governments have usually been more reactive, preferring incremental evolution.[28] Most commentators see control as largely remaining with national governments, but less so than is the case with almost all other international organisations.[29] Domestic structures, interests and political groupings thus have a major influence on EC policy development, although governments have often sought to keep EC issues off their domestic political agendas in order to preserve their own control of EC policy-making.[30] Thus the involvement of national parliaments is very limited.[31] A few member countries (notably Greece, Denmark and the UK) retain substantial bodies of opinion opposed in principle to the Community. In spite of this and the diversification of membership, the EC's institutions have managed to maintain continuity.

The Community has two main direct sources of power - legislation and funding, although there are a number of other methods of influence ranging from dialogues with member governments and interest groups to relations with other international organisations. Since the budget is relatively small and financial contributions to projects are quite modest, the chief role has been regulatory.

The legislation of the European Community takes two forms:[32]

- *Primary* - treaties which established the communities and arranged for the accession of new member states.

- *Secondary* - measures passed by the Council and Commission according to powers conferred on them by the treaties.

The principal aims and tasks of the European Community were set out in the Treaty of Rome, which included such items as the establishment of a customs union; adoption of common agricultural and transport policies; abolition of obstacles to the free movement of persons, services and capital; and the creation of a European Social Fund and European Investment Bank.[33] The European Court has established that the Articles of the Treaty of Rome have direct effect, ie they can be enforced irrespective of whether or not Member States have passed corresponding laws. The 1986 Single European Act defined the means for achieving a single internal market with free movement of goods, services, people and capital by the 31st December, 1992. It also extended the scope of EC policies in such fields as the health and safety of workers, research and environmental protection.[34] Many hope that substantial economic and employment benefits will result from the single market along the lines indicated in projections based on optimistic assumptions by Cecchini.[35] However, short-term job losses and an intensification of income differentials are also likely consequences.[36]

It has generally been easier for the Commission to promote measures which are referred to specifically in the Treaty of Rome compared with policies which relate to broader principles. For example, considerable progress has been made in the co-ordination of social insurance systems so that people who move from one member state to another retain similar entitlements (like family allowances). In contrast, the harmonisation of the contents of social insurance programmes has made little progress.[37]

The EC has three principal secondary legislative measures which have varying scope:

1. *Regulations* - must be enforced in all member states and have immediate effect. Regulations prevail over national law.

2. *Directives* - apply to some or all member states, but governments can decide how to put them into effect. Directives are given legal effect by means of changes in national law.

*3. Decisions* - apply to individual persons or states and are binding on them.

There are also recommendations and opinions which have no binding force. When there has been doubt about the direct applicability or effects of EC Law, this has often been clarified by the European Court. For example, although Directives allow some discretion in the way they are implemented, the court has determined that they can become directly effective even if the corresponding national enactments have not been passed within the prescribed time-limits. By and large, member states have accepted the supremacy of Community law, even though they may seek to delay implementation or use their own interpretations.[38] This means that individuals have rights deriving from EC law which are not clearly present in national legislation, as with regards to equal opportunities for women.[39]

### The European Community, Social Policy and Social Work

The existence and development of the European Community has had many indirect implications for social work, although until quite recently few direct consequences. Both proponents and critics of the EC would argue that the creation of a single customs union followed by trends towards economic and monetary integration has almost certainly affected overall prosperity and the distribution of wealth and poverty. One particular concern has been that the centripetal tendencies of industry, commerce and finance has been associated with an intensification of regional disparities and especially of the differences between the dynamic 'core' of the Community (in particular the Paris-Amsterdam-Rhineland area) and the 'periphery' (notably the Celtic and Mediterranean regions).

Social policy in the Community has not embraced the wide range of measures and services normally connoted by that term, but was for many years a minor by-product of economic policy dealing with employment welfare issues. The restricted notion of social policy in the Treaty of Rome has meant that the main focus of 'social' activities has been confined to social security arrangements for migrant workers; equal treatment for men and women at work; and the Social Fund.[40] On the whole, the policies have aimed to co-ordinate national policies and have not sought to harmonise them, ie influence their contents. For some people the principle of subsidiarity applies in the EC context, such that the Community should only take responsibility for matters which are beyond the scope of national governments.[41]

The European Social Fund was set up primarily to assist people working in declining areas and industries. Its prime target is vocational training (eg for disabled people, women re-entering the labour market). It has also provided resettlement grants and financed the training of social workers to work with migrants and their families. Until the 1970s it operated on a very small scale, but it was subsequently enlarged in scope and scale as part of the new concern with social aspects of the market.

In 1972 the heads of government committed the Community to the creation of a Social Action Programme.[42] The Commission subsequently developed detailed proposals, although implementation of these faltered as a result of the 1973-4 oil crisis and the ensuing economic recession. The main target of the programme was to help peripheral areas (like the Mezzogiorno in Italy) and groups of people with insecure positions in the labour market (eg disabled persons; women; school-leavers; migrant workers) - both adversely affected by the uneven growth in the EC. The main mechanisms for implementing the policy were the Social Fund, the Investment Bank and the new Regional Fund, set up in 1975 to tackle problems of unemployment, underemployment and poverty in outer rural areas and declining traditional heavy industrial districts. The combined budgets of the two Funds have grown but remain below fifteen per cent of EC expenditure. It has been argued that the development of social and redistributional policies since the 1970s has been hampered by the fact that the EC institutions were mainly intended for economic regulation and adjudication. Such policies require a greater sense of shared identity and loyalty, as they call for clear cut sacrifices of one group in favour of another.[43]

More recently, there have been pressures to give social aspects more attention in their own right.[44] The passing of the Single European Act was accompanied by recognition that the Single Market would have negative as well as positive consequences, which would be unevenly spread geographically. As before, traditional industrial areas and peripheral rural districts were likely to suffer from freer competition, with increased unemployment and depopulation as probable results unless something was done to redress the balance of differential costs and benefits.[45] Action was needed to minimise further polarisation of the EC into rich and poor. A series of proposals to provide a 'social dimension to the internal market'[46] were eventually formulated in what has come to be known as the Social Charter, although formally it is concerned only with the social rights of *workers* (Table 3).

The Charter has no legal force, but is a solemn declaration of principles. The resulting social measures are directed mainly at facilitating labour mobility (eg through harmonising social security and pension rights) and the alleviation of hardship resulting from structural change. Some governments (notably the UK)

**Table 3: Community charter of fundamental social rights of workers[47]
(The social charter)**

Listed below are summarised versions of the rights conferred by Articles of the Social Charter, with particular emphasis given to those of special relevance to social work.

*Rights*

- to work; to just conditions at work; to safe and healthy working conditions; to a fair remuneration; to organise; to bargain collectively (Articles 1-6)
- of children and young persons to protection (in relation to work) (Article 7)
- of employed women to protection (Article 8)
- to vocational guidance; vocational training (Articles 9-10)
- to protection of health; social security; social and medical assistance (Articles 11-13)
- to benefit from social welfare services (Article 14)
  
  a. promotion of provision of social welfare services
  
  b. public participation in the establishment and maintenance of social welfare services
- of physically and mentally disabled persons to vocational training, rehabilitation and social resettlement (Article 15)
- of the family to social, legal and economic protection (Article 16)
- of mothers and children to social and economic protection (Article 17)
- to work in other member states (Article 18)
- of migrant workers and their families to protection and assistance (Article 19)

have opposed the Social Charter for fear of having to concede more favourable rights to workers, whilst others (eg Denmark) were concerned that the charter might reduce rights already existing in their country.[48]

The Social Charter remains heavily preoccupied with employment-based rights, rather than with citizens' rights and social need. Thus, it does not deal with health and social services except incidentally.[49] References in the charter which seem to relate to social work concerns (such as the protection of children and the needs of disabled people) are couched largely in terms of work and training. The mechanisms for implementing the social charter consist mainly of regulation; stimulation of exchanges of information and networks of shared interests; encouragement to share solutions for common problems; and funding of action projects.[50]

*Poverty.* Since its expanded membership in the early 1970s, the EC has had anti-poverty programmes as part of the move to rectify imbalances, though some people have felt these separate actions have allowed poverty to be marginalised or been too closely tied to employment policies.[51] A programme of pilot schemes to combat poverty was organised by the Commission from 1975 to 1980 (see Appendix). Most employed professional workers and researchers, but with increasing emphasis on the involvement of volunteers. The initiatives included new forms of residential care; information and citizen's rights services; self-help child care ventures; and producer cooperatives. These were all the subject of systematic cross-national evaluation, which concluded that at least half would not have run without EC funding and that innovatory practices and participatory structures had been successfully established. The main methods used were social planning, community development and community action.[52]

After a gap of four years, a second poverty programme was set up (1985-8). This provided funds for:

• action research related to poverty

• exchange of knowledge

• collection and dissemination of comparable data.

It was directed mainly at particular disadvantaged groups, such as the long-term unemployed, the aged and refugees. In 1988-9, more direct action in the form of prototype schemes rooted in local contexts were encouraged.[53] These included integrated schemes in rural areas, for instance, which were directed at overall living conditions in the areas concerned and not confined to 'poor' people only. These schemes carried out needs and resources surveys, then fostered local participation to develop appropriate economic, social and cultural activities. For instance, two in Greece helped improve farming and tourism, whilst one in Ireland tackled youth unemployment and the isolation of elderly people. In 1989, there was a Council Decision to establish an action programme aimed at the economic and social integration of less privileged groups, with an emphasis on innovatory, preventive projects.[54] Besides these specific poverty programmes, the Community has also funded projects aimed to assist people with particular disadvantages, such as illiteracy.

Recently, the EC has shifted its concern from old poverty (linked to particular areas or relationships to the labour market like retirement) towards new poverty, ie the consequences of recession which has affected wider social groups and previously prosperous districts.[55] This distinction has been criticised and a counter-argument made that the 1980s simply broadened the range of the population subject to economic insecurity rather than substantially altered the nature of poverty and its causes.[56] Recent surveys indicate that the majority of the EC population think that measures to combat poverty are insufficient. The proportion of people who blame the poor for their situation has also decreased significantly since the mid-1970s.[57]

*Gender Equality.* The EC has given much attention to issues of gender equality in relation to employment (and associated insurance benefits) in a way which affects social workers as employees as well as their clients. Interestingly, much less attention has been given to race relations and issues of racial equality. Equal opportunities for women was one of the few items of *social* policy which did concern the EC in the 1970s, after which there was a lull until the advent of the social charter.[58] One of the factors prompting support for EC legislation in this field as in others was that countries which were more 'advanced' in equal pay (like France) feared that otherwise they would be at a competitive disadvantage.[59] This issue had the additional advantage of clear inclusion in the Treaty of Rome. Szyszczak suggests that gender issues have also 'provided a convenient vehicle for the European Community Commission to conduct its own power struggle with the Council of Ministers'.[60] At the same time, this has been a subject where the European Court has been as influential as the Commission.

The basic principle that men and women should receive equal pay for equal work is set out in Article 119 of the Treaty of Rome.[61] In the 1970s three directives were passed concerning equal pay (Directive 75/117), equal access to employment and training (76/207) and equal treatment in social security matters (78/7).[62] As in other spheres, the application to social security is confined to benefits related to employment. Nevertheless, here is an area where EC law has led to changes in national law to remove discrimination, although in some instances the changes were made reluctantly after individuals had taken a judicial route to asserting their rights via the European Court.[63] A well known example in Britain was the Court ruling which enabled married women to receive the same payments as others when looking after severely disabled persons (previously they had been excluded). Interpretations of what constitutes work of equal value or of the exempt categories of employment differ markedly from one country to the next.

Besides its legislative action, the EC has also fostered various projects, networks and conferences to further the interests of women, mainly as regards training and employment.[64] There have been two positive action programmes on behalf of women, designed to tackle structural issues neglected by the legislation on individual rights. The Social Fund has been used to train women in non-traditional skills. The European parliament has an active Committee on Women's rights and the General Directorate of Information has a Special Information Service for Women's Organisations, which issues a periodical 'Women of Europe'. Warner argues that through taking such steps the Commission 'gains political support from a large group which has never found a satisfactory response at national level'.[65]

An attempt to introduce an EC directive on parental leave failed as a result of its controversial nature, domestic political considerations in the UK and Benelux countries and the relative marginality of the issue in economic terms.[66] Several EC countries have parental leave arrangements of their own, although not as fully developed as the Commission had proposed. Parental leave at childbirth was introduced in West Germany in 1985. Paid parental leave exists also in France, Italy and Denmark (Chapter 7). Elsewhere, assistance related to childbirth is limited to mothers. Most EC countries have the same retirement age for men and women, but Greece, the UK and Portugal do not.[67]

*Migration.* The Common Market has always included the notion of a shared labour force and one of the cornerstones of the Single European Market from 1992 is the free movement of workers. EC legislation and judgements by the Court of Justice have repeatedly affirmed and extended the employment and social security rights of people working or moving to work in another member state.[68]

These rights apply, however, only to citizens of member states, which has caused concern about its discriminatory impact on migrants from outside, particularly those from the Third World. People who are legally resident in the EC but not citizens do not have the same rights to travel freely as EC citizens under the Single European Act and are subject to differing national policies as regards visas, refugee status and asylum.[69] Migrant women may find it especially difficult to obtain access to training and employment.[70] Several countries have substantial populations of recent migrants and their descendants, whether from ex-colonial territories (France, the Netherlands, Portugal and the UK) or from other parts of Europe and Turkey (Germany). In Britain, black citizens are worried that a 'fortress Europe' may be created, in which black people will lack legal protection or face constant suspicion.[71] Lobbies exist which advocate the harmonisation of immigration policies in restrictive ways.[72]

*Professional qualifications and employment.* The EC has issued a number of specific directives about the recognition of professional qualifications, but this was such a slow process that remaining occupational groups are being dealt with together in general directives. Directive (89/48/EEC) came into force in January, 1991 and applies to social work in most EC countries.[73] Thereafter, individual states cannot insist that professionals from another member state comply with their own requirements provided that the persons concerned hold qualifications covered by the Directive.[74] According to the interpretations by the Department of Trade and Industry, British social work as a whole will not count as a profession under this directive, because it does not fulfil two requirements - namely three year training and being a 'regulated' profession, although some individuals may satisfy these conditions.[75] In contrast, most member states will qualify, whilst in others (eg Ireland) pressure resulted to bring national arrangements into line with the Directive. Consequently British practitioners who wish to work elsewhere in the Community may have difficulty in having their qualifications recognised, whilst this would not apply in reverse. Harris believes that part of the problem stems from treating as one an occupation which in Britain comprises extremes of academic experience from those who qualify after six years of university study to others with two years' college-based study.[76] This in turn reflects the concern for equal opportunities of access in social work and the stress on practice competence as the key criterion for judging social work, which contrasts with the emphasis on intellectual capacities in several other EC countries. The precise implications have yet to unfold, especially since individuals would have recourse to the Treaty of Rome and Single European Act to assert rights of freedom of movement.[77]

A second general directive about professional recognition was issued in 1989. This covers professions with less than three years' training, but with the requirement for regulation retained. In Britain there has been strong resistance to the idea of establishing a national regulatory body, partly on account of concerns about elitism and fears about the interplay between professional and employer responsibilities. The recent report by Professor Parker suggests that changed attitudes and circumstances may now make a general council for social services (rather than social work) more desirable and acceptable.[78]

*The EC and Social Work.* Closer integration in the EC is likely to invoke not only a need for policies which affect social work consumers and professional mobility, but also for more specific social service measures. On the one hand, there will be a growing need to handle the consequences of cross-border movements in relation to child abusers, separated parents with custody or maintenance disputes, people with criminal records, drug handlers, etc. (Chapter 8). On the other hand, there may be pressures to diminish differences in responses, for example with respect to mental health problems, pre-school day care or the use of secure units for young offenders.

Moves towards the Single Market coupled with imbalances in supply and demand of trained social workers has led to small but significant numbers of practitioners from France, Germany and the Netherlands moving to work in the UK.[79]

## Social Work in the European Community

The remainder of the chapter highlights some key developments in social work in the countries of the EC.

*Nature of social work.* Comparisons of social work in different countries have repeatedly shown that what counts as social work in one place may not be considered in the same way elsewhere. For example, in Germany the personal social services include youth work, which is not so in most other countries.[80] There are several French occupations whose functions may be loosely regarded as 'social work'.[81] There and elsewhere may be found industrial social workers, carrying out some functions similar to those of personnel staff in Britain but with wider perspectives and a more pro-active stance.[82] On much of the continent, though not in the British Isles, there exist social pedagogues, a profession which parallels and overlaps with social work. Social pedagogy (Chapter 3) is something of a hybrid between social work and community education, with an emphasis on social education and stimulation.[83] Lorenz shows how the very diversity and ambiguity of social work may be a strength rather than a weakness, enabling the profession to straddle administrative and functional boundaries and to adapt to changing circumstances (Chapters 3, 11). In most countries, social work became more politicised in the 1970s, but it is now broadly accepted that it has a dual role mediating between individuals and society (represented mainly by bureaucratic agencies) to facilitate both personal change and social reform.[84]

*Organisation of Services.* The role and functions of social workers vary widely amongst European countries, as does the extent of overlap and co-operation with other professional groupings. For example, in the UK social work has for many years been separated from social security functions, whereas in places like France and the Low Countries many social workers are attached to social assistance or family allowance offices (Chapter 10).[85] Here they have an important discretionary role in assessments and recommendations about entitlements to financial help.[86] They still tend to carry out full social assessments and to offer counselling, but most contacts include making payments. At local level, social work and health services are normally separate, but not in Italy, the Republic of Ireland or - within the UK - Northern Ireland.[87] The French system of circonscription involves co-ordination and support of varied social service and health professionals by people called 'responsables'.[88] These are nearly all women with social work training and they organise partnership agreements between professionals.

In much of the EC, many personal social services functions are provided by private or religious institutions, whilst public provision is quite limited - the reverse of the British situation.[89] There are further differences in that non-governmental organisations may be funded by the State (as in Luxembourg and the Netherlands) or raise funds by such means as church taxes, subscriptions, charges and lotteries (eg Germany).[90] Some are profit-making. The extent of regulation as well as funding by public bodies varies considerably. Financial responsibility, quality control and service delivery may be unified or separated. In several countries, social services in quite small areas are provided by a wide diversity of organisations, which some regard as undesirable fragmentation. French social workers in the same office may be paid by different organisations (eg the State, Social Insurance companies, voluntary funds). Some voluntary and church organisations (like Caritas and the Red Cross) operate in several EC countries.[91]

In most countries there has been a trend towards decentralisation, sponsored by critics of state welfare bureaucracy from the left (community empowerment), the right (value for money and consumer sovereignty) and indeed the centre (popular participation).[92] This confluence of conservative and radical critiques of social work is noted in several chapters in this book (Chapters 3, 5, 7).

*Social Work Education and Training.* Brauns and Kramer have analysed the dimensions along which social work education and training varies amongst European countries (Chapter 4).[93] They note that most professional training occurs outside Universities but there has been a trend towards academisation. For instance, in the 1980s, Italy, Spain and Greece passed legislation attaching social work to universities, although some courses retain links with the Church.[94] Brauns and Kramer identify a number of other general trends including increased professionalisation, regulation, genericism (except in France) and secularisation. Despite these convergences, a remarkable diversity often persists. In Belgium, social work training is not only sharply divided between French and Flemish-speaking populations, but takes place in institutions run by Central Government, local authorities or 'private' organisations.[95] The last grouping includes denominational institutes and workers' colleges. Before 1974, Portuguese social work was largely organised by the Catholic church, but since then the state has taken over much of the responsibility for social work education.[96]

By contrast with the UK situation, social work education in many countries is carried out largely by non-social workers (such as lawyers and psychologists) and/or by part-time staff.[97] In several EC countries, there is little or no quality or quantity control over entrants to social work training, whilst others have quite strong controls.[98] The duration and types of placement vary greatly, too.[99] In Germany and the UK, research has shown that many students experience 'practice shock' when they move into employment. This is linked with questioning of the value of their prior training and an enhanced awareness of organisational issues in social work.[100]

Although there have been influential indigenous thinkers, it is evident that by and large theories underpinning European social work education have mainly been adapted from North America (Chapters 3, 4). It will be interesting to see whether the greater communication between social work practitioners and academics stimulated by EC developments may lead to a more coherent and distinctively European approach.

Since 1975 there has been a European liaison committee concerned with social work training, with the purpose of fostering cooperation, student exchanges and freer circulation of social workers.[101] In order to achieve these objectives, the committee has recommended measures to harmonise training, such as encouragement of fluency in second languages, courses on International Law and the extension of courses to four years. Training courses in most countries are now paying greater attention to socio-economic factors, management and computerisation.

Links between social work teachers and students in different countries have been growing quite rapidly.[102] Most involve pairs of institutions, but there are some multi-national programmes. The EC's Erasmus programme sponsors such educational networks. Potential benefits include learning ideas about services and policies which it may be possible to apply back home; obtaining a different perspective on one's own practice assumptions; refreshing innovations in curriculum design and assessment.

*Community Work.* This has been the form of social work which has received most sponsorship from the EC itself, notably in the Programmes against Poverty (Chapter 5). The strategies have included social surveys in Ireland; large-scale service planning in Padua; more local or specialised social planning in France and Germany; community development in western Ireland, Edinburgh and Brussels; and finally community action in France.[103] The Social Fund has also supported experimental family centres.

In most countries, community work has exerted an increasingly important influence on social work activity.[104] During the 1970s this was 'the most highly valued form of social work' in Spain, with a focus on organising self-help associations and neighbourhood groups.[105] Local commitment to community development approaches in Portugal have been strengthened by interchanges with European colleagues (Chapter 5). In the Netherlands ninety per cent of community workers are employed by local authorities and Dutch agencies have increasingly accepted their role in facilitating joint action by 'State' and 'Street'

(ie government and local residents), as in Rotterdam's urban renewal programmes.[106] In rural Greece, traditional patterns of multiple households and
social support have needed increasing support as a result of economic change and
out-migration of younger people (Chapter 6).[107]

*Services for Families with Young Children.* In view of the conventional
division of responsibilities for young children, the needs of families in the early
stages of their life-cycle raise issues of gender, as well as of financial support,
day care facilities and special needs. For some years, the employment rates of
mothers of young children has ranged widely in the EC, with Ireland having the
lowest proportion of women in the working population and Denmark the highest.[108] Denmark also has considerably more day care places for children under
three than any other EC member. There workplace nurseries are publicly funded
and open to local people as well as employees.[109] Indeed Denmark may be
regarded as a representative within the EC of the Scandinavian model it shares
with its non-EC Nordic neighbours (Chapter 7). The high level of Danish financial
support and day care provision for families with young children has achieved
broad public acceptance, but interestingly there is a widespread desire for policies
which would enable both mothers and fathers to work part-time during the early
years of parenthood. France is the only EC country which provides cash grants
to assist with child care costs, in addition to tax relief.[110]

The EC Commission and Council have both made broad declarations in favour
of family policies in which the interlinked issues of day care for children and
equal opportunities play a prominent part, but these have so far not been
developed into an action programme. Child care provision for the under-threes
is regarded as a priority area.[111]

*Elderly People and Community Care.* EC legislation has little to say about
elderly people and their needs, except insofar as they are regarded as elderly
workers, eg proposals for a common retirement age. National governments
throughout the EC have taken a growing interest in community care in response
to cost and demographic factors (Chapter 10). There have been common trends
in Europe towards greater diversification and co-ordination of domiciliary services, although the latter has been more problematic in countries like Greece
where there are a multiplicity of church and voluntary organisations involved.[112]
Until recently, social care for elderly people has tended to receive less attention
in countries like the UK and Ireland where social work responsibility has been
submerged in generic departments giving priority to other client groups, especially families and children.[113] Dutch services, which are based on a network of
specialist non-governmental agencies regulated by the State and financed through

compulsory insurance schemes, have achieved very high standards.[114] In Brittany an integrated EC funded programme of housing and domiciliary services helped many elderly inhabitants to remain in their own homes.[115]

A cross-national comparative research project dealing with the social and medical care of people aged 75+ has shown that to varying extents, all nine EC countries involved in the study have attempted to shift from a focus on hospital care to broader health service planning, involving better support to people in their own homes.[116] This is easier where there are organisational links between the agencies responsible for health care, housing, social services and income maintenance. For example, in France the commune office of Aide Social provides cash assistance, practical aids and services as well as managing old people's homes and home helps. However, non-profit voluntary organisations also play a significant role in domiciliary care under contracts as part of the circonscription system outlined earlier.[117] In Germany, voluntary agencies provide both home help and nursing care in conjunction with the public sector, as well as imaginative rehabilitation programmes.[118]

*Disabled People.* For some time now, attempts have been made all over Western Europe to integrate disabled people more fully into normal education and work, [119] but practice on the ground is very variable. Usually children with less severe disabilities are nowadays encouraged to integrate in mainstream day care, except in Greece. Italian nurseries give priority to disabled children.[120] Danish schools are obliged to have places on school committees for parents of children with disabilities when appropriate provision is needed.[121] Social pedagogues play an important part in Danish respite and residential care, which also emphasise parental involvement in planning.[122] In West Germany, there is greater acceptance of institutional care for severely mentally handicapped children than in Britain, perhaps because the stress is on stimulation and education rather than medical routines.[123]

Italy has been in the forefront of de-institutionalisation and normalisation policies for adults. Supported work programmes are also well developed in Italy, which pioneered co-operative small businesses. These allow for part-time work and less demanding schedules within contexts which are otherwise 'non-sheltered'.[124] The Lega per il Diritto al Lavoro degli Handicappati has fought for disabled people to have equal rights as citizens, particularly as regards employment.[125] The Netherlands has specialist social workers for people with mental disabilities and they are employed by three organisations forming a National federation.[126]

During the 1980s the EC has given particular attention to the needs of disabled people and created two action programmes with demonstration projects.[127] The European Social Fund has subsidised projects which assist in the rehabilitation of disabled people and also helped finance a network of innovative centres. In 1983, the EC created a Bureau for Action in favour of the Disabled, which set up the Accord project to help schemes evaluate and publicise themselves.[128]

In 1988, the HELIOS programme was established by the EC to promote social integration and employment of disabled people.[129] Networks have been established to develop and evaluate local model projects. There is also a computerised information system concerning disability (HANDYNET). Staff from participant projects share their experiences through seminars, publications and HANDYNET. There is also provision to assist cross-national training and offer technical advice.

*Mental Health.* Most EC countries have initiated policies of closing large mental hospitals and developing community care but often the passing or implementation of mandatory legislation has been hampered by controversy or inadequate resources.[130] No such inhibitions affected the dramatic attempt made in this direction by Italy. There in 1978 a revolutionary law was passed to deinstitutionalise mental patients. The law required that assessment and treatment, even if compulsory, should be community-based whenever possible or else involve admission to a general hospital ward rather than large public institutions.[131] Hospital care was to be replaced by sheltered housing, group flats and psycho-social centres.[132] Community mental health centres employing medical staff, psychologists and social workers were to be set up to offer day care, emergency treatment and a limited number of residential places. However, it proved difficult to extend such programmes over the whole country in the short space of time allowed. Consequently, this Italian experiment is now acknowledged to have been at best a partial success. It lacked the necessary support to relatives in most areas and was poorly equipped to deal with certain groups, such as those with senile dementia.[133] As a result, a process of partial re-institutionalisation has occurred, although compulsory admissions have been much reduced without any apparent linked increase in suicides or prison admissions.[134]

*Adult Offenders.* The Treaty of Rome makes no mention of crime and the EC has neglected illegal economic activities, except those of the most dramatic kind. For example, interior and justice ministers and officials meet periodically to coordinate attempts to combat drug-trafficking and terrorism.[135] Yet Heidensohn and Farrell argue that offending is closely linked to the socio-economic circumstances which the EC seeks to modify and could well be exacerbated by the effects of the Single Market.[136] Tutt believes EC policy implementation is rife with fraud and law-breaking.[137] Cross-national studies show that most EC countries have had similar trends in recorded crime rates; in the typical offender profile (young, male, poor, urban); and in the nature of victimisation.[138]

In most EC countries social work with adult offenders and their families is organised within the national justice system, often with accountability to a Justice Minister.[139] By contrast, these functions are carried out in England and Wales by the Probation Service, which is funded by Central Government but run separately from both the justice and social services systems. In Scotland similar responsibilities (for writing court reports; probation; prison after-care etc.) are carried by generic social workers integrated in local authority area teams. There have been criticisms of both systems for developing insufficient expertise, so that in 1990 the British Government floated the idea of training probation officers outside the social work education system.

Greece and the Netherlands have the lowest rates of imprisonment per 100, 000 population in the EC.[140] The UK has the dubious distinction of being first in the league table, and Scotland has a particularly high percentage of adults in prison.[141] The UK and Ireland also have exceptionally high proportions of young people in prison.[142]

*Juvenile Justice.* The UK provides an interesting contrast in juvenile justice systems within its own borders. The Juvenile Court system of England and Wales tends to follow a 'justice' or legally oriented model, whilst in Scotland the Children's Hearings System operates more on 'welfare' lines with lay members of the community making all disposals (except in the most serious offences) according to the needs of the child and family rather than the nature of the offence. The French system is somewhat intermediate between these two.[143] The juge des enfants is legally trained and has powers similar to an English magistrate, but has a welfare perspective, procedural flexibility and a monitoring role akin to those of a Scottish Hearing. There is a presumption in favour of non-custodial ('educational') measures.[144]

Most of Western Europe has witnessed attempts to divert juvenile offenders from custody and indeed from the justice system altogether, in the belief that punitive measures are not only detrimental to children, but may reinforce rather than diminish law-breaking behaviour. Whereas some places have successfully implemented policies of minimal use of custody (eg Emilia Romagna in Italy) the UK has continued to have high usage of institutions for young offenders, which Pitts attributes to the failure to depoliticise juvenile crime.[145] West Germany policy has been much influenced by the 'Ambulante Bewegung' or non-confinement movement, which includes elements of what are known in Britain as Intermediate Treatment, Alternatives to Custody and Diversion (Chapter 9). As elsewhere, questions have been raised whether such measures assist people and prevent problems from getting worse or whether 'net-widening processes' mean that youngsters with minor or no problems are unnecessarily involved.[146]

France also relies largely on community measures, since there are no closed institutions specifically for juveniles.[147] Experimental neighbourhood summer programmes were set up in the early 1980s to direct the energies of actual and potential delinquents into sporting, artistic and cultural activities. There followed a drop in the recorded crime rates in the areas concerned, so these schemes have now been established in most urban areas, with a strong orientation towards community involvement in crime prevention councils.

*Drugs.* Dependency on drugs is commonly associated with other problems, such as AIDS, prostitution and stealing. For instance a Spanish survey found high rates of HIV infection and intravenous drug use amongst prostitutes.[148] In the Netherlands there has been a switch from policies aimed at prevention through strong warnings in public education towards stances which seek to deglamorise and destigmatise drug-taking.[149] This shift in approach was influenced by studies showing dramatic publicity to be ineffective. In Amsterdam a longitudinal study has been carried out to evaluate the impact of AIDS prevention measures on drug users. This suggested that intensive counselling and advice about risk-taking behaviour, accompanied by access to such things as clean injecting equipment, methadone and condoms, could lead to safer sex practices. Other studies have shown that needle exchanges do not lead to increased drug use, though they tended to attract people who are more socially integrated than 'non-ex-changers'.[150] In order to protect prostitutes from AIDS and sexually transmitted diseases, an informal drop-in mobile unit has been used in Utrecht to give information and medical advice and provide condoms. Details of safe sex were successfully transmitted through prostitute networks, whilst workers became better informed about prostitutes' behaviour and knowledge.[151] There is concern in some quarters that illicit drugs will spread more easily from such 'soft' regimes following the removal of border controls.[152]

*Child Care, Child Abuse and Adoption.* British child care policy, insofar as it has been subject to outside influences, has looked almost exclusively to North America, with occasional recent glances at developments in Australia and New Zealand. Apart from specialist fostering of teenagers with its roots in Swedish practice,[153] there has been very little interest shown in European models. Yet there is undoubtedly much that could be learned. A small study carried out by the National Children's Bureau showed that far more young adults who have been in public care continue to gain support in France and the Netherlands, compared with the abrupt transition to independence which has been generally expected in the UK.[154]

Since 1945 Britain has been used to several major shifts in child care philosophy being embodied in law, but this has not been the case in a number of other countries (Chapter 9).[155] The emphasis by the Irish constitution and church on family rights has made it harder for the interests of the child to achieve such prominence in law as in the UK. Many West European countries have higher rates of children in care than the UK, although most have also experienced declining numbers taken into care over the last ten to twenty years.[156] Social workers with responsibility for child care may be confined to public local authorities (Denmark); mainly work in private and voluntary agencies (Netherlands); or be well represented in both government and non-government organisations (Ireland; West Germany).[157] Greek foster care is organised through semi-public agencies. Denmark is unusual in that decisions to remove children from their parents are made by local politicians rather than magistrates. The EC poverty programme has included projects aimed at prevention (eg family centres) and others concerned with training and co-ordination in child protection work.[158]

In the UK, child care work and indeed social services in general has become dominated by concern about child abuse, with sexual abuse receiving major attention in recent years. The British approach has been characterised by formal social controls and an early recourse to legal orders - a policy response prompted by repeated public outcries and critical inquiry reports.[159] This contrasts markedly with the situation in the Netherlands, where the emphasis has been much more on gaining voluntary co-operation (Chapter 8). The prime co-ordinating role for all cases of suspected abuse lies with the Confidential Doctor (Vertrouwensartsen) Service. Social workers have important support and therapeutic functions. Some are employed by the government in the Confidential Doctor Bureaux, but many work in small independent child protection or family guardianship agencies.[160] Most cases referred to the Bureaux are already known to welfare professionals, so that usually their main function is to advise about and orchestrate help rather than initiate it.[161] Wherever possible, treatment is arranged without legal intervention and only rarely is criminal prosecution considered.[162] As a result, the focus of work and recording is more on family and environmental problems, with much less attention to the details of abuse than in Britain. At the same time, more attention is given to emotional and cognitive abuse.[163] Dutch research has shown physical abuse to be more common in working-class areas, but in middle class neighbourhoods there is more psychological abuse. The Triangel in Amsterdam offers intensive and multi-disciplinary residential programmes for families at severe risk and has been able to avert permanent substitute care for many of the children.[164]

The Dutch model has been copied in Belgium and Germany. The French system, too, has a non-adversarial stance and channels child abuse referrals through a single agent, in this case a legal rather than a medical one - the juge des enfants, who has wide-ranging powers. Court social workers carry out the measures required by the 'juge'.[165] The French 1989 Child Protection Act emphasised the key information-gathering and co-ordinating roles of social workers.[166] In Ireland, there has also been a reluctance to use the courts or custodial measures except in extreme cases.[167] Germany has no system of abuse registers as in Britain and France. Partly as a result, social work efforts have mostly concentrated on cases where there have been criminal convictions, although voluntary agencies have established preventive programmes which aim to minimise legal involvement and enhance family independence.[168]

Adoption laws have been introduced at markedly different dates in countries of the EC and all have undergone later modification (eg France, 1804; Italy, 1865; England, 1926; Ireland, 1952; Portugal, 1966). Several countries like France and Belgium distinguish 'simple' and 'full' adoption, whilst others like the UK and Netherlands recognise only the latter.[169] In much of continental Europe, adoption of indigenous children is nowadays very limited and in some countries adoption is virtually synonymous with intercountry adoption.[170] In the Netherlands and Denmark, only authorised agencies can handle such adoptions, but in Italy most are arranged privately.[171] A large research programme based in Utrecht has concluded that most children adopted from overseas have fared well, although with some problems of identity confusion, but the long-term outcomes in adulthood are not yet known.[172] The British (and North American) use of adoption to provide permanent substitute family care for older or disabled children in public care has not been imitated elsewhere in the EC.[173] In Denmark, this 'invisibility' of adoption in child care planning is associated with a strong concern for parents' rights and family ties, but the result appears to be that some children drift in care with negligible contact with relatives and little active review.[174]

## Conclusion

No single book can cover all the issues related to social work and the EC. What we can hope to do is to whet people's appetites to find out more; to indicate some lessons from other countries about how things might be done differently at home, whilst acknowledging what we share; and to widen our horizons about the nature of social problems and their potential solutions.

## References

1. Bamford, C. G. and Robinson, H. (1986), *Geography of the European Community*. Longman, Harlow.

   Shanks, M. (1977), *European Social Policy: Today and Tomorrow*. Pergamon, London.

2. Higgins, J. (1981), *States of Welfare*. Blackwell, Oxford.

   Oyen, E. (1990), *Comparative Methodology*. Sage, London.

3. Sorrentino, C. (1990), 'The Changing Family in International Perspective' *Monthly Labour Review*. March, 41-58.

4. Boh, K. (1989), 'European Family Life Patterns - A Reappraisal'. In Boh, K., Bak, M., Clason, C., Pankratova, M., Quortrup, J., Sgritta, G. B. and Waerness, K. (Eds.) *Changing Patterns of European Family Life*. Routledge, London.

   Cherlin, A. and Furstenberg, F. F. (1988), 'The Changing European Family' *Journal of Family Issues*. 9, 3, 291-297.

5. Eurostat. (1988), *Demographic Statistics*.

6. Harding, S., Phillips, D. and Fogarty, M. (1986), *Contrasting Values in Western Europe*. Macmillan, London, 213.

7. Heidenheimer, A. J., Heclo, H. and Adams, C. T. (1983), *Comparative Public Policy*. St. Martins Press, New York.

   Kaim-Caudle, P. R. (1973), *Comparative Social Policy and Social Security*. Martin Robertson, London.

   Kamerman, S. and Kahn, A. J. (1981), *Child Care, Family Benefits and Working Parents*. Columbia University Press, New York.

8. Flora, P. (1981), 'Solution or Source of Crises? The Welfare State in Historical Perspective'. In Mommsen, W. J. (Ed.) *The Emergence of the Welfare State in Britain and Germany 1850-1950*. Croom Helm, London.

   Jones, C. (1985), *Comparative Social Policy*. Tavistock, London.

   Munday, B. (Ed.) (1989), *The Crisis in Welfare*. Harvester Wheatsheaf, Hemel Hempstead.

9. Roebrook, J. M. (1989), 'Netherlands'. In Dixon, J. and Scheurell, R. P. *Social Welfare in Developed Market Countries*. Routledge, London.

   Thane, P. (1982), *Foundations of the Welfare State*. Longman, London.

10. Ford, R. (1987), 'Social Welfare Provision in the Federal Republic of Germany'. In Ford, R. and Chakrabarti, M. (Eds.) *Welfare Abroad*. Scottish Academic Press, Edinburgh.

11. Holloway, J. (1981), *Social Policy Harmonisation in the European Community*. Gower, Aldershot.

12. Curry, J., (1980), *Irish Social Services*. Institute of Public Administration, Dublin.

13. Birks, C. (1987), 'Social Welfare Provision in France'. In Ford, R. and Chakrabarti, M. (Eds.) *Welfare Abroad*. Scottish Academic Press, Edinburgh.

    Cannock, M. (1987), 'Helping les Miserables' *New Society*. 81, 1282, 14-15.

14. Munday, B. (Ed.) op. cit.

    Oyen, E. (Ed.) (1986), *Comparing Welfare States and their Futures*. Gower, Aldershot.

15. Eaton, L. (1990), 'Spanish Cocktail' *Social Work Today*. 16.8.90, 13.

    Rossell, T. and Rimbau, C. (1989), 'Spain - Social Services in the Post-Franco Democracy'. In Munday, B. (Ed.) *The Crisis in Welfare*. Harvester Wheatsheaf, Hemel Hempstead.

16. Grunow, D. (1986), 'Debureaucratisation and the Self-Help Movement: Towards a Restructing of the Welfare State in the Federal Republic of Germany'. In Oyen, E. (Ed.) *Comparing Welfare States and their Futures*. Gower, Aldershot.

17. Craven, E., Rimmer, L. and Wicks, M. (1982), *Family Issues and Public Policy*. Study Commission on the family, London.

    Hill, M. (1989), *The Pros and Cons of Developing a Co-ordinated Family Policy*. SCAFA, Edinburgh.

18. Birks, C. op. cit.

    Higgins, J. (1986), 'Comparative Social Policy' *Quarterly Journal of Social Affairs*. 2, 3, 221-242.

19. Muller, C. W. (1989), 'Germany, West'. In Dixon, J. and Scheurell, R. P. (Eds.) *Social Welfare in Developed Market Countries*. Routledge, London.

    Roebrook, J. M. op. cit.

20. Ferrara, M. (1986), 'Italy'. In Flora, P. (Ed.) *Growth to Limits*. Walter de Gruyter, Berlin.

21. Ford, R. op. cit.

22. Bradshaw, J. and Piachaud, D. (1980), *Child Support in the European Community*. Bedford Square Press, London.

23. Heinze, R. G., Hinrichs, K. and Olk, T. (1986), 'The Institutional Crisis of a Welfare State. The Case of Germany'. In Oyen, E. (Ed.) *Comparing Welfare States and their Futures*. Gower, Aldershot.

24. Ferrara, M. (1989), 'Italy'. In Dixon, J. and Scheurell (Eds.) *Social Welfare in Developed Market Countries*. Routledge, London.

25. Parry, R. (1990), *Privatisation*. Research Highlights No.18. Jessica Kingsley, London.

26. Nugent, N. (1989), *The Government and Politics of the European Community*. Macmillan, London.

    Parker, G. (1981), *The Logic of Unity*. Longman, Harlow.

    Steiner, J. (1988), *Textbook on EEC Law*. Blacktone Press, London.

27. Lodge, J. (1989), 'EC Policymaking: Institutional Considerations'. In Lodge, J. (Ed.) *The European Community and the Challenge of the Future*. Pinter, London.

28. Wallace, H. (1983), 'Negotiation, Conflict, Compromise: the Elusive Pursuit of Common Policies'. In Wallace, H., Wallace, W. and Webb, C. (Eds.) *Policy Making in the European Community*. Wiley, London.

29. Brewster, C. and Teague, P. (1989), *European Community Social Policy: Its Impact on the UK*. Institute of Personnel Management, London.

   Nicoll, W. and Salmon, T. C. (1990), *Understanding the European Communities*. Phillip Allan, Hemel Hempstead.

30. Bulmer, S. (1983), 'Domestic Politics and European Community Policy-Making' *Journal of Common Market Studies*. 21, 4, 349-363.

   Webb, C. (1983), 'Theoretical Perspectives and Problems'. In Wallace, H., Wallace, W. and Webb, C. (Eds.) *Policy Making in the European Community*. Wiley, London.

31. Wilson, R. (1985), 'Westminster and Brussels: The Relationship of Parliament to the EEC' *Public Administration*. 63, 235-240.

32. Marshall, E. A. (1982), *General Principles of Scots Law*. W. Green & Son, Edinburgh.

33. Steiner, J. op. cit.

34. Nicoll, W. and Salmon, T. C. op. cit.

   Nugent, N. op. cit.

35. Cecchini, P. (1988), *The European Challenge 1992*. Wildwood House, Aldershot.

36. Cutler, T., Haslam, C., Williams, J. and Williams, K. (1989), *1992 - The Struggle for Europe*. Berg, New York.

37. Holloway, J. op. cit.

38. Wallace, W. (1983), 'Less than a Federation, More than a Regime'. In Wallace, H., Wallace, W. and Webb, C. (Eds.) *Policy Making in the European Community*. Wiley, London.

39. Collins, L. (1980), *European Community Law in the United Kingdom*. Butterworths, London.

40. James, E. (1982), 'The Role of the European Community in Social Policy'. In Jones, C. and Stevenson, J. (Eds.) *Year Book of Social Policy in Britain 1980-81*. RKP, London.

   Quintin, O. (1990), *The Social Dimension of the European Community*. Paper presented to the Social Policy Association, University of Bath.

41. Wallace, H., Wallace, W. and Webb, C. (Eds.) (1983), *Policy Making in the European Community*. Wiley, London.

42. Shanks, M. op. cit.

43. Wallace et al., op. cit.

44. Vandamme, J. (1985), 'From European Social Policy to "L'Espace Social Européen"'. In Vandamme, J. (Ed.) *New Dimensions in European Social Policy*. Croom Helm, London.

45. Lodge, J. (1989), 'Social Europe: Fostering a People's Europe'. In Lodge, J. (Ed.) *The European Community and the Challenge of the Future*. Pinter, London.

   Pepinster, C. (1990), 'EC Report Says Britain Faces 1992 Job Losses' *Observer*. 14.1.90.

46. Delors, J. (1989), 'Programme of the European Commission for 1989' *Bulletin of the European Communities*. Supplement 2.

47. Commission of the European Communities (1990), 'Community Charter of Fundamental Social Rights of Workers' *Social Europe*. 1, 45-50.

    Commission of the European Communities. 'The Charter of Fundamental Social Rights' (1989), *Bulletin of the European Communities*. 22, 5, 9-11.

48. George, M. (1989), 'Charter Accounts' *New Statesman and Society*. 2, 62, 22-23.

49. Bell, H. (1990), '1992: Implications for Health and Social Services' *European Information Service*. 108, 17-22.

    Hadjpateras, A. (1986), 'Charting the Course of Poverty' *Social Work Today*. 7.12.89, 26.

    Leibfried, S. (1990), *European Models of Welfare and the Wider International Order*. Paper presented to the Social Policy Association, University of Bath.

50. Commission of the European Communities (1989), *Communication from the Commission Concerning its Action Programme Relating to the Implementation of the Community Charter of Basic Social Rights for Workers*. Office for Official Publications of the European Communities, Luxembourg.

51. Brown, J. C. (Ed.) (1984), *Anti-Poverty Policy in the European Community*. Policy Studies Institute, London.

52. Dennett, J., James, E., Room, G. and Watson, P. (1982), *Europe Against Poverty: The European Poverty Programme 1975-80*. Bedford Square Press, London.

53. Van Loo, D. (1989), 'Poverty: A New Programme Proposed by the European Commission' *Social Europe*. 2, 66-69.

54. Commission of the European Communities (1989), 'The Poverty Programme' *Social Europe*. Supplement 2.

    Commission of the European Communities (1989), 'Commission Communication to the Council on a Medium-Term Action Programme to Foster the Economic and Social Integration of the Least Privileged Groups'*Bulletin of the European Communities*. Supplement 4.

55. Brown, J. C. (Ed.) op. cit.

56. Room, G., Lawson, R. and Laczko, F. '"New Poverty" in the European Community' *Politics and Policy*. 17, 2, 165-176.

    Room, G. (1990), *New Poverty in the European Community*. Macmillan, London.

57. Eurobarometer (1989), *The Perception of Poverty in Europe in 1989*. Office for Official Publications of the European Communities, Luxembourg.

    Jowell, R., Witherspoon, S. and Brook, L. (1989), *British Social Attitudes: Special International Report*. Gower, Aldershot.

58. Hoskyns, C. and Luckhaus, L. (1989), 'The European Community Directive on Equal Treatment in Social Security' *Politics and Policy*. 17, 4, 321-335.

59. Warner, H. (1984), 'EC Social Policy in Practice: Community Action on Behalf of Women and its Impact on Member States' *Journal of Common Market Studies*. 23, 2, 141-167.

60. Szyszczak, E. (1987), 'The Future of Women's Rights: The Role of European Community Law'. In Brenton, M. and Ungerson, C. (Eds.) *Yearbook of Social Policy 1986-7*. Longman, London, 50.

61. Mazey, S. (1988), 'European Community Action on Behalf of Women: The Limits of Legislation' *Journal of Common Market Studies*. 17, 1, 63-83.

62. Mossuz-Lavau, J. (1988), *Women of Europe: Mirroring the Course on Women's Rights in Europe (1977-1987)*. Commission of the European Communities, Brussels.

63. Hoskyns, C. and Luckhaus, L. op. cit.

   Millar, J. (1989), 'Social Security, Equality and Women in the UK' *Policy and Politics*. 17, 4, 311-319.

64. Commission of the European Communities (1988), *Women of Europe*, 56.

   Commission of the European Communities (1988), *Equal Opportunities*. Supplement to Women of Europe, 23.

   Commission of the European Communities (1988), *Women of Europe: 10 Years*. Supplement to Women of Europe, 27.

   IRIS (1989), *Bulletin 2*. June-August.

65. Warner, H. op. cit.

66. Cohen, B. (1988), *Caring for Children*. Commission of the European Communities, London.

   Rutherford, F. (1989), 'The Proposal for a European Directive on Parental Leave: Some Reasons Why it Failed' *Politics and Policy*. 17, 4, 304-310.

67. Eurolink (1990), *Eurolink Age Bulletin*. March.

68. Holloway, J. op. cit.

69. Gordon, P. (1989), *Fortress Europe*. Runnymede Trust, London.

   Kahn, R. (1989), *Migrants et Travail en Europe*. Presses Interuniversitaires Européens, Paris.

70. Prondzynski, I. (1989), 'The Social Situation and Employment of Migrant Women in the EC' *Politics and Policy*. 17, 4, 347-354.

71. Sanders, C. (1989), 'Race Apart' *New Statesman and Society*. 2, 68, 25-26.

   Sivanandan, A. (1988), 'The New Racism' *New Statesman and Society*. 1, 22, 8-9.

72. Flynn, D. (1990), 'Fortress Europe - Foreigners Needn't Apply' *Community Care*. 28.9.90, vi-vii.

73. Barr, H. (1989), 'Odd One Out' *Community Care*. 20.7.89, 20-21.

   Bechillon, C. de (1990), 'Une Réponse Professionelle' *La Revue Française de Service Sociale*. 156, 46-52.

   Lunn, T. (1989), 'Watching the Directives' *Community Care*. 5.10.89, 16-17.

74. Barr, H. (1989), *Social Work in its European Context*. CCETSW, London.

75. Department of Trade and Industry (1989), *Rights of Establishment: European Community Directive on a General System for the Recognition of Higher Education Diplomas*. DTI, London.

76. Harris, R. (1989), 'Outside Looking In?' *Community Care*. 7.12.89, 16-18.

77. Hall, T. (1990), *Social Work Education and Training in the UK and EC Developments*. Paper presented at the SEC/CCETSW Conference 'Update on Europe', June.

Pisarski, W. (1989), 'The CQSW and 1992' *Social Work Today*. 17.8.89, 25.

78. Parker, R. (1990), *Safeguarding Standards*. NISW, London.

79. Fry, A. (1989), 'Crossing the Channel and the Language Barrier' *Social Work Today*. 9.11.89, 9.

Owen, M. (1989), 'Casting the Net in Europe' *Social Work Today*. 10.8.89, 9.

80. Munday, B. (1990), *Social Services in the European Community and the Implications of 1992*. Reports of a Meeting of Social Services Representatives, University of Kent.

81. Thévenez, A. and Désigueux, J. (1985), *Les Travailleurs Sociaux*. Presses Universitaires de France, Paris.

82. Googins, B., Reisner, E. and Milton, J. (1986), 'Industrial Social Work in Europe' *Employee Assistance Quarterly*. 1, 3, 1-23.

83. Jervis, M. (1990), 'A World Apart' *Social Work Today*. 19.4.90, 20-21.

84. Flora, I. M. A. (1986), 'Social Work Education in Portugal'. In Brauns, H-J. and Kramer, D. (Eds.) *Social Work Education in Europe*. Eigenverlag des Deutschen Vereins für Öffentliche und Private Fürsorge, Frankfurt-am-Main.

Villa, F. (1987), 'Il Lavoro Sociale comme Professione' *Studi di Sociologica*. 25, 3, 322-348.

85. Leaper, R. (1982), 'Cash and Caring: Belgium, Britain and France' *Social Policy and Administration*. 16, 3, 187-212.

Leaper, R. (1988), 'Cash and Care in a European Perspective'. In Becker, S. and MacPherson, S. (Eds.) *Public Issues, Private Pain*. Social Services Insight Books, London.

Rodgers, B., Doron, A. and Jones, M. (1979), *The Study of Social Policy: A Comparative Approach*. George Allen & Unwin, London.

86. Knegt, R. (1987), 'Rule Application and Substantive Justice: Observations at a Public Assistance Bureau' *Netherlands Journal of Sociology*. 23, 116-125.

87. Curry, J. op. cit.

Gilligan, R. (1989), 'Policy in the Republic of Ireland: Historical and Current Issues in Child Care'. In Carter, P., Jeffs, T. and Smith, M. (Eds.) *Social Work and Social Welfare Yearbook 1*. Open University Press, Milton Keynes.

88. Henderson, P. L. and Scott, A. (1989), *The Circonscription System in French Social Services: Its Relevance to the UK*. ESRC Report, National Institute of Social Work, London.

89. Brauns, H-J. and Kramer, D. (1989), 'West Germany - the Break Up of Consensus and the Demographic Threat'. In Munday, B. (Ed.) *The Crisis in Welfare*. Harvester Wheatsheaf, Hemel Hempstead.

90. Flamm, F. (1980), *Social Welfare Services and Social Work in the Federal Republic of Germany*. Eigenverlag des Deutschen Vereins, Frankfurt-am-Main.

Munday, B. op. cit.

91. Flamm, F. op. cit.

Rossell, T. and Rimbau, C. op. cit.

92. Deacon, A. (1985-6), 'Strategies for Welfare: East and West Europe' *Critical Social Policy*. 5, 2, 4-26.

93. Brauns, H-J. and Kramer, D. (Eds.) (1986), *Social Work Education in Europe*. Eigenverlag des Deutschen Vereins für Öffentliche und Private Fürsorge, Frankfurt-am-Main.

94. Lorenz, W. (1986), 'Social Work Education in Western Europe: Themes and Opportunities' *Issues in Social Work*. 6, 2, 89-100.

   Lorenz, W. (1988), 'Some Comparative Dimensions in Social Work Education'. In *Report from the European Directive Workshop*. CCETSW, Stoke Rochford, Lincs.

   King, J. (1990), 'An Olympic Struggle' *Community Care*. 834, 6.10.90, 20-23.

   Sone, K. (1990), 'Homage to Catalonia' *Community Care*. 832, 20.9.90, 20-23.

95. Remion, G. and Messiaen, P. (1986), 'Social Work Education in Belgium'. In Brauns, H.-J. and Kramer, D. (Eds.) *Social Work Education in Europe*. Eigenverlag des Deutschen Vereins für Öffentliche und Private Fürsorge, Frankfurt-am-Main.

96. Flora, I. M. A. op. cit.

97. Barr, H. (1989), *Social Work in its European Context*. CCETSW, London.

   Schiller, H. (1983), 'Current Situation and Trends in European Social Work Education' *International Social Work*, 26, 1-6.

98. Coleman, R. (1990), 'An Analysis of a Social Work Course in the Federal Republic of Germany' *Social Work Education*. 9, 1, 44-53.

   Munday, B. (1989), 'Conclusion', in Munday, B. (Ed.) *The Crisis in Welfare*. Harvester Wheatsheaf, Hemel Hempstead.

99. Braun, J. (1982), 'Social Work Education in the Federal Republic of Germany' *International Social Work*. 25, 2-13.

100. Barbour, R. (1984), 'Social Work Education: A Training in Pessimism or Parable?' *Social work Education*. 4, 1, 21-28.

   Davies, M. (1984), 'Training: What We Think of it Now' *Social Work Today*. 15, 24.1.84, 12-16.

   George, J. and Koch, U. (1986), 'Do the "Twain" Meet After All? Attitudes of Social Workers in Europe and Asia' *International Journal of Social Work*. 29, 29-42.

101. Commission of the European Communities (1989), *Social Work Training in the European Community*. Office for Official Publications of the European Communities, Luxembourg.

102. Cannan, C. (1985), 'Linking up with a West German Social Work Course' *Issues in Social Work Education*. 5, 2, 117-126.

   Cannan, C., Coleman, R. and Lyons, K. (1990), *Links and Exchanges*. CCETSW, London.

   Lyons, K. (1990), 'The European Dimension in Social Work Training' *Issues in Social work Education*. 9, 2, 93-95.

103. Dennett, J., James, E., Room, G. and Watson, P. op. cit.

104. Curry, J. op. cit.

   Ford, R. op. cit.

105. Andreau, C. R. and Poch, T. R. (1986), 'Social Work Education in Spain'. In Brauns, H-J. and Kramer, D. (Eds.) *Social Work Education in Europe*. Eigenverlag des Deutschen Vereins für Öffentliche und Private Fürsorge, Frankfurt-am-Main.

106. Raspe, A. (1987), 'Street and State in Community Work: Some Developments from the Past 20 Years' *Community Development Journal*, 22, 4, 287-293.

107. Taylor, R. (1985), 'Studying the Elderly Cross-Culturally' *Ageing and Society*. 5, 297-222.

108. Mazey, S. op. cit.

109. Phillips, A. and Moss, P. (1984), *Who Cares for Europe's Children*. Office for Official Publications of the European Communities, Luxembourg.

Jensen, J. J. (1990) *Childcare in Denmark*. Paper presented to the Childcare in Europe Conference, Edinburgh.

110. Moss, P. (1988), *Child Care and Equality of Opportunity*. Commission of the European Communities, Brussels.

111. Commission of the European Communities (1984), *Day Care Facilities and Services for Children under the Age of Three in the European Community*. Office for Official Publications of the European Communities, Luxembourg.

Commission of the European Communities. *Communication from the Commission on Family Policies*. Com(89)363 final, Brussels.

112. Amman, A. (1981), *The Status and Prospects of the Aging in Western Europe*. Eurosocial Occasional Paper, 8, Vienna.

Illsley, R. and Taylor, R. (Eds.) (1984), *Individual Choice and Enabling Structures*. Official Publications of the European Communities, Luxembourg.

113. King, J. 'The Poor Relation?' (1989), *Community Care*. 23.11.89, 19-22.

114. Lunn, T. 'Public Ends, Private Means' (1990), *Community Care*. 30.11.90, 15-17.

115. Dennett, J., James, E., Room, G. and Watson, P. op. cit.

116. Hunter, D. (1986), *Age Care Research in Europe*. University of Bath.

117. Bartlett, N. (1989), 'Caring, the French Way' *Community Care*. 9.11.89, 20-22.

118. Jervis, M. (1990), 'Self-sufficiency in Residence' *Social Work Today*. 3.5.90, 20-21.

Tester, S. (1989), 'Focus on an Ageing World' *Social Work Today*. 24.8.89, 22.

119. Birks, C. op. cit.

Lunn, T. (1990), 'Public Ends, Private Means' *Community Care*. 30.11.90, 15-17.

Mara, G. (1989), 'Youth and Disability' *Eurosocial*. 34, 11-17.

120. Ghedini, O. P. (1990), *The Network of Childcare Services in Italy*. Paper presented to the Childcare in Europe Conference, Edinburgh.

Moss, P. op. cit.

121. Fish, J. (1987), 'Disability and Social Policy: An International Perspective'. *Children and Society*. 2, 114-122.

122. Philpot, T. (1989), 'Bringing Home the Bacon' *Community Care*. 16.11.89, 21-24.

123. Sluckin, A. (1987), 'Focus on Europe: Further Education Needed for People with Mental Handicap' *Practice*. 1, 1, 63-70.

124. Commission of the European Communities (1984), *The Economic Integration of the Disabled: An Analysis of Measures and Trends in the Member States*. Office for Official Publications of the European Communities, Luxembourg.

Fish, J. op. cit.

125. Tudor, K. (1989), 'The Politics of disability in Italy' *Critical Social Policy*. 25, 37-54.

126. Netherlands Ministry of Welfare, Health and Cultural Affairs (1986), *Fact Sheet on Welfare Policy for the Disabled*. Rijswijk.

127. Olivier, P. (1986), *Analysis of Current Needs and Initiatives in the Field of Adaptation of Vocational Training for Young Handicapped People to the New Employment Realities*. Office for Official Publications of the European Communities, Luxembourg.

128. Mangen, S. (1985), *Mental Health Care in the European Community*. Croom Helm, London.

129. Commission of the European Communities (1989), *Helios*. 1.

Commission of the European Communities (1989), 'Helios: A New Step Towards the Integration and Independent Living for Disabled People in the European Community' *Social Europe*. 2, 62-65.

130. Mangen, S. op. cit.

131. Ramon, S. (1985), 'The Italian Psychiatric Reform'. In Mangen, S. (Ed.) *Mental Health Care in the European Community*. Croom Helm, London.

132. Jones, K. (1989), 'Community Care: Old Problems and New Answers'. In Carter, P., Jeffs, T. and Smith, M. (Eds.) *Social Work and Social Welfare Yearbook 1*. Open University Press, Milton Keynes.

133. Jones, K. and Poletti, A. (1984), 'The Mirage of a Reform' *New Society*. 69, 1137, 10-11.

Jones, K. and Poletti, A. (1985), 'Understanding the Italian Experience' *British Journal of Psychiatry*. 146, 341-347.

Jones, K. and Poletti, A. (1986), 'The "Italian Experience" Reconsidered' *British Journal of Psychiatry*. 148, 144-150.

134. Ferrara, M. op. cit.

Ramon, S. op. cit.

135. Gordon, P. op. cit.

Nugent, N. op cit.

136. Heidensohn, F. M. and Farrell, M. (1990), *Social Welfare and Social Change in Europe: The Challenge of Crime*. Paper presented to the Social Policy Association, University of Bath.

137. Tutt, N. (1989), *Europe on the Fiddle*. Christopher Helm, London.

138. Van Dijk, J., Mayhew, P. and Kilias, M. (1990), *Experiences with Crime Across the World*. The Hague, Kluwer.

139. Cartledge, G. (1988), *Probation Work Across Europe - A Comparison*. Paper presented to the Conference on 'Crime in Europe - Practice, Policy and Prospects', University of York.

140. Audit Commission (1989), *The Probation Service: Promoting Value for Money*. HMSO, London.

Hood, R. (Ed.) (1989), *Crime and Criminal Policy in Europe*. Proceedings of a European Colloquium, University of Oxford, Oxford.

141. NACRO (1986), *NACRO Briefing*. National Association for the Care and Resettlement of Offenders, London.

142. Blagg, H. and Smith, D. (1989), *Crime, Penal Policy and Social Work*. Longman, London.

143. Tonkin, B. (1988), 'A Bench without Tears?' *Community Care*. 14.7.88, 25-26.

144. King, M. and Petit, M-A. (1985-6), 'Thin Stick and Fat Carrot - the French Juvenile Justice System' *Youth and Policy*. 15-6, 26-31.

King, M. (1988), *How to Make Crime Prevention Work*. NACRO, London.

145. Pitts, J. (1988), *The Politics of Juvenile Crime*. Sage, London.

146. Hudson, J. and Galaway, B. (Eds.) (1989), *The State as Parent*. Kluwer, Dordrecht.

147. King, M. op. cit.

Pitts, J. (1990), *Working with Young Offenders*. Macmillan, London.

Pitts, J. (1990), 'Prevention is Better than Crime' *Social Work Today*. 10.5.90, 30-31.

148. Estebanez, P. E. (1990), 'Prostitution and AIDS in Spain'. In Plant, M. (Ed.) *Aids, Drugs and Prostitution*. Tavistock/Routledge, London.

149. Netherlands Ministry of Welfare, Health and Cultural Affairs, (1988), *Drugs*. Rijswijk.

150. Buning, E. (1989), 'Aids Related Interventions Among Drug Users in the Netherlands' *International Journal on Drug Policy*. 1, 5, 10-13.

151. Kleinegris, C. M. and Verbrugge, M. (1989), *Huiskamer Aanloop Prostituees*. English Version Project Report, Utrecht.

Venema, P. U. and Visser, J. (1990), 'Safer Prostitution: A New Approach in Holland'. In Plant, M. (Ed.) *Aids, Drugs and Prostitution*. Tavistock/Routledge, London.

152. Heidensohn, F. and Farrell, M. (Eds.) (1991), *Crime in Europe*. Routledge, London.

153. Hazel, N. (1981), *A Bridge to Independence*. Blackwell, Oxford.

154. Slade, M. and Smith, P. *A Comparative Study of Young People Leaving Care in Britain*. National Children's Bureau, London, forthcoming.

Stein, M. 'Leaving Care'. In Kahan, B. (Ed.) (1989), *Child Care Research, Policy and Practice*. Hodder & Stoughton, London.

155. Gilligan, R. op. cit.

Kelly, G. (1989), 'Patterns of Care: The First Twelve Months'. In Hudson, J. and Galaway, B. (Eds.) *The State as Parent*. Kluwer, Dordrecht.

156. Brauns, H-J. and Kramer, D. op. cit.

Curry, J. op. cit.

Christopherson, J. (1989), 'European Child-Abuse Management Systems'. In Stevenson, O. (Ed.) *Child Abuse: Professional Practice and Public Policy*. Harvester Wheatsheaf, London.

157. Davies, M. and Sale, A. (Eds.) (1989), *Child Protection in Europe*. NSPCC, London.

Southon, V. (1986), *Children in Care: Paying their Families*. DHSS, London.

Doek, J. E. and Slagter, S. (1979), *Child Care and Protection in the Netherlands*. Werkverband integratie Jeugdwelzijnswerk, Utrecht.

158. Dennett, J., James, E., Room, G. and Watson, P. op. cit.

159. Frost, N. and Stein, M. (1989), *The Politics of Child Welfare*. Harvester Wheatsheaf, London.

Stevenson, O. (1989), *Child Abuse: Professional Practice and Public Policy*. Harvester Wheatsheaf, London.

160. Christopherson, J. (1981), 'Two Approaches to the Handling of Child Abuse: A Comparison of the English and Dutch Systems' *Child Abuse and Neglect*. 5, 369-373.

Netherlands Ministry of Welfare, Health and Cultural Affairs (1989), *Fact Sheet on Child Abuse*. Rijswijk.

161. Baneke, J. W. (1983), 'The Dutch Approach to Child Abuse'. In Leavitt, J. E. *Child Abuse and Neglect: Research and Innovation*. Martinus Nijhoff, The Hague.

162. Sluckin, A. and Dolan, P. (1990), 'Tackling Child Abuse in the EEC' *Journal of Social Work Practice*. 4, 2, 98-102.

163. Christopherson, J., op. cit.

164. Findlay, C. (1988), 'Child Abuse: The Dutch Response' *Practice*. 1, 4, 374-381.

165. Davies, M. and Sale, A. (Eds.) op. cit.

166. Seailles, L. (1990), 'Interrogations autour de la Nouvelle Loi sur la Protection des Enfants Maltraités' *Revue Française de Service Sociale*. April, 53-62.

167. Gilligan, R. op. cit.

168. Sluckin, A. and Dolan, P. op. cit.

169. Rieg, A. (1985), 'Introduction Comparative' *Revue Internationale de Droit Comparé*. 3, 511-524.

Curry, J. op. cit.

170. Hoksbergen, R. (Ed.) (1986), *Adoption in Worldwide Perspective*. Lisse, Swets and Zeitlinger.

171. Selman, P. (1990), *Inter-Country Adoption*. Paper presented to the Social Policy Association, University of Bath.

172. Loenen, A. and Hoksbergen R. (1986), 'Inter-country Adoption: The Netherlands. Attachment Relations and Identity' *Adoption and Fostering*. 10, 2, 22-26.

173. Hill, M., Lambert, L. and Triseliotis, J. (1989), *Achieving Adoption with Love and Money*. National Children's Bureau, London.

174. Southon, V. op. cit.

# Chapter 2

# Welfare States in the European Community

## Richard Parry

Social work in European Community countries must be located within their wider social policy contexts. These comprise political, social and economic variables which go well beyond legal and financial matters. Contemporary social work is an advanced expression of the idea of a welfare state, one which assumes a high level of public involvement in the economic and social formation of its citizens. It is common to see this as an ameliorative and positive process, but in fact it is neither uncontroversial nor irreversible. This chapter discusses the historical growth of welfare states, the management of resources in them, and the political and sociological factors behind the reconstruction of the welfare state in the 1970s and 1980s.

### The Growth of Welfare States

Welfare states are those in which social policy has been incorporated into the predominant routines of state activity. Put most simply, social policy involves the interaction between the state and the individual in such spheres as education, social care and protection, and income maintenance. It revolves around the choice of instruments to achieve social end states like happiness, health, security and education. The production of outputs like houses, school places and pension rights is part of social policy, but it does not exhaust the concept and cannot be an end in itself in the long term.

This definition implies two distinctions: between the state's achieving policy aims through coercion of others or by its own direct action, and between services in cash and in kind. The state can mandate - require by law or regulation - individual and corporate behaviour, including the purchasing of services through insurance. It can equally put itself in the role of direct supplier and employer, with attendant risks and benefits. The movement of money - the traditional task of social security - is supplemented by services in kind received through an intermediary, such as a doctor, teacher or social worker.

These distinctions make social policy a complex political and economic matter. Politically, it may be regarded as a partially contested concept, found in all industrialised states but supported to varying degrees by the ideology of governments. The degree of contest does not fall on a continuum between left and right, or socialism and capitalism; it is cut across by attitudes towards 'big government' and the 'nanny state', and by European religious traditions. The main sources of variation comprise the number, nature and position of institutions standing between the individual and the state. Hence the cost of the welfare state is not necessarily minimised in right-wing political cultures, where also the state may intervene extensively in society and become a vehicle for social change. State services may be sponsored as guarantors of social stability and reproduction, in a way which is functional to capitalist economic development. The welfare state is expected to deal with dynamic issues and problems arising from social development. This creates stress and potential destabilisation if the demands on the welfare state exceed its capacity to meet them.

Economically, social policy is not insulated from the supply and demand mechanisms of the market. Most social policies are 'merit goods' or 'quasi-public goods' - that is, they will be supplied in a rudimentary fashion if left to the free market but in insufficient quantity to meet the long-term needs of the individual or the needs of society. But it is never straightforward to determine what the role of the state should be. All sorts of possibilities exist for distorting the market by subsidies or regulation; by mandating individuals and their employers; and by charging for services the state produces or compelling contributions to them. This is why 'privatisation' in social policy is much harder to define than in industrial policy. Shifts in government generosity and alterations of eligibility can reduce greatly the value of state welfare to the individual within a framework of deep state involvement.

These shifts occur in relation to a continuum of activities in which the division of public and private responsibility runs broadly from most to least public through national security, police, education, social security, health care, personal social services and labour market services to housing. These are ranked only imperfectly in terms of importance to the individual or indispensability of the state. Their order is determined rather by the political framework in which public policy debate takes place. Those areas which relate to the legal system, security framework or to economic policy may receive 'undeserved' prominence. Those where a tradition of private or voluntary provision has produced a 'mixed economy of welfare' may suffer cuts that bear hardest on the most disadvantaged citizens. The decisive breakthrough for social policy in Europe came in the period from 1880 to 1914, when for the first time governments sought to secure the individual welfare of their citizens as well as the physical security or economic structure of their states. Several events happened at the same time and interacted with one another. Some were political, some economic, some philosophical. Particularly noteworthy was the enactment of sickness, accident and old age insurance in Germany in the 1880s under Chancellor Otto von Bismarck (the initial speech by the Kaiser to the Reichstag provided the cause for centenary celebrations of the welfare state in Berlin in 1981). The German example was followed in most European countries (though not until 1912 in Britain), not so much through direct emulation as a common response to political and economic pressure.

National unification and a stable political structure (especially in Germany after 1871) had allowed rapid urbanisation, industrialisation and a speeding-up of economic growth. The coming of mass democracy through the extension of the vote to most men (though not women) by 1914 ensured the responsibility of governments to parliament, and electoral competition between political parties. The growing labour movement (trades unions and associated socialist parties) had not yet taken power but posed a threat to conservative forces. National public education often represented a takeover by the state from the church. Above all, there was a break with liberal ideas which had previously posited that the relief of need would interfere with economic laws unless done in a repressive way which implied individual guilt. Now, some individual misfortunes were seen as insurable contingencies whose risks could be spread and averaged across the population. Even though private instruments might be used to administer services, the power of the state became the guarantor of insurance rights.

These preconditions allowed the introduction for at least part of the workforce of insurance schemes against the interruption of earnings for physical reasons. But not until well into the twentieth century was there general provision for medical care expenses and universal income maintenance not based upon employment status. The pace of the broadening of coverage from sickness to retirement to unemployment varied and in many countries there were sudden jumps in coverage. It can be argued that the most important expansion of coverage occurred either in the 1920s and 1930s or the 1950s and 1960s.[1] Whereas the inter-war years saw a significant extension to new risks and groups, it was only in the early postwar years that coverage was completed. This in turn created pressure for the consolidation and unification of schemes, which took place in the 1960s and 1970s. Welfare was now seen as a common right of citizenship rather than as means of differentiating between sections of the population.

Over time, Anglo-Scandinavian notions of 'social citizenship' have come to dominate the continental 'Bismarckian' pattern of minimalist benefits. T. H. Marshall's famous idea[2] of a progressive ascent from legal to political to social citizenship, the latter providing welfare guarantees without diminishing any other rights, is too simple and neglects the illiberal and coercive tendencies of many modern states. But it does capture a general European tendency to provide wider income guarantees and rights to vocational preparation. France's new income maintenance scheme of 1988 (*revenue minimum d'insertion*) combines the two themes in its provision of money linked to training for the one million long-term unemployed and the non-disabled who have never worked.

The comparison of social policies across Western Europe naturally reveals elements of similarity and diversity, but taken as a whole the range of policies found is wider than the socio-economic homogeneity would suggest. The traditional notion that there has been uniform modernisation through urbanisation and industrialisation is less plausible than the recognition of the diversity and multi-dimensionality of growth associated with religious and geographical variations and political choices. The differences between the Protestant north and Catholic south of Europe are particularly clear. Reviewing the results of his major cross-national study of expenditure data, Flora[3] suggests that two main variables produce diversity:

i) the degree of penetration of welfare by the state and the room for manoeuvre it grants to other entities;

ii) the degree of fragmentation of the welfare state according to social and political differentiation, induced by such factors as federal political structures, the degree of confessional split within the churches, and the occupational distribution of the workforce.

The homogeneous aspects of welfare states are most apparent at two levels: in the ultimate role of the state as guarantor, and in the nature of the transaction between the producer and consumer of welfare. In between, there is a multitude of options about administration and finance and of balances between public and private provision. Nor is money the only currency: laws, customs and political expectations all play a part. The growth of welfare states is a by-product of political and economic development, but it is not pre-determined in detail, and can take a variety of forms according to the circumstances of each nation.

For example, Germany and Belgium have a multiplicity of institutions administering compulsory health insurance, whereas Britain, Italy and Denmark have favoured public sector administration. The Catholic church has an important role running its own educational institutions in the Netherlands, whereas it is excluded in nominally more Catholic France. Education is rigorously centralised in France but is devolved to the Länder in Germany. Social work, a separate profession in Britain, is usually allied to health care elsewhere in the European Community. Whether or not the client notices, the distribution of service responsibility is an important political factor.

## Resource Management in Welfare States

The prime resource of the welfare state is the spending of public money raised through taxation. This money consists of two economic components: government final consumption of goods and services, and transfer payments for final consumption by others. Principally, the former type consists of payments to em-

### Table 1: Social spending in European Community Countries

| | Total Expenditure social as % of GDP | Social security transfers | Total public | Public consumption |
|---|---|---|---|---|
| | *(1981)* | *(1987)* | *(1987)* | *(1987)* |
| Belgium | 38 | 21 | 52 | 16 |
| Netherlands | 36 | 26 | 60 | 16 |
| Denmark | 33 | 16 | 58 | 26 |
| Germany | 32 | 16 | 47 | 20 |
| France | 30 | 22 | 52 | 19 |
| Italy | 29 | 17 | 51 | 17 |
| Ireland | 28 | 5 | 55 | 18 |
| UK | 24 | 14 | 46 | 21 |
| Greece | 13 | 14 | 43 | 20 |
| Spain | n/a | 16 | 42 | 14 |

Note: full data are not available for Luxembourg and Portugal.

Sources: OECD, Social Expenditures 1960-1990 (1985) Table 1 (for later data on a narrower definition see OECD, *The Future of Social Protection* (1988); *Historical Statistics 1960-87* (1989) Tables 6.2, 6.3 and 6.5).

ployees, the latter takes the form of social security payments under a variety of schemes not necessarily administered by the state. These payments are spent by their recipients and so are recycled into the economy. Hence there is no inherent limit on the extent of the 'recycling' of money that the state can mandate through the tax and benefit system.

Table 1 illustrates the impact of these two economic categories. The purchase of goods and services influences the 'real economy' of production and employment.

The payment of wages and purchases of land and equipment may become a 'non-market' element in the economy, lacking competitive restraint on price and volume. Politically, it creates vested interests who need the state as an employer or purchaser. In contrast, transfers reallocate spending resources in the economy, usually ameliorating previous inequalities of income. In terms of economic impact they cannot be separated from the tax system, but in terms of political salience there is a vast difference between the concepts of 'welfare spend' and 'tax cut'.

The state has a large presence in modern economies. In 1987 the ratio of public expenditure to Gross Domestic Product (GDP) for all European Community countries exceeded fifty per cent for the first time. Social expenditure - defined as spending on social security, health and education, but excluding housing and tax reliefs - doubled from fifteen to thirty per cent of GDP between 1960 and 1981. Social security transfers, mostly pensions, are on average twenty per cent of GDP. Education is tending to fall and health rise as a share of the social policy total, since the expenditure consequences of mass provision were confronted earlier in the former service.

There are marked variations between countries. Belgium, the Netherlands and Denmark have the highest total spending, with particularly high transfers in the Netherlands (twenty six per cent of GDP) and of final consumption in Denmark (twenty five per cent of GDP, a level second only to Sweden in Europe). This illustrates how welfare states can develop in two directions - the 'money movers' and the 'service producers'. The latter, notably Denmark and the United Kingdom, are the more truly 'welfarist' because they have incorporated welfare into the institutions of state activity.

## The Relationship between Growth and Welfare

EC countries have reached very different levels in their welfare expenditure as well as in their organisational structures. It is remarkable that countries with similar economies cannot be assumed to have similar resource inputs, let alone outcomes like life expectancy or unemployment. Scandinavian academics who start from a pro-welfare perspective explain this in terms of political commitment to welfare and full employment, especially through the influence of labour unions and left-wing parties.[4] In its most developed form this can amount to the 'decommodification' of labour, in which the state provides an adequate income to all, in or out of work. The answer to questions like Therborn's 'Why are some people more unemployed than others?' is held to be that nations wedded to a liberal tradition fail to recognise the dynamic benefit of social and economic protection. Right-wing thinkers are much more sceptical about interfering with the spontaneous workings of economic markets and social norms.

The debate often revolves around notions of value and waste. A great deal of apparent growth can be accounted for by isolating relative price movements, changes in the demographic composition of the population, and extensions of coverage. For instance, wages typically rise faster than average in the health care sector; a high proportion of children or elderly people relative to the wage-earning population necessitates higher social spending; and changes in school-leaving or retirement ages are expensive to finance. OECD data show that in the 1960s 3.2 per cent of the 7.3 per cent annual average growth in welfare's share of national economies was less than 'real' in these senses. The political effort required to finance the spending is less than the perceived benefit received. Unless governments can be persuaded to alter their national accounting systems so that they are better able to measure social values and dynamics, social policy remains dependent on general notions of the strength of economies, as assessed by international capital markets.

Demographic changes have an important influence on growth, because most economic planning assumes a stable ratio of wealth-producers to the total population. The 'demographic wave' or 'baby boom' of the 1950s and 1960s caused a bulge of around twenty five per cent, putting a burden on the educational system in the 1970s, on entry to employment in the 1980s, and eventually on retirement provision around 2020. Since the 1960s the birthrate has fallen to below the replacement level of 2.1 children per woman, to run at between 1.4 and 1.8 in most European countries. Only Ireland, Spain and Greece are achieving replacement birth rates, while Germany and Denmark have the lowest birth rates. Only immigration has prevented the German population from falling since the early 1970s. The ratio of all persons of working age to elderly people will fall from the present 5:1; that of actual wage-earners to pensioners, already little more than 2:1 in most of Europe, may reach 1:1 next century, at least in Germany, with the possibility of an 'inter-generational crisis'. This is counterbalanced by increased female participation in the workforce, now averaging fifty per cent throughout the EC and ranging from thirty nine per cent in Ireland to seventy five per cent in Denmark. This compares with nearly eighty per cent in Sweden (which is in effect nearly one hundred per cent allowing for childbirth and the care of infants) but this raises its own questions about the care of the elderly and the provision of labour in the domestic economy.

An indicator which unites expenditure and demographic variables is the extent of public employment. There is a wide cross-national variation influenced by the labour-intensity of services. For instance, in Britain only three per cent of all social policy employees are needed to run the social security system, compared with eighteen per cent in Germany.[5] Many health employees are, in formal terms, either self-employed or on the staff of hospitals owned by charitable or religious agencies. But they may be regarded as quasi-public employees because of their dependence on state funding and reimbursement. Opinions differ about the use of publicly funded occupational groups to perform social care tasks. In one sense this is a natural expression of the division of labour in advanced economies, but it also produces burdens on public finances as wage costs tend to drift upwards.

At certain levels of state activity, there tends to be resistance to running the social services through state mechanisms of taxing, spending, employment and regulation. It may become attractive to use the domestic or non-monetary economy or even the unofficial economy (also known as black, hidden or shadow) in which money is exchanged but not declared to the authorities. As a rough estimate, about half of the time 'worked' by most people is in the domestic economy, and the black economy amounts to three to five per cent of GDP.[6]

There are obvious economic reasons why the unofficial economy should grow. Taxation and means-testing encourages the concealment of earnings; productive efficiency may be greater in the unofficial and domestic economies. But there are also sociological factors. Non-official production may enhance social integration and the quality of consumer-producer relationships. It may express frustration with the 'welfare state bargain' of high taxes in return for high benefits. European social policy runs the risk of becoming a victim of its own success in securing comprehensive coverage and generous transfers. In the search for the right combination of scale and uniformity, on the one hand, and individuality and self-expression on the other, welfare states have lost the sense of how much they wish to pay for.

## Political and Sociological Factors in Social Policy

Ever since Emile Durkheim analysed the concept of 'anomie' as a condition of modern society, the welfare state has aroused high expectations that it can be more than the sum of its parts, and can guide the 'public household' into the reconciliation of class and group conflicts. Economic complexity can lead to social disintegration; there are casualties of economic change but also great demands for the care and development of the ordinary citizen and family. These demands can only be met through the political system, which operates imperfectly.

Much of the debate about the politics of the welfare state revolves around the success of the political system in translating popular preferences into policy. A simple model would posit a direct transference of demands into action. Party programmes would be constructed to express the demands; voters would choose between them; and an optimal policy would be secured through coalition-building and the working-out of detailed policies in consultation with interest groups. Inevitably, as with economic competition, a degree of imperfection is inherent in the process. Packages of proposals are uneasy compromises, and there is unequal participation in the political process. Significant clienteles of social policies may be excluded altogether, and interest groups may protect producers rather than consumers.

This becomes clear if we assess social policy through the most common image of political competition - left versus right, with working class representatives challenging capitalist interests. As social policies are in principle an exchange between the economically strong and weak (which, of course, may be the same individual at different stages of the life-cycle) they might seem to fall into a natural location in the struggle between left and right. The evidence does not support this, however.

The first problem is that the initial development of welfare states predated the coming to power of left-wing parties. The first national social insurance schemes tended to be under liberal or conservative (especially Catholic) governments. National public education systems are in no sense left-wing artifacts. Even after socialist parties were given a share in office, the evidence is that 'cumulative left power has had no effect on welfare effort or output . . . whatever influence left parties have is indirect and weak'.[7] But in the more recent past there is greater evidence that the turnover of governments does produce an observable effect, with commitment to public welfare falling when left-wing governments are removed from office. This was clearly observable following the advent of conservative-dominated governments in Germany, Belgium, the Netherlands and Denmark in the early 1980s.

The cross-national study by Francis Castles concluded that 'partisan control of governments is a major determinant of policy outputs',[8] but through right-wing governments having a negative impact on expenditure rather than left-wing ones having a positive impact. This may be explained by suggesting that while the structure of welfare states receives support from most political parties, over the long-term the level of input has turned into a matter of political controversy in which the effect of a change of government may be observed. Walter Korpi's study of sickness insurance emphasises the subtlety of the causal process. He found that left party participation in government was a significant factor in extending benefits, but 'left strength' in the form of votes and density of union membership was capable of generating strategic action by non-socialist governments.[9]

The complex nature of attitudes to the welfare state is also evident in data on public opinion. When asked whether they support public spending on welfare services, most Europeans are inclined to say yes. And yet, quite reasonably, they want it both ways. Goals which may be in conflict (eg choice; economy; generosity; protection against abuse) are desired simultaneously. Stein Ringen writes of a tendency for people to be ideological conservatives but operational liberals.[9] They place a different value on different services (retirement and health benefits being most valued, unemployment benefit least). The level of support varies between nations, but the gradient is similar: for instance in a 1985 survey eighty six per cent in Britain but only fifty four per cent in Germany agreed that it was definitely a government responsibility to provide health care for the sick; forty five per cent and twenty four per cent saw a similar responsibility to provide a decent standard of living for unemployed people.[10] Table 2 shows the similarity

**Table 2: Attitudes to welfare state spending (1985 survey)**

| % wanting more state spending on: | Britain | Italy | Germany |
|---|---|---|---|
| Health | 88 | 81 | 52 |
| Old age pensions | 75 | 76 | 46 |
| Education | 75 | 63 | 40 |
| Unemployment benefits | 41 | 57 | 35 |

Source: British Social Attitudes survey (1989) p.41.

of the hierarchy of demands for extra spending in Britain, Italy and Germany: health first, then pensions, education and finally unemployment benefits. Criticism takes the form of scepticism rather than hostility to welfare, which is a difficult emotion to handle politically as it may lead to precipitate changes of policy or government in a way that exaggerates the underlying preferences of the electorate. This was the problem of the 'welfare backlash' of the 1970s.

There is an anti-welfare undercurrent in many European countries, in which social fears are transformed into a dislike of 'scroungers' or of government inefficiency. Populist or protest parties (like the Progress Parties of Denmark, the National Front in France and the Republicans in Germany) have an electoral potential of ten to fifteen per cent of the vote upwards in certain circumstances. But tax revolts like Proposition 13 in California in 1978, when voters cut property taxes, or the insurance premium cut of 1988 in the same state are not really possible within the structure of European politics, because single-issue referenda are not an acceptable device on non-constitutional matters.

## Perspectives for the 1990s

The dramatic political events of 1989 pointed up the dangers of relying on models of social policy that derive from the mid-1970s, when international recession was combined with an arms race and the long-term prospects for socialist ideologies still seemed plausible. It was easy to detect crisis symptoms then, which were in part a delayed reaction to comfortable notions about the sustainability of welfare. Fifteen years later, it is clear that the crisis was somehow overcome, and we need to understand why.

In the first place, the financial arithmetic looks better. Four European Community countries (Italy, Greece, Belgium and the Netherlands) run large public sector deficits but these have all been reduced as a share of national income in the 1980s. It may be difficult to achieve the tax increases or spending cuts necessary to reduce the deficits but the consensus for doing so is present.

Two more general themes are evident: a move towards liberal democracy throughout Europe, and a reassertion of the primacy of work values in economic and social life. The Southern European countries of Greece, Spain and Portugal reasserted democratic forms in the mid-1970s and have sustained them through political disturbance and changes of government. Their social services developed fast, and there was a political push towards contributory benefits in order to promote equity and propriety in public administration. The revolutions of 1989 in Eastern Europe demonstrated the lack of political appeal of even a reformed socialism and the poor quality of many of the social services claimed to be an advantage of the old regimes. Labour-intensive child care might have been good, but matters of technical or financial complexity (health services or income maintenance) were not functioning well. Only East Germany had a substantial contributory pension scheme, whose benefits were boosted to West German levels by the treaty of May 1990. The incorporation of the GDR into the Federal Republic and hence the European Community is a unique possibility; elsewhere in Eastern Europe the achievement of levels of social protection found in the EC will be a much slower and more uncertain process.

The second theme of work values, of a kind of conformity to capitalist package deals, has accompanied retrenchment in Western welfare states. This exploited the mixed public/personal funding of welfare to shift the balance in the personal direction. Even marginal cuts in the state's contribution to the cost of income replacement or medical bills can yield significant savings for governments, who have been tempted into such packages, as in two initiatives to reduce health costs in 1987: the Blum plan in West Germany and the Séguin plan in France. The converse of this were the cuts in marginal tax rates introduced in several countries in the late 1980s. A new consensus that the highest rate of tax should not be above about fifty per cent was sustained by European Community regulations on the free movement of capital. It has forced a greater use of indirect taxation and made it difficult to increase the level of social security contributions, for these need to be aggregated with income tax to produce an indicator of the total burden on the individual.

What this can produce is a crisis of the insurance principle in which the state's role becomes that of reducing burdens rather than providing services. For instance, in Germany there is extensive opting-out of the state health insurance scheme by the higher-income groups who are free to do so and find the private insurance premiums cheaper - an example of the 'creaming-off' seen as a notorious feature of pre-universal insurance. At the same time, the provision of services in kind is threatened by pressures to cut back the size of public bureaucracies and deliver services through non-state institutions. This has happened most explicitly in Britain, where welfare has been squeezed for non-welfare reasons, in the form of economic liberalisation and deconcentration of the state's monopoly position as employer and taxpayer. Intermediate institutions like voluntary organisations are a necessary part of this Conservative vision, but they play a different role from the historical interest groups of other European nations. They are now set up as contrivances to help dismantle the state, or rather conceal its presence behind a network of regulation and subvention. The interconnectedness of European societies and economies is tending to produce imperatives inimical to welfare, leaving only consumption commodities purchased through power in the labour market. Even though the level of welfare is vastly higher than in the mid 19th century, there is a certain reversion to philosophical notions of that time which tended to neglect the value of comprehensive and secure provision used to reinforce social harmony. The catholic notion of 'subsidiarity' - that the state should do only what smaller-scale entities cannot - is widely cited in support of these moves.

The challenge for social policy in the 1990s lies in two areas. First, it must reinforce the technical security of the system, so that financial arrangements do not fall victim to expenditure and demographic crises. Especially in health, techniques for financing and managing complex systems have proved inadequate. Secondly, the relationship between narrowly-defined cash transfers and wider public policy needs to be better understood. Successful social policy requires a stable balance between generations, labour market categories, and types of service. Rather than see welfare as an intense political, economic and sociological problematic, it might be better to treat it as a stable and self-regulating aspect of modern societies, delivering essential services which all will rightly demand. If European Community nations can set clear objectives and develop the technical means of achieving them, some of the historical dynamic that had faltered in the recent past might be recaptured. The process may be aided by the inspiration of the positive international climate set by a reduction in the arms race, the full potential for national self-determination in Europe, and the harmonisation throughout the European Community of the best practices of individual nations.

## References

1. Flora, P. and Alber, J. (1981), 'Modernisation, Democratisation and the Development of Welfare States in Western Europe'. In Flora, P. and Heidenheimer, A. J. (Eds.) *The Development of Welfare States in Europe and America*. Transaction Books, London.

   Heclo, H. (1981), 'Towards a New Welfare State?' In Flora and Heidenheimer op. cit.

2. Marshall, T. H. (1950), *Citizenship and Social Class*. Cambridge University Press, Cambridge.

3. Flora, P. (1986), Introduction to *Growth to Limits* Vol. 1. de Gruyter, Berlin

4. Esping-Andersen, G. (1990), *The Three Worlds of Welfare Capitalism*. Polity Press, Oxford.

   Korpi, W. (1983), *The Democratic Class Struggle*. Routledge and Kegan Paul, London.

   Therborn, G. (1986), *Why Some People are More Unemployed than Others*. Verso, London.

5. Rose, R. (1985), *Public Employment in Western Nations*. Cambridge University Press, Cambridge.

6. Rose, R. (1985), 'Getting By in Three Economies: the Resources of the Official, Unofficial and Domestic Economies'. In Lane, J.-E. (Ed.) *State and Market*. Sage, London.

7. Wilensky, H. (1981), 'Leftism, Catholicism, and Democratic Corporatism: the Role of Political Parties in Recent Welfare State Development'. In Flora and Heidenheimer op. cit., 355.

8. Castles, F. (1982), *The Impact of Parties*. Sage, London, 88.

9. Korpi, W. (1989), 'Power, Politics and State Autonomy in the Development of Social Citizenship: Social Rights During Sickness in Eighteen OECD Countries since 1930' *American Sociological Review*. 54, 309-328.

Ringen, S. (1987), *The Possibility of Politics*. Clarendon Press, Oxford.

10. British Social Attitudes Survey. (1989), *Special International Report*. Gower, Aldershot.

# Chapter 3

# Social Work Practice in Europe: Continuity in Diversity

## Walter Lorenz

The question of the unity of the social work field is as old as the profession itself but the closer integration of European countries poses it with renewed poignancy. In essence, it asks whether social work is simply a collection of practices whose development depended on specific historical conditions, or whether it has eman-cipated itself from these historical ties and can determine its own boundaries. In the first case, the trans-national compatibility of social work depends on external, political and legal conditions largely outside its control. On the other hand, if the profession has gained autonomy and realised its critical potential vis-à-vis these outer constraints, then social workers themselves can be in charge of establishing the unity of the field, although there is then always the danger of one of the elements making 'imperialist' claims to represent 'true' social work.

However, it will be hypothesised in this chapter that the enmeshment with historical and political processes is the very essence of social work as a profession oriented towards bringing about social change. Social workers are neither mere functionaries of bureaucracies nor mere therapists and counsellors. The political, social and legal context in which their clients' difficulties arise is their primary domain, although this context never determines the social work agenda entirely. The following comparative observations aim therefore not just at highlighting the diversity of social work; they also relate this diversity back to questions concern-ing the nature and boundaries of social work by looking at the various ways it is demarcated, conceptualised and implemented.

The identity of something like 'European social work' is hard to recognise and can certainly not be established by administrative or linguistic procedures. But just as the identities of the almoner, the probation officer and the child care worker have in the British case somehow found their (not undisputed) common expression in the title of social worker without blurring all the distinct areas of responsibility and corresponding principles of practice, so it might be possible to recognise common features in social work across Europe without disregarding distinct competencies. Furthermore, diversity and diffuse boundaries, rather than being a sign of social work's inferior, 'immature' professional status[1] may emerge as central positive characteristics of a professional field that has a critical mandate in society and therefore has to examine constantly its 'relevance' to that changing scenario.

The problem therefore is not how to overcome the diversity and to find a term or concept general enough to capture all the different manifestations. Rather, efforts must be concentrated on evaluating the significance of the variations in practice. There are examples of social work professionals carrying out at times identical functions and yet bearing different titles (eg Sozialarbeiter/Sozialpäda-goge in Germany, éducateur/animateur in France). There are titles that appear identical in different languages and suggest an identity of functions whilst different legal and organisational frameworks render the forms of practice quite incompatible. For example, some of the statutory functions of a German social worker or 'Sozialarbeiter' and of the Danish equivalent, the 'Socialraadgiver', are clearly those of a British social security officer. Finally some tasks are the prerogative of social workers in one country but in others are carried out by members of other professions (eg nursery nurses, occupational therapists) or indeed by unqualified volunteers.

In order to understand the significance of cross-national differences in the practice and the titles of social work, it is necessary to consider a combination of determinants simultaneously. Social work's inevitable links with social policy make it appear a historically conditional discipline. The development of an autonomous training tradition helped to underpin its professional independence, although this remains relative not least on account of the central ethical maxim of enhancing self-help abilities in clients. This conjures up the possibility of making the profession redundant or merging it with the activities of volunteers in wanting to represent more closely the needs of the users of services. It appears useful, therefore, to conduct these international comparisons by investigating how social work in a particular national context relates to the forces mapped along the following *three axes*, recognising that these influences do not represent impurities or distortions, but are inseparable from the essence of social work:

1. principles of social policy

2. educational traditions

3. responses to articulated needs

## Social work and social policy

Social work is an intrinsic part of a country's social policy structure. This manifests itself not just in the regulations determining daily tasks but also in the broader public perceptions of the social work role.

*a) General features and traditions of social policy and their effect on social work*

Where social work has developed as part of an (until recently) taken-for-granted notion of a welfare state as in Britain, it can be portrayed more readily as a coherent whole than in countries like Germany or Ireland where the welfare functions of the state are limited by the principle of 'subsidiarity'. This principle is a centre-piece of both the liberal concept of state-society relations and of Roman Catholic social teaching (Encyclical 'Quadrogesimo anno' of 1931). It states that the responsibility for securing well-being should rest with the smallest, most immediate 'social unit' of which an individual may be part (the family, the neighbourhood, the church community, the self-regulated association and only finally the state). Support by the bigger unit should be confined to enhancing the initiative of the smaller unit and must not aim at replacing it. In Germany particularly this principle helped to consolidate the position and influence of the so-called 'free welfare associations' of the main religious groupings (Catholic, Jewish, Protestant) and of other associations like the Red Cross and the Labour Movement. In consequence, personal social services in Germany tend to be distributed over an unusually wide variety of agencies and organisations. This is also true in the Netherlands, where sectoral interest groups (like churches, trade unions, political parties) led to a 'pillarisation' ('verzuiling') of society which is in turn reflected in ideologically segregated social services.[2] In societies following this model of social policy the state sector employs social workers only to carry out narrowly defined statutory responsibilities especially in relation to child care and to income maintenance. A notable example are social workers within the youth office in Germany who de facto fulfil family support functions. However, there is much more scope for imaginative differentiations of social work tasks and methods within the voluntary agencies, some of whom operate in competition with each other. It may also be that in such fragmented systems the 'blame' for continuing social problems is shared among several professions or pinned on the 'smaller unit' ie 'the family', whereas social workers within an integrated welfare structure are more susceptible to becoming the sole scapegoats.

*b) De-centralisation*

The push towards de-centralisation and local and regional autonomy in countries that had previously been very strongly centralised (like France, Greece, Italy, Portugal and Spain) has also had a profound effect on the nature of social work. Not only has the profession grown numerically as a result, it has also had to become more responsive to the changing expressions of need to which it became more directly exposed. In Italy this is enshrined in Law 833 of 1978 which de-centralised health and social services (Unita Sanitaria Locale, USL), whilst in France regional health and Social Service administrations (DRASS) were created in 1977 and a Decentralisation Act passed in 1982. In Italy the law afforded opportunities for the establishment of inter-disciplinary community teams in which social work plays a significant part, equal to that of psychologists and the medical personnel, giving the workers considerable autonomy and scope to respond to local requirements. In Greece regional centres are designed to have all main central government departments represented, including social welfare and regional health centres. The question is however whether this model confines social work functions within a 'health' framework (albeit defined as social health) or whether it re-defines the whole notion of 'health' precisely through the co-operation of social professions as attempted in some parts of Italy ('Unita *Socio*-Sanitarie Locali', USSL) and in Catalonia in Spain.[3]

*c) Statutory Frameworks*

There appear to be wide discrepancies between European countries in the extent to which social work tasks are actually sanctioned or prescribed by law. Ireland and Germany may be taken to represent opposite ends of the scale. In Ireland the involvement of social workers in statutory responsibilities with respect to child care and mental health is largely a matter of custom and practice. Social workers are not mentioned explicitly in any piece of legislation.[4] Whilst new child care legislation is in preparation, up to now legislation from 1908 (predating the emergence of social work and Irish independence from Britain) has been used to sanction the duties of social workers in relation to taking children into care. By contrast, social workers in German statutory services are caught up in a process of increasing 'legalisation' ('Verrechtlichung'), ie the tendency to regulate progressively more individual situations of need through statutory provisions.[5] On the one hand this affords the individual citizen the right to claim assistance in specific circumstances (eg adaptations and aids for people with various disabilities) and allows social workers to mobilise resources accordingly. On the other hand it embroils social workers in a dense net of regulations which can become the prime reference point for intervention. Social workers in Germany acting 'on behalf of the state' are part of an elaborate system of public administration whose duties are minutely prescribed by law at local, regional, state and federal level all within the framework of the written constitution (Grundgesetz). They have to remain conscious that as public servants their interventions have statutory character and can be subjected to legal scrutiny. This situation, though in much more pervasive form, resembles the conditions created in the UK for the first time by the introduction of 'approved social workers' in the mental health field. Social workers play a central role in 'individualising' the general provisions of social welfare legislation which cannot cover every eventuality. German social workers in the public sector are directly involved in the administration of welfare benefits, as elsewhere in the EC (eg Denmark, France, Greece, Italy). Thus, Grundger observed that

> 'The efficiency of the social security policy (in Germany) rests not only on social insurance and other welfare assistance measures, but decisively on the individualising task of the personal social services to supplement and adjust these measures'.[6]

*d) Social workers as public servants*

The nature and structure of public services of a country has also a significant bearing on whether social workers are employed on the strength of their professional training and qualifications, or whether they are employed for managerial functions which could be carried out by people from a cluster of training backgrounds. In countries like Greece, Italy and Spain, public employees in higher grades need to be university graduates whereas social work training does not yet extend into the 'graduate' programmes of universities. Hence graduates from disciplines like sociology, psychology, law or general arts are advantaged over qualified social workers in relation to higher positions in social services.[7]

In the absence of any clear guidance from the statutory sector, many posts in the non-statutory field are not reserved for qualified social workers and functions may overlap with those of educators, pedagogues, psychologists, nurses and other medical and para-medical personnel. For instance, a survey of social work positions advertised in Germany in 1988 found that only seventy per cent specified a qualification in social work or social pedagogics as essential. The remaining thirty per cent were open to other professionals, particularly pedagogues (ten per cent), therapeutic pedagogues (six per cent), and psychologists (four per cent).[8] This trend seems to be strengthening compared to previous studies.

As far as shared responsibilities are concerned, an Italian study found a considerable overlap between psychologists, social workers and community health workers (assistenti sanitari), particularly in tasks like groupwork, liaison with institutions, psycho-social diagnosis to establish resource needs and identifying eligibility for welfare subsidies.[9]

It appears therefore that social work has limited control over its field but receives its mandate largely from the general structure of services or more cynically from the gaps in service provisions.

*e) Impact of recent social policy changes*

In most European countries the 'crisis in welfare' and the associated fiscal restrictions during the 1980s had a major impact on the development of forms of social work practice. The central dilemma is that at the same time as public resources became more restricted (eg in relation to hospital beds, residential places or income maintenance payments) the demand for these services increased due to demographic changes and to growing unemployment with its concomitant social problems. Consequently, the task of social workers in allocating these scarcer resources on a professional basis has become more difficult. Social work functions may often have to concentrate on administrative tasks leaving less room for counselling or preventive work (eg in Germany).[10] Social work posts have not been cut as a result of tighter fiscal policies everywhere. For instance Spain continued to expand its newly created public social services vigorously in the 1980s.[11] In Germany the rapid growth of the 1970s slowed down, but no direct reductions in overall posts were reported.

By contrast, in Ireland there has been a loss of nearly ten per cent of social work posts, even though a substantial expansion had been planned at the end of the 1970s. Similarly a packet of reforming measures for the establishment of comprehensive services at local level in Italy never came to full fruition due to fiscal constraints, leaving a very uneven pattern of service distribution.[12]

This meant that on the whole social work functions in public services narrowed their scope to acute crisis work rather than realising their preventive potential. This heightened their social control element and widened the discrepancy between workers perceived as part of the tightfisted welfare bureaucracy and professionals in the independent sector with a more benign image. The voluntary services were less directly affected by these restrictions. Thus in Germany the only real growth occurred in this sector. More jobs were advertised by church employers (forty six per cent) than in the public sector (seventeen per cent) according to Sauer et al.[13]

In terms of 'community orientation' or more specifically the development of 'community social work', social policy decisions had a crucial though highly ambivalent effect. Moves towards de-centralisation often implied greater responsiveness to the needs of users of social services, not just as individuals but as groups and as people who identify with a geographical area. In this regard, the Italian 'experiment' with psychiatric de-institutionalisation and 'democratic psychiatry' was not an isolated development but had its parallel in the establishment of multi-disciplinary community health care teams and in the setting up of integrated schools. Indirectly, the withdrawal of resources from state residential care and other economies in the provision of health and institutional care meant that social workers of necessity had to shift their expertise more decisively from mediating between individuals and institutions to negotiating with informal support networks within 'the community'. In several countries, notably the Netherlands and Germany, this trend coincided with the emergence of self-help initiatives, some of which imply a direct critique of the dominance of the state bureaucracy. The community orientation represents therefore a strange confluence of conservative and 'radical' ideologies which will be discussed further in the final section.

## Educational Traditions and Professional Identity

Social workers occupying identical positions sometimes come from very different training backgrounds. Despite the attempts by the core of European 'pioneers' in social work training, together with their American counterparts, to 'internationalise' social casework in the 1920s and early 1930s it cannot be assumed that their model represented the standard form of social work. The relationship between social work practice and social work training has always been a two-directional affair. Education comes in a sense after practice, systematises, categorises and analyses developments in the field, yet it also has its own traditions, dynamics and rationale. For instance, the influence of pedagogical concepts on forms of continental European social work practice has been as important as that of disciplines like sociology and psychology.

In Belgium, Denmark, France, Germany and the Netherlands two distinct though intersecting professional groupings, social work and social pedagogy, make up what in English is termed 'social work'. The collective title 'travailleurs sociaux' in France encompasses 'assistantes sociales', éducateurs spécialisés and 'animateurs', signifying that social work has several conceptual strands.

How this overlap came about historically is perhaps best illustrated by tracing briefly the development of 'Sozialpädagogik' in Germany where today the boundary between social work and social pedagogy has become unclear even for Germans. In the climate of Bismarck's social policy towards the end of the 19th century academic circles promoted idealistic notions of a 'renewal of society' through educational campaigns aimed not only at universal schooling but at adult education, cultural renewal and youthwork.[14] These social-pedagogical concerns found an intellectual base in education departments of German universities particularly in the 1920s while simultaneously the new Weimar constitution gave social pedagogy a key role in social policy. This helped to 'pedagogise social work' when earlier on 'pedagogy had been socialised',[15] making German social work from the outset less dependent on psychotherapeutic concepts than in Britain and the USA. After the collapse of the Hitler regime the framework of the Weimar youth and welfare legislation was left largely intact in the re-building of West German society and the slowly emerging personal social services saw the distinction between social work and social pedagogy initially preserved. Staff in kindergartens, nurseries, youth organisations and residential institutions tended to receive the social pedagogy type education while workers in public welfare organisations trained in social work.

The gradual merger of the professional groupings occurred in the 1970s. An emphasis on 'process' gained prominence in both 'progressive education' and 'radical social work' which helped to reduce the conceptual and methodological differences. Moreover from a more pragmatic view, social pedagogy meant access to university level education through its attachment to education departments, whilst the vocational opportunities in the 'social' field in turn promised to open up employment opportunities for university trained pedagogues whom the school system could no longer absorb.

Pedagogy as the skill of developing a person's inherent potential need not be confined to education or to young people at all, although working with youth remains one of its most prominent applications. The fact that the titles Sozialpädagoge or éducateur/animateur can extend to responsibilities in the areas of community action, adult literacy, leisure activities for all ages, music, art and occupation therapy indicates that their identity rests with their methodology rather than their organisational structure. It is much harder to establish this professional unity where the title derives from a field of practice ('youth and community worker', 'child care worker', 'adult literacy worker'). Pedagogy provides a framework utilised by both conservative and socialist ideologues. English-speaking readers associate the notion of 'pedagogy' perhaps more readily with Freire's

*Pedagogy of the Oppressed* which of course has its roots in this tradition but the potential of pedagogy as a tool for social engineering has persisted since the days of Bismarck.

The existence of the dual titles in Germany epitomises a latent tension inherent in all European countries. What is particular to the German situation is only the degree of interchangeability the two strands have reached. 'Éducateurs' (with various specifications such as éducateur spécialisé, éducateur de jeunes enfants, éducateur social) are also found in Belgium and France, and have their equivalents elsewhere (the 'educatore especializzato' in Italy, socio-educational workers in Denmark). They work in residential institutions, day care centres, projects for people with special needs and in community initiatives. The Dutch Ministry for Social Work, set up in 1952, was re-named in 1965 as Ministry for Culture, Leisure and Social Work (Cultur, Recreatie en Maatschappelijk Werk) and later still for Welfare, Health and Culture, which illustrates the fluid boundaries of the state's welfare concerns. As yet there is no recognised umbrella title to capture this diverse field ('community education' is an approximate equivalent), but the field itself is no more diverse than that marked by the title 'social work'.

Seen from a methodological perspective, the boundary disputes between professional groupings within the 'family' of social work occupations are not petty territorial claims but express the ongoing quest in the social professions for a central theoretical model capable of dealing with the complexity of practice. The suspicion remains probably on both sides that by not upholding a particular theoretical tradition and position, the profession would lose its autonomy and turn into a bureaucratic tool for the administration of welfare policies. This autonomy is at times tied to (but by no means secured by) the university status of the discipline of pedagogy above all in Germany, Italy and to some extent in France. However in a country like Ireland the status differential is reversed: all social work training takes place at the university level, whereas social care education, in many ways the direct equivalent to social pedagogy, is offered by non-university higher education institutions.[16]

In France the differentiation of pedagogical training patterns has been taken even further with the creation in 1979 of the qualification of 'animateurs' (socio-cultural workers in community centres, leisure and social action projects) competing sometimes for the same ground as the 'éducateurs'.[17] Comparisons with the British tradition of 'youth and community work' training spring to mind revealing a significant though not a total correspondence. The differences arise once again not just from the variations in fields of activity (animateurs work with all age groups and extend their competence into the fields of play therapy or rehabilitation for people with disabilities) but much more significantly from the distinct theoretical starting positions: animateurs originated in a climate of political critique of the case-work model of social work.

Taking titles and qualifications together with their respective training avenues as a criterion for professional identity (rather than the activities prescribed by employing agencies) opens up once more the vexed question, whether the field of 'social work type activities' is defined by an outer perimeter or by a core. How are we to decide whether probation work lies within the field and nursing, occupational therapy, career counselling or consumer advice lie outside?

There exists something like a methodological consensus as far as casework approaches are concerned which may offer opportunities for cross-national understanding, but it is worth examining whether this is based purely on methodological, politically neutral principles. The consensus has as much to do with the adaptation of the 'social diagnosis' approach promoted by Mary Richmond to European conditions (Alice Salomon's work was seminal in Germany in the 1920s[18]), as with the internationally backed (re-)construction of social work education in several European countries after World War II. Social work methods based on the notion of encouraging self-help and 'client self-determination' gained prominence by virtue of the fact that prospective trainers from countries like Italy, Greece, the Scandinavian countries and to a lesser extent also Germany and Ireland had to be trained abroad, which meant in the USA or in the UK where this case-work model had been firmly established, ironically with contributions from emigré Europeans like Salomon and Friedländer.[19] Initiating social work education programmes was also part of a political programme of democratising the social infra-structure of countries recovering from the devastation of Fascism and war.[20] It could be speculated that pedagogical methods within social work were not only not available in the English-speaking countries hosting the training for trainers, they were also ideologically suspect because of their non-individualist orientation. Re-educating the masses had been the corner stone of fascist propaganda; the task was now to build up the autonomous, 'self-determining' capacities of individuals.[21]

## Social Work as a Response to Articulated Needs

In spite of continuing boundary problems with other occupational groups and internal conceptual ambiguities, professionalisation has assisted social work in forming a fairly coherent identity, not least by putting professional practice at a distance from the functions of untrained volunteers. However, recent demands for de-professionalisation have called into question the justifications for this distance. The critique of elitist implications of professionalisation arose specifically from the student movements of the 1960s and this left its mark on the social work professions in most West European countries. This political discourse exposed the dishonesty of the assumed neutrality of the professional and sought to fill this conceptual vacuum with explicit political norms and values.[22] Its intention was to make social work more responsive to the needs of its users, challenging it to address the processes responsible for producing structural inequalities and thereby to reduce the element of social control it was in danger of exercising 'inadvertently'. For instance, after the revolution in Portugal in 1974 social workers were generally criticised for their technocratic orientation and this critique was officially adopted by some of the social work schools, as in Lisbon.[23] In the wake of these self-critical processes any uncertainties over the status of the social work profession appear as much self-induced as the product of imposed political and fiscal restrictions.

The resulting 'fluidity' between professional expertise, political campaigning and self-help organisation seems to have established itself in two broad areas across several European countries: community action (including youthwork, women's action, work with refugees and other minority groups) and therapeutic initiatives (with people with drug dependencies, in the psychiatric field and other areas of 'problematic behaviour'). The most celebrated example of the latter kind was perhaps the Italian movement of 'psichiatria democratica' with its aim of dissolving institutional barriers, be they buildings or organisations. This affected parts of the psychiatric profession even more tangibly than the social work profession.[24] Organisationally, these tendencies located themselves within the 'newer' manifestations of social work such as social pedagogy in Germany, animateurs in France, or socio-cultural 'Opbouwwerk' in the Netherlands.

It is ironic that social work's professional aspirations have more recently been made the butt of conservative critiques with the intention of introducing tighter administrative controls on the core statutory activities and delegating other functions increasingly to volunteers. Perhaps nothing highlights social work's status insecurity more than the use of volunteers in personal social services as they are a reminder of social work's pre-professional past. And yet, the use of volunteers in the 'caring' field is currently expanding in countries which otherwise have a high level of professionalisation, notably Belgium, Germany and the Netherlands. This trend is intrinsically linked to the notion of 'community care' and the politically ambivalent function this concept has assumed. On the one hand, there had been a decisive move from within the social work profession to make its work more responsive to the community, to involve clients in larger areas of decision making and more recently to have the ethnic characteristics of the community represented in the ranks of the professionals. This slowly opened up opportunities for members of ethnic minority groups to be recruited into areas of social work (second generation immigrants in France and the Netherlands, migrant workers in Germany). On the other hand there are self-help movements emerging which take a definite anti-professional stance ('expertocracy'). In particular the women's movement, welfare rights, youth and community work, streetwork and drug treatment projects have produced this picture in highly developed welfare societies.

However, it has to be recognised that overall the growing participation of non-professionals in the wider social care field, whilst being methodologically challenging, does not seem likely to reduce the number and significance of social work professionals. On the contrary, self-help initiatives sometimes break a path for the subsequent professionalisation of a field, not least by sharpening the articulation of needs in society. State or larger voluntary organisations will in time respond by creating posts for 'accountable' professionals and putting them in charge.[25,26]

The experience of the effects of the 'crisis of the welfare state' in virtually all European Countries showed that, by not being entrenched in a high-status professional model and by being confronted with the necessity to re-evaluate constantly its boundaries both towards other professionals and towards untrained practitioners, social work may actually endure changing political and social scenarios rather well.

## Evaluation and Outlook

The significance of a particular variety of social work practice in the countries touched upon cannot be understood as a product of any one of the dimensions selected. An understanding of the character and meaning of any form of social work needs to make reference to the 'underlying dynamics' ie the interaction between social policy, professional autonomy and consumer demands, rather than rest with their 'frozen' manifestations (such as titles, job descriptions, employ-ment and career structure). This means for instance that it may be as important to look at the methodology applied in a voluntary project as at its voluntary status in order to assess the extent of its involvement in social control. Social work within a church organisation need not at all mean 'conservative' work practices or a denial of welfare rights. Indeed, some of the more 'radical' forms of social work practice can be found in church-funded projects, as in Germany or the Netherlands.

Equally, the complexity of factors that make up the identity of a professional activity indicate that it is constantly in flux and that any professional group barricading itself behind fixed and rigid criteria does so at its peril. This is not to say that changes should be accepted uncritically - on the contrary. Only the realisation that a form of practice is always more than the application of a particular set of theories, more than the implementation of administrative directives, more than an immediate response to expressed needs can lead to a realistic and ethically as well as politically justifiable interpretation of professional autonomy and of 'practice-relevant' training. Greater opportunities for getting to know other forms of European social work in an integrated Europe are a live laboratory setting for the study of these complex relationships and above all an invitation for the critical re-evaluation of one's own tradition and practice.

In conclusion, there are no clear 'trends' emerging in this brief review of themes in European social work practice, but the following developments may be of significance across national boundaries:

• There is a continued and perhaps increasing emphasis on individualised welfare service delivery despite the growth of universal welfare entitlements. The mediation between socio-political structures producing their own functional rationality[27] and the constituency of people affected by them is a key part of any modern welfare system and recognised as such by governments in Europe regardless of their political persuasion. This development has led in turn to growing expectations of improved individualised assistance for vulnerable groups (the elderly, children, migrant and refugee groups), whereby it remains an open question which of these are to be met predominantly through professionals or through volunteers.

• Welfare benefits work and therapeutic interventions seem to have become more polarised, either as functions within agencies or between distinct professional groups. This trend is related to a re-emerging split and a politically ambiguous relationship between public and private welfare services which creates opportunities for higher professional status within the latter thus eroding the autonomy and self-confidence of the former even further.[28]

• Resource constraints on public social services force them to concentrate more and more on crisis work. As prevention remains an unrealised ideal this highlights the precarious position of social work in society and its symbolic function in the management of social conflict. Consequently, the link between social work practice and participation in social policy formulation remains tenuous.

Everything that can be said about social work remains relative: to political, social and legal conditions; to the concepts developed in allied disciplines; to changing users of social services. Social workers will have to learn to live with more of that relativity as cultural, ethnic, legal and political norms interact ever more acutely across Europe. The position of a profession placed socially and politically on the boundaries between so many divisions should make it eminently capable of conceptualising and assisting in these further frontier crossings faced by the people of Europe.

## References

1. Stevenson, O. (1986), 'The Personal Social Services'. In Wilding, P. (Ed.) *In Defence of the Welfare State*. Manchester University Press, 123.

2. Van Schedelen, M. P. C. M. (1984), 'Consociationalismus, Pillarisation and Conflict Management in the Low Countries' *Acta Politica* 19, (special issue).

3. Rossell, T. (1987), *L'Entrevista en el Treball Social*. Euge, Barcelona.

4. Gilligan, R., Kearney, N., and Lorenz, W. (1987), 'Intermediäre Hilfesysteme personenbezogener Dienstleistungen in der Republik Irland'. In Bauer, R., and Thränhardt, A.-M. (Eds.) *Verbandliche Wohlfahrtspflege im Internationalen Vergleich*, Westdeutscher Verlag, Opladen.

5. Voigt, R. (1980), *Verrechtlichung*. Konigstein.

6. Gründger, F. (1987), 'Brauchen wir eine ökonomik der sozialen Dienste?' *Soziale Arbeit*. 36, 12, 445-450.

7. Rossell, T., and Rimbau, C. (1989), 'Spain - Social Services in the Post-Franco Democracy'. In Munday, B. (Ed.) *The Crisis in Welfare*. Harvester, Hemel Hempstead, 105-123.

8. Sauer, P., Metzmacher, U., and Groll, D. (1988), 'Wer vergibt die Jobs von morgen? Eine Analyse von Stellenanzeigen für den Bereich der sozialen Arbeit' *Soziale Arbeit* 37, 9, 314-321.

9. Bernardi, L., De Sandre, I., Giraldo, S., Grigoletti, P., and Niero, M. (1985), *Professionalità sociale e innovazione*. Capelli, Bologna, 138-140.

10. Sudbrink, S., Sagebiel, J., and Nolte, J. (1989), 'Erwachsenenhilfe im Sozialamt' *Soziale Arbeit*. 38, 1, 9-16.

11. Gründger, op. cit.

12. Rebuffat, P. (1982), 'La politica ed il servizio sociale nelle prospettive della Pubblica Amministrazione'. In Ruggeri, F. (Ed.) *Assistente Sociale - processi di cambiamento politica dei servizi*. Nuova Guaraldi, Florence.

13. Sauer et al., op. cit.

14. Wendt, W. R. (1989), 'Hundert Jahre "Sozialpädagogik", Erinnerungen an ihre politischen Anfänge' *Soziale Arbeit* 38, 5, 158-164.

15. Wendt, W. R. (1985), *Geschichte der sozialen Arbeit*. Enke Verlag, Stuttgart.

16. Lorenz, W. (1986), 'Social Work Education in Ireland'. In Brauns, H.-J., and Kramer, D. (Eds.) *Social Work Education in Europe*. Deutscher Verein, Frankfurt, 293-320.

17. Ion, J. and Tricart, J.-P. (1984), *Les Travailleurs Sociaux*. Editions La Découverte, Paris.

18. Salomon, A. (1926), *Soziale Diagnosis*. Heymanns, Berlin.

19. Friedlander, W. A. (1975), *International Social Welfare*. Prentice-Hall, Englewood Cliffs.

20. Myrdal, A., Altmeyer, A. J. and Rusk. D. (1955), *America's Role in International Social Welfare*. Columbia University Press, New York.

21. *Training for Social Work* (1958). Third International Survey, United Nations, UN Publications, New York, 83.

22. Thiersch, H. (1981), 'Die Zukunft der Sozialarbeit und der sozialen Berufe'. In Projektgruppe Soziale Berufe (Ed.) *Sozialarbeit: Ausbildung und Qualifikation; Expertisen*, Juventa, Munich, 20-38.

23. Athayde Flora, I. M. (1986), 'Social Work Education in Portugal'. In Brauns, H.-J. and Kramer, D. *Social Work Education in Europe*. Deutscher Verein, Frankfurt, 437-450.

24. Ramon, S. (1983), 'Psichiatria Democratica: A case study of an Italian Community Mental Health Service' *International Journal of Health Services*. 13, 2, 307-324.

25. Kramer, J. (1986), 'Ehrenamtliche Mitarbeit - persönliches Bedürfnis oder politischer Bedarf?' *Soziale Arbeit*. 35, 9, 334-337.

26. Pasquay, N. Windisch, M. and Bubenheim, D. (1988), 'Zum Bedarf an Sozialarbeitern/Sozialpädagogen' *Soziale Arbeit*. 37, 11, 407-414.

27. Habermas, J. (1976), *Legitimation Crisis*. Heinemann, London.

28. Baron, R., and Landwehr, R. (1989), 'Zum Wandel beruflicher Identität - der Verlust bürgerlichen Selbstbewusstseins in der sozialen Arbeit'. In Olk, T. and Otto, H.-U. (Eds.) *Soziale Dienste im Wandel 2*. Luchterhand, Neuwied, 139-167.

*Chapter 4*

# Social Work Education and Professional Development

## H.-J. Brauns and David Kramer

Although the European Community has expended much energy in the pursuit of greater cultural, political and economic integration, member countries still tend to know very little about each other in the field of social work. Basic data on the education of social workers in the various national contexts - not to mention comparative analyses - are still all too rare.

In 1986 we edited a comprehensive description of social work education in Europe.[1] The information in the present overview has been taken, with some modification, from that volume; it was not possible to update all the information for this overview, as would have been desirable.

### Instead of a Definition of Social Work

The term 'social work' often covers widely divergent conceptions and realities. The taxonomical imprecision which is endemic in social work practice and education has direct consequences for our overview. It is not possible to state flatly how many schools of social work there are in Europe. Moreover, professional social work practice includes persons who were trained in a variety of different institutions with varying educational programs.

We apply the definition of social work education used by the International Association of Schools of Social Work (IASSW) to define eligibility for membership. The IASSW recognises only institutions of tertiary education, whose training qualifies for the practice of social work according to the respective national guidelines. This formal criterion excludes, eg 'youth and community work' in the UK and Ireland and 'Erziehungswissenschaften' in West Germany. With respect to France and Belgium, we focus on the education of the 'assistant(e) de service social' (France) and the 'assistant(e) social(e)' (Belgium).

There is a certain circularity in a definition of a profession which itself makes reference to national guidelines whose criteria remain unspecified. Such a defini- tion - although slightly better than nothing - can only be functional. Much work remains to be done before a definition of social work and social work education in Europe can be formulated with prescriptive authority.

## Social Work Education within the National Systems of Education

In all the countries under consideration, the education of social workers takes place within the tertiary system of education and mostly at the undergraduate level. Ireland and the UK also offer the possibility of a (first) qualification in social work for graduates and non-graduates. Belgium, France, and the Nether- lands offer highly specialised courses of study (see Table 1). Luxembourg, too, with no schools of social work of its own, has licensing regulations which favour the highly specialised courses offered by most of its neighbours. In all the other countries, students receive a generic qualification which formally qualifies them for the wide range of social work practice. However, this is the result of a long and contested process which has led from specialisation to greater generalisation.

### Table 1: Specialisation and central regulation of training*

| | Generic | Central Regulation | |
| --- | --- | --- | --- |
| | | Type | Body |
| B (Belgium) | no | Regulation | Education |
| D (West Germany) | yes | None | - |
| DK (Denmark) | yes | Regulation | Legislation |
| E (Spain) | yes | Regulation | Legislation |
| F (France) | no | Regulation | Legislation |
| GB (Great Britain) | yes | Accreditation | CCETSW |
| GR (Greece) | yes | Regulation | Education |
| I (Italy) | yes | None | - |
| IRL (Ireland) | yes | Accreditation | CCETSW |
| L (Luxembourg) | no | Regulation | Health |
| NL (Netherlands) | no | Regulation | Government |
| P (Portugal) | yes | Regulation | Education |

* For the sake of convenience our tables use the abbreviations of international automobile regis- trations.

Countries like West Germany, Ireland and the UK adopted the generic approach recently, and the issue is still controversial.

At least two countries do entirely without centralised supervision of social work education (West Germany and Italy). The most centralised form of oversight seems to exist in Ireland and the UK where the Central Council for Education and Training in Social Work (CCETSW) closely monitors the requirements and content of courses as well as degrees and certification. Some countries regulate social work education in varying measure through legislation (eg Denmark, France or Spain), while others (Belgium, Greece, Luxembourg, the Netherlands, Portugal) delegate authority for oversight to the Ministry of Education or of Health. Such arrangements guarantee the comparability of courses through more or less detailed curricular regulations (eg France and Spain), or - as especially in Ireland and the UK - through prerequisites and criteria for courses of study and examinations, validation and recognition of degrees and professional licensing. A certain tension seems to exist nearly everywhere between centralised regulation and institutional autonomy, although the balance between the two is drawn differently in every country.

## Institutions of Social Work Education

There are a total of at least 387 institutions offering social work education in the twelve EC member countries. This figure, which should be regarded as an order of magnitude rather than as a hard fact, comprises only distinct institutions, not various faculties, divisions, departments etc. within a single institution. In other words, it ignores the fact that in West Germany and in the UK, for example, social workers are sometimes educated in different departments of the same institution. By the same token, it also does not include institutions in France and Belgium which educate for professions other than that of 'assistant(e) social(e)'. Thus we are aware of at least 160 educational institutions in France which offer various specialisations within the social professions, but only fifty two of these are included in our compilation (Table 2).

Social work education is offered exclusively by publicly financed institutions in Denmark, Greece, Ireland and the UK. Dutch schools of social work are private institutions. All other countries are characterised by a mixture of private and public institutions. In some countries private status and religious orientation are closely related. In Portugal and Spain there is a numerical preponderance of educational institutions with some affiliation to the Roman Catholic Church. In the remaining countries, public institutions are more numerous.

## Table 2: Schools of Social Work

| | Number | | | Character | | Date First School Established |
|---|---|---|---|---|---|---|
| | *Total* | *University* | *Extra* | *Private* | *Public* | |
| B | 23 | - | 23 | 4 | 19 | 1920 |
| D | 49 | 5 | 44 | 16 | 33 | 1899 |
| DK | 6 | 1 | 5 | - | 6 | 1937 |
| E | 28 | 28 | - | 24 | 4 | 1932 |
| F | 52 | 2 | 50 | 41 | 11 | 1907 |
| GB | 86 | 33 | 53 | - | 86 | 1896 |
| GR | 3 | - | 3 | - | 3 | 1945 |
| I | 98 | 7 | 91 | 79 | 12 | 1928/45 |
| IRL | 3 | 3 | - | - | 3 | 1934 |
| L | - | - | - | - | - | - |
| NL | 36 | - | 36 | 36 | - | 1896 |
| P | 3 | - | 3 | 2 | 1 | 1935 |

## Table 3: Social work education in the educational system

| | Tertiary Sector | Institutional Setting | | 1st Qualification | |
|---|---|---|---|---|---|
| | | *university* | *extra-u.* | *undergrad.* | *grad.* |
| B | x | - | x | x | |
| D | x | x | x | x | |
| DK | x | x | x | x | |
| E | x | x | - | x | |
| F | x | x | x | x | |
| GB | x | x | x | x | x |
| GR | x | - | x | x | |
| I | x | x | x | x | |
| IRL | x | x | - | x | x |
| L | x | - | x | x | |
| NL | x | - | x | x | |
| P | x | - | x | x | |

The trend toward integration of social work education into the tertiary system of education - and the increased qualitative, quantitative and, particularly, financial challenges which this implies - have exacerbated the inherent difficulties of organisation and funding social work education under private auspices. In some countries private institutions benefit from considerable public subsidies (eg West Germany). In general, however, the relative contribution of private institutions has declined with the 'academisation' of social work education. This process is well underway in Greece and similar developments seem likely in Italy and Spain.

Social workers are educated exclusively at universities in Ireland and Spain. They are educated both at universities and in other types of institutions in Denmark, France, West Germany, Italy and the UK, but only in the UK are university and extra-university education accorded a status which is ostensibly equal. Elsewhere social work education takes place exclusively in extra-university institutions of higher education (Belgium, Greece, the Netherlands, Portugal).

In the majority of countries the situation can be described as an incomplete transition towards 'academisation' - a transition, however, whose outcome is still

**Table 4: Characteristics of schools of social work**

| | Student Body | Academic Autonomy | Independent/ Department | Research | Tasks Graduate MSW | DSW |
|---|---|---|---|---|---|---|
| B | 200 | no | I | no | yes | no |
| D | 150-1200 | yes | both | yes | no | no |
| DK | 100-300 | yes/no | I | no/yes* | no | no |
| E | 100-500 | yes | D | no | no | no |
| F | 100-200 | yes/no | both | no/yes* | no | no |
| GB | 40-150 | yes | D | yes | yes | yes |
| GR | 300-600 | yes | D | yes | no | no |
| I | 20-240 | yes | both | no/yes* | no | no |
| IRL | 50-100 | yes | D | yes | yes | yes |
| L | - | - | - | - | - | - |
| NL | 300-1600 | yes | I | no | no | no |
| P | 260-400 | yes | I | yes | no | no |

\* 'yes' restricted to university institutions.

not entirely certain. Most common is the type of independent institution offering only courses in social professions (Belgium, Denmark, France, Italy, the Netherlands, Portugal). Otherwise, social work education is offered as one option among several in a university or extra-university setting.

Relatively small institutions with 100-200 or even fewer students are widely typical of social work education (Belgium, Denmark, France, Ireland, Italy, Spain, the UK). In Greece and Portugal the institutions have approximately double this number of students. West Germany - and to some extent the Netherlands - are unusual in that many of their institutions (or faculties) of social work education encompass more than 500 students and sometimes as many as 1,000 or 1,200 (Table 4).

Not all institutions of social work education enjoy rights of autonomy and self-government with respect to decisions on personnel, academic questions and finances. Autonomy appears to be the greatest where the courses are offered at universities. In countries where they are offered in institutions more or less resembling the secondary school system the characteristics of academic freedom often seem to be lacking (Belgium, Denmark, France). The possibilities for research also vary greatly in the national settings. The trend towards academisation here also appears to be dominant. In most countries research is now included in the legal mandate of social work education (West Germany, Greece, Ireland, Portugal, the UK). However, social work research is still in its infancy or at least it often still falls far short of meeting normal social scientific expectations. It remains the exception that post-graduate and doctoral courses are offered by institutions of social work education (as distinct from neighbouring disciplines such as 'educational science', sociology or psychology).

Continuing education for professionals is widely available. This is certainly a positive expression of the close ties between education and practice in the field of social work.

## The Nature of Social Work Education

Despite being anchored in divergent national, legal and social systems, social work education in EC countries operates within fairly similar structures, which often produce quite similar problems. The basics of the social sciences and of the legal and administrative system are taught everywhere. Likewise, the organisation, functions and methods of social work are on every national training agenda. Finally, complementary disciplines such as statistics, empirical social research and foreign languages have their place in most national curricula. Characteristic of social work education is a considerable amount of variation in the length, organisation, timing and supervision of the placements. However, the rule seems to be that at least one-third of the training for social work should be in placement; only Denmark requires less. The basic training of social workers usually lasts for three or four years. However, the UK and Ireland also offer one- and two-year courses for graduates and a two year diploma course for non-graduates with appropriate job experience. One year courses are being phased out.

In some countries the education of social workers rests upon a long tradition. The first courses were instituted prior to World War I in France, Germany, the Netherlands, and the UK. Formal training was begun between the World Wars in Belgium, Denmark, Ireland, Italy, Portugal and Spain. Greece, where courses were first organised after World War II, was a latecomer (see Table 2). Everywhere the scope of social work education has greatly widened since World War II in keeping with the expansion of the Welfare State.

**Table 5: Characteristics of the undergraduate programme**

|  | Duration Years | Field Work % | Fees* | Qualification |
|---|---|---|---|---|
| B | 3 | 30 | 5,000 | Diplôme d'État |
| D | 3/4 | 33-50 | free | Diplom-Sozialarbeiter |
|  |  |  |  | Diplom-Sozialpädagoge |
| DK | 3/3,5 | 20 | free | Socionom/Socialraadgiver |
| E | 3 | 40 | 60,000 | Diploma |
| F | 3 | 50 | 500 | Diplôme d'État |
| GB | 4 | 50 | free | BSW |
| GR | 3,5 | 45 | free | ptychion |
| I | 3 | 30 | 100,000 | Diploma |
| IRL | 3/4 | 50 | 850 | B. Soc. Sc. |
| L | 4 | 30 | - | Diplôme d'État |
| NL | 4 | 30 | 1,000 | Diploma |
| P | 4 | 40 | 35-60,000 | Diploma |

* per year in the respective national currency unless otherwise noted.

Many of the courses have been substantially reformed since 1970. Various reasons are given for the recent reforms. The need to respond to changes in professional practice seems to have been the dominant motive in Italy and the UK. In other countries the reform of social work education appears to have been incidental to a comprehensive reform of the educational system. Often the reforms seem to have started at the organisational or institutional level without really penetrating to questions of content. This seems to be the case in West Germany, Greece and the Netherlands.

*Post-Graduate Courses*

The varying organisation and structure of social work education within the European Community make it difficult to generalise about possibilities of post-graduate qualifications. The following remarks are restricted to post-graduate degrees in social work, not in various related disciplines.

**Table 6: Second degrees and doctoral programs in social work:**
**Admission requirements, degrees, duration**

|  | *Admission Requirements* | *Duration* | *Degree* | *Doctorate* |
|---|---|---|---|---|
| B | Diplôme d'État | 2 | licence | no |
| D | - | - | no | no |
| DK | Diploma, 5 years | 1 year | no | no |
| E | - | - | no | no |
| F | Diplôme d'État | 600 hrs* | diplôme supérieur | no |
|  | Diplôme Universitaire | 2 years | licence | no |
|  | licence | 1 year | maitrise | no |
| GB | SSD** 1 year, interview | 1 year | Master | yes |
|  |  | 2 years | Master | yes |
| GR | - | - | no | no |
| I | - | - | no | no |
| IRL | SSD** 1 year, interview | 1-2 years | Master | yes |
| L | - | - | no | no |
| NL | - | - | - | no |
| P | - | - | no | no |

\* in-service training over a period of two years
\*\* Social Science Degree (BA, BSc, MA etc.)

Post-graduate qualifications are available in Denmark, the UK, Belgium and France. An undergraduate qualification in social work or social science is a standard prerequisite for such courses. Ireland and the UK also require personal interviews and at least one year of professional experience for admission. In these two countries the possibility also exists for graduates in other subjects to enroll in a two-year course in social work. However, the professional qualification thus achieved corresponds to the standard undergraduate degree or diploma in social work. Ireland and the UK offer the possibility of a doctoral degree in addition to other post-graduate diplomas or master's degrees (Table 6).

*Degrees and Diplomas*

With the successful conclusion of an undergraduate or post-graduate course of studies, the student receives certification of an academic qualification from the institution at which the course was undertaken. In some countries, where courses of differing length are offered, graduates may receive different types of certification (Belgium, France, Ireland, the Netherlands, the UK). In general, academic certification is equivalent to a license of professional qualification, but some

**Table 7: First qualification in social work**
**(professional qualification in parenthesis)**

| | |
|---|---|
| B | Assistant social (because of specialisation there are also other qualifications) |
| D | Diplom-Sozialarbeiter and/or -Sozialpädagoge (Staatliche Anerkennung) |
| DK | Socialraadgiver, Socionom, Socialformidler |
| E | Diplomado en Trabajo Social |
| F | Assistant de service social (because of specialisation there are also other qualifications) |
| GB | Diploma, Bachelor or Master of Social Work (Certificate of Qualification in Social Work - CQSW) |
| GR | Ptychion in Social Work (License) |
| I | Diploma d'assistente sociale, Diploma universitario di servizio sociale |
| IRL | Bachelor/Master of Social Science, Diploma in Social Work (CQSW) |
| L | Assistant d'hygiène sociale or assistant social |
| N | Diploma Hoger Beroepsopleiding in the various areas |
| P | Diplomado em Serviço Social (Assistente social) |

countries require professional licensing in addition to the academic certification. As a rule, this license is granted by a government ministry (West Germany, Greece, Luxembourg) or a special licensing body (Ireland and the UK) (Table 7).

*The Student Body*

Yearly admissions to social work courses in the twelve countries under consideration reach approximately 27,000 (including an estimated intake of 2,000 for Italy). The majority of beginning students are female. In most countries the proportion of women in the student body is over two-thirds. The schools in the Netherlands constitute an exception in that approximately an equal number of men and women are present in the student body. On the other hand, in France, Greece, Italy, Portugal and Spain very few men study social work. Here the percentage of female students is often around ninety per cent or greater.

Even when all due allowance is made for imprecisions in compilation, wide variations in the national ratio of students of social work to overall population are

## Table 8: Student body

|     | Annual Intake | % Women | Student Population | Graduates Population | Total Pop. (Mill.) | Intake/ (1:1000) |
|-----|------|------|------|------|------|------|
| B   | 1800 | 75 | 5400 | 1500 | 9.87 | 5,480 |
| D   | 8000 | 66 | 37000 | 7000 | 61.34 | 7,660 |
| DK  | 340 | 80 | 970 | 345 | 5.16 | 15,170 |
| E   | 1300 | 90 | 3900 | ? | 37.18 | 28,600 |
| F   | 2000 | 95 | 6000 | 2000 | 53.48 | 26,740 |
| GB  | 3500* | 67 | 6450* | 3440 | 55.82 | 15,940 |
| GR  | 370 | 89 | 1000 | 169 | 9.36 | 25,290 |
| I   | ** | 90 | 6000 (est.) | ** | 56.91 | - |
| IRL | 150* | 80 | 550 | 40 | 3.36 | 22,400 |
| L   | 10 | - | - | 5 | 0.36 | 36,000 |
| NL  | 7200 | 56 | 26400 | 5900 | 14.03 | 1,940 |
| P   | 330 | 90 | 950 | 210 | 9.87 | 29,090 |

* including undergraduate, graduate, and non-graduate
** no exact data available

apparent. Small countries like the Netherlands and Belgium have the highest ratio of social work students to overall population. Interestingly, West Germany is the only large country among those having one social work student per less than 10,000 population. Most European countries have one student of social work for between 15,000 and 30,000 of population (Table 8).

Few figures are available on the social characteristics of the student bodies. In West Germany the percentage of students from working class families in social work education is approximately twice as high as among students in general. The indications are that social work education is not a typical academic field (ie with the overwhelming majority of students coming directly from secondary schools). Rather it is characteristic of this course of study that many of its students have already gathered work experience and are often older than standard student cohorts. In some countries this tendency is encouraged by mechanisms such as an obligatory minimum age of admission or required job experience (Table 9).

### Table 9: Admission requirements for undergraduates

| | For Secondary School Leavers | | | | | Other* |
|---|---|---|---|---|---|---|
| | Diploma or Certificate(s) | Entrance Exam | Minimum Age | Interview | Prof. Experience | |
| B | x | - | - | - | - | yes |
| D | x | - | - | some | sometimes | some |
| DK | x | - | 20 | - | 9 months | yes |
| E | x | - | 18 | x | - | yes |
| F | x | x | - | x | - | yes |
| GB | x | - | - | x | - | yes |
| GR | x | x | 17 | - | - | - |
| I | x | - | 18 | x | - | some |
| IRL | x | - | 19 | x | - | yes |
| L | x | x | - | - | - | yes |
| NL | x | - | 18 | - | - | yes |
| P | x | - | 18 | - | - | - |

* applications possible without secondary school diploma

All countries regard the national secondary school-leaving certificate which qualifies for university studies as the standard of admission. In addition, many countries require further proof of personal suitability. Applicants are often obliged to submit to interviews, psychometric tests or special admission examinations. In some countries it is possible for people without the standard secondary school-leaving certificate but with appropriate job experience to gain admission to courses in social work.

*Faculty*

The varied composition of staff reflects the diverse, interdisciplinary focus of social work education. Integration of considerable placement elements is secured by the use of practitioners as advisors or supervisors. The weight of these and other groups in the faculty varies from country to country.

Teaching staff generally include academic social workers, social scientists and active social work professionals. Almost all countries distinguish to some degree between these groups. This is symptomatic of the fact that in nearly all countries social work does not yet enjoy (or has not long enjoyed) full academic recognition. Thus the curious situation arises in many countries that social workers as teachers in courses on social work are relegated to a lower status than representatives of other academic disciplines. In some countries this seems to be a transitional problem which the formal academic recognition of social work training will eventually resolve (eg Ireland and the UK). However, in a number of countries the partial academisation of social work education first caused the problem to appear and the present immobility in this process admits of no easy solution (West Germany, Greece, Italy, the Netherlands, Spain). It seems to us self-evident that the equal participation of social workers is desirable.

Status and remuneration of staff depend on many factors. Some staff are employed on a full-time basis, others part-time. As a rule, all schools have a 'core' of permanent, full-time faculty members. Spain is a problematical exception in that schools there usually only have one or two permanent faculty members, while the rest of the teaching staff are only engaged on the basis of honoraria. As a permanent arrangement this situation is probably incompatible with quality education. Some countries report that staff are encouraged to participate in social work practice and all make use to a large degree of the teaching services of social work professionals on a part-time basis.

Social work appears to have a relatively large proportion of women among teaching staff. However, academisation has had effects here as well. The proportion of men is higher among teachers from disciplines other than social work. The experience in West Germany may be symptomatic. The integration of social work education into the tertiary educational system with its traditional academic standards of employment has led to the hiring of many more men than women since 1971. Presently women in positions of institutional leadership are still rare exceptions in West Germany.

## Social Work, Social Movements and Social Reform

The early history of social work shows a clear connection between social work as a profession and the social movements of the time. In those countries in which modern social work began to take shape prior to World War I, it derived its main impulses from the women's movement. The 'founding mothers' of social work regarded the embryonic profession not only as a lever for social reform but also as an instrument of emancipation for women. This was no longer so clearly the case in countries in which social work developed between the wars or after World War II.

Interesting questions for historical research present themselves. Does this have to do with the 'decline' and 'diffusion' of the women's movement between the wars? Or with the economic disarray of the classical European bourgeoisie from which early social workers had been largely recruited? Or with a 'generalisation of social distress'? In fact, all these and other factors as well, may have been involved. Much more research will be required before definitive statements can be made on this matter. In any case, it is clear that today, despite a renaissance of feminism in parts of Europe, a close connection between social work and the women's movement no longer exists in a form comparable to the situation prior to World War I.

From the very beginning the churches have played a significant role in the development of social work. Throughout Europe, Catholic and Protestant organisations were active in the founding of institutions for social work education. In many cases the churches have maintained a considerable engagement to the present.

During the early years of social work practice, there was a close connection between the organised workers' movement and social work in many parts of Europe. More research will be needed to clarify why the connection between social work and social movements such as the women's movement or the workers' movement has become quite tenuous, while the connection to the churches - though diminishing - has proved more durable.

There is historically a strong connection between social work education and the process of social reform. Legally mandated social services seem to have a particularly strong impact both on social work practice and education. But in a more general sense, an interdependence of social work education and social policy trends can be postulated. The 'crisis of the Welfare State' which is perceived in many advanced industrial countries has already had far-reaching qualitative and quantitative effects on social work education. Economic downturns in countries such as Belgium, Denmark, West Germany, and the UK have undermined public confidence in Welfare State instruments and have facilitated cuts in social expenditures. In this situation social work often seems to be on the defensive: criticism of social work mounts while the problems with which it is confronted fester. Resignation and embitterment among social service professionals are often the result. However, there appear to be certain exceptions which deserve careful examination. In Greece and Spain social work is still a 'growth industry'. It is an open question, whether social work will eventually run up against its own specific 'limits to growth' in these countries as well.

## 'Europeanisation' of Social Work

As we have seen, the origins of social work education in Europe are rooted deeply in the national history of the various countries. The women's movement, the churches and the workers' movement all played a role. However, the search for international cooperation was also a factor which should not be forgotten. The founding of the International Association of Schools of Social Work in Paris 1928/29, under the leadership of extraordinary personalities like Alice Salomon, was an important milestone. International cooperation in the field of social work suffered setbacks under the influence of ultra-nationalism, Fascism and National Socialism between the wars and especially as a result of World War II and the subsequent division of Europe into antagonistic blocs. After World War II, American experts and ideas played a key role in the (re)construction of social work and social work education and practice in much of Europe during the post-war period. This development probably reflected not only the strength of the United States at the time but also the relatively developed state of the American social work profession.

The first post-war generation of teachers of social work in Europe was educated to a remarkable extent in the USA. This, perhaps, accounts for the fact that the 'classical' American methodological triad of casework, group work and community work still enjoyed a quasi-canonical status in Europe even after it had come under increasingly critical scrutiny in the USA itself.

In recent years certain trends seem to point in the direction of a 'Europeanisation' of social work methods. Roughly parallel developments can be observed in many European countries. The search for a 'holistic' or unified approach to social problems seems to be replacing reliance on the three 'classical' methods. The focus in Europe seems to be shifting toward a new, more comprehensive type of 'community social work' which incorporates elements of all the three 'classical' methods while rejecting what is felt to be their 'individualistic orientation'.

One can only speculate as to the reasons for this development. Much more research will be necessary to reveal the deeper meaning of the 'Europeanisation'. Possible contingent factors are: momentum towards European political unity, a growing criticism of American practices and policies, the professionalisation of social work, educational and social reforms in Europe, sheer faddishness.

## Professionalisation through Academisation

The status of social work education in the various national systems of education seems to be an indicator of the degree of professionalisation which has been achieved. Social work education is involved in a secular process of transition from the secondary to the tertiary level of education. In most countries social work education is situated in a curious position within the tertiary system, but outside the universities. However, even in countries where it has received full university recognition, the status of social work education is sometimes still overlaid with ambiguity (eg in the UK social work education still co-exists in university and extra-university institutions). Other countries are considering the integration of social work with the established academic disciplines on the one hand and with the social work profession on the other (eg, West Germany, the Netherlands, Spain). Nevertheless, the process of professionalisation through academisation of training appears to us to be inevitable and - in the final analysis - desirable. It is, however, remarkable that each country seems determined to make its own mistakes in this connection rather than learning from the errors of others.

The process of professionalisation through academisation seems to be related to 'secularisation' of social work education. The trend throughout Europe seems to be overwhelmingly in the direction of increasing state responsibility for previously private or church-related institutions. This process can be clearly observed in West Germany, Greece, Italy, and Spain. It appears that the financial demands of modern social work education increasingly exceed the resources which non-governmental organisations can - or are willing to - devote to it.

In general, professionalisation of social work seems to parallel increasing male participation. The percentage of male social workers and social work students is quite large in some, but not all countries in which social work is most strongly professionalised (West Germany, the Netherlands and the UK). However, there are so many anomalies in the international scenery that one should not jump to early conclusions.

A notable feature of recent years in highly developed European countries is a blurring of the boundaries between professional social work and other forms of intervention. The renaissance of self-help initiatives and other types of voluntary work is certainly related to the financial crisis of the 'Welfare State', but it also seems to imply a criticism of the bureaucracy which professionalism often entails. In many countries public criticism of professional social work can no longer be ignored. However, even within the profession there seems to be a growing sense that self-help and voluntary efforts need to have a greater role in social work practice.

One indication of the uncertainty of professionalisation within an increasingly academised social work education is the unequal status of faculty members with social work degrees in many countries (Belgium, West Germany, Greece, Spain). Perhaps this, too, is a transitional problem, which will disappear in the future as social work teachers take advantage of doctoral level degree opportunities within their own discipline. In any case, it is not surprising that many countries with highly professionalised social work establishments either already have created possibilities for doctoral degrees in social work or are debating the issue seriously.

The tenuousness of social work professionalisation can also be observed on the job-market, where social work graduates compete with an array of others, including sociologists, psychologists, teachers and even people with legal training. Social workers are not only experiencing increased competition from better established academic disciplines for basic grade jobs, but are often at a distinct disadvantage for leadership positions. In some countries competition also exists with other qualifications for social services, such as the 'educatore specializzato' in Italy and 'administrative civil servants' (Verwaltungsbeamten) in West Germany and Denmark.

## Social Work between Theory and Practice

European social work is torn between its striving for academic status and the demands of daily practice. This tension, which is deeply rooted in the history of the profession, finds expression in an uneasy coexistence between eclectic social sciences on the one hand and a specific form of vocational training on the other. No European country seems to have found an entirely satisfactory solution to the quandary. Even Great Britain, with its long and venerable tradition of university education for social workers, still appears to be struggling with this problem. The balance between academic and vocational orientations is struck in widely varying ways in the different countries.

All countries show a degree of reverence for the vocational side of social work education by requiring practical placements and by incorporating practicing social workers in the teaching staff. By the same token, most countries make gestures in the direction of subsuming the social-scientific disciplines under a problem-orientation ostensibly derived from practical necessity. Some efforts seem quite promising in this regard. Denmark and West Germany are experimenting with projects as the integrative centres within courses. Other countries, such as France, Ireland, the UK and, once again, Denmark, encourage full-time teaching staff to renew personal experience in the field.

However, the difficulties of integrating theory and practice are not merely a result of 'over-academisation'. Social work education can also be 'under-academic', ie, lacking in scientific foundation. This tends to be the case in countries in which teaching is done primarily on a part-time basis by active social work professionals and/or other itinerant academics who have neither time nor opportunity to reflect on their practice and teaching in the light of current research.

This situation is exacerbated by a general dearth of specific, reliable research in the field of social work. Thus it is, among other things, a concern for the quality of education (not merely practice) which leads to complaints from all parts of Europe about insufficient support for social work research. In fact, dissatisfaction with the state of research in the field of social work seems to be one of the uniting links in social work education in Europe.

There is certainly no easy answer to the question of why there is so little first-rate research in the field of social work. We are convinced that the tension between theory and practice and the uncertain state of professionalisation provide part of the answer. However, more mundane factors probably play a role as well. In West Germany, for example, full-time staff must teach eighteen hours per week, despite their nominal status as 'professors'. This incredible teaching load, which exceeds that of colleagues in some so-called less developed countries (eg Greece) obviously acts as a deterrent to serious research. And yet, social work research is found wanting even in countries with reasonable teaching loads. We suspect that certain deeply ingrained psychological mechanisms militate against social work research: methodological insecurity, prophylactic resignation, sporadic indolence and affected lugubriousness. In short, many social work educators seem to feel more comfortable in sackcloth and ashes than in the library.

The institutions for mediating the tension between theory and practice are as varied as the countries in Europe. Centralised regulation and local autonomy are the two poles between which a spectrum of possibilities unfolds. The UK has created a centralised, non-governmental certifying agency which promulgates minimum standards of education and monitors their observance. West Germany, at the other extreme, has an exquisitely decentralised system of institutional autonomy (in which, however, the various provincial governments constantly meddle in inscrutable ways). Some observers associate the results with Humboldt, others with humbug. In France, Spain and Denmark standards of social work education are prescribed by statute at the national level, while Belgium entrusts a government ministry with the task of supervising the issuing of separate guidelines for Flemish and French-speaking schools.

Each of these approaches has its advantages and disadvantages. The British solution gives employing agencies a degree of influence which many Europeans would view as excessive; however, it also makes possible a great deal of professional flexibility. Countries relying strongly on legislation are necessarily much less flexible, unless (as seems to be the case in some Mediterranean countries) room is left for 'para-legal' fudging with the letter of the law.

Despite the differences in approach, the majority of countries appear to have some mechanism for enforcing a semblance of national standards with respect to educational structure and content. It would be very useful to have more research on the varieties of approach and the differential rates of success or failure. However, measured by the criticism of social work education which is uttered by employers in the UK on the one hand and West Germany on the other, it appears that the actual results of diverse organisational schemes may not be all that different from each other.

## Training, Education, Further Education

Many European countries obviously believe that effective social work requires personal qualities which are not necessarily reflected in academic transcripts. In Ireland, Spain, the UK and some other countries prospective students undergo interviews and other forms of subjective evaluation. Low teacher:student ratios discourage anonymity and ensure a personal relationship between staff and students. Here again, however, West Germany is on the cutting-edge of an arguably dull sword. Whereas most European 'schools of social work' have around 200 students, it is not rare for West German and Dutch 'schools' to be three to five times as large. Furthermore in West Germany, selection procedures are based on the assumption that personal traits should be excluded from the admission process. Not surprisingly, such antics have begun to generate their own corrective. Prospective students have begun staying away from social work courses in West Germany in droves, even though more students are crowding into German higher education than at any time in history.

Three general directions are discernible among countries which presently offer instruction beyond undergraduate level:

*   academic post-graduate courses (leading often to a MA or Ph.D degree);

*   thematic specialisations (particular fields of work, client groups or methods);

*   intensified qualifications for management.

This is an area which certainly calls for increased international cooperation. The large challenges with which social work is confronted already transcend national boundaries, and this process can be expected to intensify in the future. Long-term unemployment, labour migration from the countryside to the city and from less-developed to more-developed areas, demographic shifts and changes in values are issues which confront all the countries of Europe. Post-graduate education would therefore seem to be an ideal area for European social work education to cultivate elements of a trans-national professional identity.

## Conclusions

Some of the most significant trends in European social work education have been described:

*   academisation

*   secularisation

*   an increasingly 'generic' approach

*   'Europeanisation'.

Widespread public scepticism towards social work has become apparent in many highly developed countries in recent years. While this is often attributed exclusively to the financial 'crisis' of the Welfare State, we see it as also inextricably bound up with an 'identity crisis' of social work itself. Competition from voluntary and self-help initiatives on the one hand and from other professions on the other hand is forcing professional social work in many countries to specify its unique contribution and to justify its cost. Having become accustomed to automatic expansion during the post-war period, many social workers find this process annoying and even painful. It is noteworthy that the social work 'boom' seems to be over in precisely the most economically advanced countries. In most European countries, the social work profession has clearly entered a phase in which consolidation is necessary.

One promising strategy of consolidation at the level of methodology may emerge from the community social work discussion in West Germany, France, Italy and the UK. Social workers may be able to carve out a professional niche for themselves as planners, organisers and facilitators of social change. However, if such a professional stance is to be credible, social work education will have to replace its tendency towards lamentation and muddle with well-designed, scientifically founded, practically oriented curricula equal to the task.

## Reference

1. Brauns, H.-J. and Kramer, D. (1986), *Social Work Education in Europe. A Comprehensive Description of Social Work Education in 21 European Countries*. Eigenverlag des Deutschen Vereins für öffentliche und private Fürsorge, Frankfurt-am-Main.

*Chapter 5*

# Community Development in Europe*

## Charlie McConnell

In 1990 the European Foundation for the Improvement of Living and Working Conditions published the findings of the first stage of a major research project on Social Change.[1] This research was based upon fieldwork and interviews with initiatives in several countries within the European Community. The overall aim of the study was to examine the importance of local community life and to determine the factors which influence the ability of people to cope with and to respond actively to changing social and economic conditions.

The initial phase of the research consisted primarily of a literature review, discussions with policy-makers and the creation of a framework for carrying out fieldwork involving several European countries. This fieldwork phase commenced in 1990.

One of the main areas of investigation concerned local community action, i.e. 'the capacity of people to organise themselves with or without professional help to improve the local conditions and to participate and negotiate with authorities and other resource holders'.[2] The research study was one of the first in Europe to look at the effects upon peripheral and marginalised localities of the social and economic changes in the lead up to 1992. It identified a tremendous diversity of forms of local action within member states.

Two interesting findings have emerged from the research. The first concerns definition. Whilst all countries use concepts of local life, there was no universal concept of the locality or of community. There is therefore a lack of consistent language for comparison. For example in terms of scale, local or community can mean anything from a small village of a few thousand people to a county or

---

\* *In this paper I am using Community Development to describe a type of professional intervention that aims at involving local people in the regeneration of their communities. The paper draws upon the findings of a recent study published by the European Foundation for the Improvement of Living and Working Conditions and upon a 1989 Council of Europe Resolution and Conference on Community Development.*

department of a million or more inhabitants. Furthermore within one country there can be several kinds of local authorities responsible for social welfare and social development at different levels, with varying levels and responsibilities. In some countries there are evident conflicts between central and local government, whilst some local government systems have undergone extensive change in recent years. One can identify the existence of a variety of authorities and agencies with different social welfare responsibilities affecting any given locality, though with common problems of coordination of services.

Secondly the study identified common stimuli to people participating in local action. In all countries studied, this was influenced by factors such as unemployment, poverty and poor housing. The potential for community action can be regarded as existing more or less everywhere and the problems which generate it are common too. As the research report states, 'it is a normal human attribute to seek to make a constructive response to the situation which people find themselves sharing'.

Technical support for local community action in the form of community development interventions differs widely in Europe. The availability of specialist and technical skills for facilitating and enabling local people to organise is more widespread in northern Europe than in the south. But in all the countries studied there is a relative marginalisation of publicly funded community development agencies. Throughout the 1980s funding has been short term and experimental. This has made it difficult for community development agencies to engage in long term support and development of community action. There has to date been little *strategic* planning and funding for community development by public authorities which would facilitate the involvement of local people in the regeneration of their communities.

Also in 1989, the Council of Europe endorsed a resolution on community development proposed by the Standing Conference of Local and Regional Authorities of Europe.[3] This resolution was based on a report entitled *Self Help and Community Development in Towns.*[4] The report included contributions from local authority associations in several EC countries - Denmark, Federal Republic of Germany, Spain, Portugal and the UK. It also included contributions from Sweden and Switzerland outwith the EC. This study was concerned with the relationship between community development and local authorities. It noted that some local authorities had pursued a variety of initiatives (including decentralisation) in order to foster new relationships with the consumers of their services.

The report highlighted that local governments throughout Western Europe were modifying their style and organisation of service delivery and beginning to identify common problems when building more effective relationships between themselves and their consumers. Common patterns were emerging in the larger urban centres whereby community groups were seeking technical support, in order to be able to respond to this new climate permeating local authorities. The report pointed to community development as providing much of that support. It went on to describe examples from different member countries where local authorities' funding of community development programmes has encouraged community groups to organise around issues of concern, to present their case and to negotiate more effectively with council departments. The involvement of the local community in planning and service delivery is being recognised widely as having a number of advantages to local authorities, not least because local authority service providers are able to communicate with the communities they serve and understand their needs better.

What is apparent as we enter the 1990s is that local community action and participation is emerging higher on the agenda of European institutions and associations such as the Standing Conference of Local and Regional Authorities. For several years now the European Commission has been concerned to identify new ways of involving people, particularly those from the more disadvantaged and marginalised parts of the European Community, with a range of funding programmes available for local authorities and non-governmental organisations (NGOs) notably through the Social Fund and Poverty Programmes (See chapter 1 and Appendix). There seems to be a growing, albeit slow, recognition at European, national and local government level that social, economic and political integration, cohesion and development of the European Community will require the involvement and participation of all its citizenry.

There is a long tradition of representative democracy within many EC states, yet wider concepts of participatory democracy and of an empowered active citizenry though fashionable in terms of rhetoric are still comparatively young in terms of practice. The notion of state funding either directly or indirectly through non-governmental organisations for community development workers to facilitate this empowerment remains experimental, to be handled with care. Where funding has been made available, whether from the Commission, national states or local authorities, it has usually been through the conduit of short term social welfare programmes.

I should now like to look in a little more detail at the relationship between community development and social work in five member countries of the European community - Portugal, Spain, the Netherlands, Ireland and the UK. The title community development worker is not necessarily used as a job description in each of these countries. Whilst the Council of Europe resolution helps us in harmonising our definition and understanding, the European Foundation research noted earlier highlights that we still have quite a long way to go in promoting community development as the general description of this activity. A number of European wide networking initiatives are currently taking place with this objective in mind and I shall return to this later.

## Community Development in Portugal

Present Portuguese society still has a level of socio-economic development and a structural role in the world system which is intermediate.[5] The question raised by the integration of Portugal into the EC is whether she will be promoted to the ranks of the most advanced member states or will have her position consolidated as a poorer (or less developed) country in European terms and an intermediate one in a world context.

The change in the political regime in 1974 saw the late introduction of a welfare state. As a result, social provision is adequate in some cases and conspicuous by its absence in others, making the situation of disadvantaged social groupings all the more tenuous. One indication of the survival of the effects of the corporatist regime which existed up until 1974 and which are associated with the country's semi-peripheral condition, is the fact that public administration and large sections of the population have still not really taken the existence of social rights and of a welfare state to heart. In this respect the shortcomings in state provision have to be compensated for by self help practices undertaken by families or at neighbourhood level by voluntary organisations.

Family and informal neighbourhood structures in Portugal are still very strong and display a vitality within the welfare system. Self help has always been a dimension of that provision. In the past this was essential in order to protect people against oppressive policies and the lack of sufficient welfare provision by the state. This should be seen much more in terms of a compensatory self help culture rather than a participatory political culture. In recent years, however, social work professionals have been working in these communities trying to develop local networks between people. For example in order to provide support for young unemployed people, new organisations are being developed by field social workers with young people. Social workers in Portugal increasingly spend time and effort in organising new forms of community action where the problems of particular targeted groups can be voiced and solved.

Portuguese social workers are in this sense building upon the tradition of self help within Portuguese society. However, a new phenomena has begun to emerge whereby professionals are also trying to develop a more direct and active relationship between local groups on the one hand and local authorities and government departments on the other. This involves working with local people either defending certain services or raising issues about the quantity and quality of welfare service provision. Professional practice in this area of community action is often intended to reinforce and revitalise existing forms of self help and stimulate participation by new social groups. A number of city local authorities, notably in Oporto and Lisbon, have begun to give support to community development interventions of this type.

In Lisbon policies have been developed by the city authority, concerned to involve local communities in the resolution of their own problems. One example is the funding of an action research project for community development in the Chelas district of Lisbon concerned with the social effects of a regeneration scheme.

A number of European Commission schemes have also provided opportunities in recent years for the funding of community development interventions. Funding available from the second poverty programme has helped in promoting community development and in persuading institutions to accept concepts such as public participation. However, this is despite the continued existence of a quite centralised welfare bureaucracy and administrative structure.

The growing interest in community development and participation is not a recent development in Portugal. Indeed social work training schools such as the Co-operativa de Ensino Supero Servico Social did much to promote this type of work in the 1970s and 1980s. But what seems to be emerging is a new found interest and confidence within parts of the social work profession towards community development styles of intervention. This interest has in part been stimulated by growing exchanges between practitioners in Portugal and northern European countries notably the Netherlands and UK.

At the same time some professionals within the social welfare sector believe that the development of the welfare state in Portugal, which is still deficient in many senses and far lower in terms of minimum standards in comparison to other European community countries, may have come to a halt.

## Community Development in Spain

Whilst practitioners and politicians in North-West Europe were often critical of the achievements and nature of their welfare systems, Spain like Portugal was still at the stage of seeking to develop a comprehensive welfare state during the late 1970s and 1980s.

In 1975 following Franco's death Spain emerged as a parliamentary democracy. The Socialist party came to power in 1982 and secured membership of the European Community. As in Portugal, at no time during the last two centuries has Spain enjoyed such lengthy democratic rule. The period since democratisation has also coincided with the recession in the international economy leading to lower economic growth rates and considerably higher unemployment and poverty. This has also diminished labour demand and reduced migration.

In the 1960s a number of economic migrants from Southern Spain moved to the industrially developing areas in the North. Since the late 1970s many have returned to establish their own enterprises or retire. This too had some effect upon attitudes and behaviour including for example growing labour union affiliation, new social organisations and growing demand for social welfare services. Therefore it is important to address Spanish community development and community action in the context of the North/South divide.

Spain has marked regional diversity, and considerable autonomy is given to the regions in the fields of personal social services and community development. It is the local and regional authorities who generally fund community development programmes. There are therefore large regional disparities between social welfare provision within Spain and a truly national welfare state has not been created. The Basque country, for example, has taken the leading role in becoming the first autonomous region to establish an allowance for deprived families. Community development in the social services within certain regions in the North is beginning to grow. In relation to urban renewal, town planning and housing improvements there has recently been a growing interest in community development and self help. Examples include the provincial department of Zaragoza and the autonomous community of Aragon.[7] The city of Barcelona, with support from the European Social Fund, has launched a three year integrated neighbourhood development programme, a central part of which involves the participation of local organisations.[8]

Many people in Spain have experienced a growing disenchantment with the political class, illustrated by the low turn out rates in elections. National institutes concerned with social work, including community development, such as IN-TRESS in Barcelona have argued for a growing role for community development in that interface between central and local government institutions and local communities.[9]

Again there is a long tradition of self help in Spain. There exists an extensive voluntary sector often organised around single issues. A recent example is the growth of organisations to support minority ethnic communities such as gypsies with the Asociación Societariado General Gitano taking a lead. In March 1990 over thirty national Spanish voluntary organisations met in Madrid to discuss a proposal to establish a social action network to promote new forms of social development in the European context. Spanish agencies have also begun to engage in community development exchanges with other EC countries.

## Community Development in the Netherlands

In both Spain and Portugal, community development in the social service sector is patchy with no official figures available as to funding and numbers of community development workers. By contrast community development in the Netherlands has been an institutionalised part of social service provision for a number of years. In the 1970s a strong position had been achieved with over 3,000 community development workers operating throughout the country, within both the social services and voluntary sector. The Netherlands has a highly sophisticated and well developed welfare state. However after several years of conservative government policies and extensive cuts in public expenditure on social welfare, community development has been seriously reduced. In 1990 it is estimated that there are barely 700 community workers operating in social service and voluntary sector agencies. As one Dutch speaker at a recent conference on community development stated, the Netherlands isn't the Netherlands any more.[10]

There has been a major crisis in the provision of community development training by institutes of higher education. Re-organisations of the Dutch collegiate system have removed community development as a separate field of study. By 1990 three of the four postgraduate schools for community development in the Netherlands had stopped accepting new students and the national educational institute for community development (LOCO) is now the only postgraduate school to offer this field of study. In the near future the institute will lose its government subsidy and become privatised. Also there is now no specialist community development training in the social service sector.[11]

In a number of cities, community development organisations have disappeared completely as a result of direct cuts in government spending or reorganisations by local authorities. Community development workers, who throughout the 1970s and early 1980s were seen as a basic provision by social service departments in disadvantaged areas, have been replaced by traditional social workers or those working on short term contract with specific groups such as the young and migrants.

Public participation is strongly rooted in the Dutch political culture and it is ironic that at the very same time of these cuts in public social service expenditure, there has also been a growing trend towards introducing decentralised planning and to extend public participation, particularly at local government level. It is here that community development is now finding opportunities for local government support. Cities like Rotterdam, The Hague and Nijmegen have been able to enhance public expenditure through decentralisation policies and practice and maintain and support community development organisations. So it seems that in the Netherlands there are contradictory messages in official public support for community development. Direct central government support through the social services has clearly been seriously cut back, whilst local authorities in many parts of the country are taking over the lead through identifying community development as a central process in decentralisation and public participation programmes.

New issues and social problems are confronting community development workers in the Netherlands with a growing emphasis upon urban renewal and tackling environmental problems. In the late 1980s Werkplaats Opbouwwerk Noord-Nederland conducted research into the current state of play of community development in the Netherlands and identified the social problems and conditions that were seen as of most importance. A focus upon environmental issues and the prevention of industrial pollution was seen as the major priority for community development workers in the 1990s.

Clearly there has been a period of soul searching and analysis amongst community development workers in the Netherlands in recent years. NIMO - the Dutch institute for community work[12] - has noted that it is a progressively ageing profession with community development workers working with the same employers for several years. A product of the 1960s and 70s has had to adapt to new challenges in the 90s.

Ideas from Dutch practice, particularly on regional support centres to promote community development, have been widely disseminated in Europe. Dutch practitioners have also taken a lead in Europe-wide networking.

## Community Development in Ireland

Community development in Ireland has survived, developed and diversified in the 1980s but its funding base still remains precarious. In terms of its practice theory it has been highly influenced during this period by British Community Work literature, adapted to the particular social and political context of the Irish Republic. As in the Netherlands, community development workers have shifted their emphasis from neighbourhood work to specific issue based work, particularly on training and employment and on work with women or with minority groups.

This change in practice has reflected the major social and economic changes that occurred in Irish society during the 1980s. Economic inequalities have persisted and deepened.[13] As in other countries, there have also been major public expenditure cuts, with a national rate of unemployment of over seventeen per cent in the late 1980s. The opportunities provided by membership of the European Community have been mixed. At a conference of Irish community development workers held at the end of the decade concerns were expressed about the peripheral nature of Ireland and its economy.[14]

In social welfare terms it was also a decade of debate around social and moral issues. In particular referenda were held concerning proposed amendments to the constitution to include the rights of the unborn and to remove prohibition on divorce. Issues concerning women's rights and the church and the state have been highlighted. Politically too the decade has been one of fragmentation and an increase in social polarisation. The events in Northern Ireland were forced back onto the agenda in the Republic following the 1981 hunger strikes. Political parties have also been moving towards a left/right division.

There has been a long tradition in Ireland of religious and voluntary sector support for community development but often of a somewhat conservative, self help type. As with Portugal the second European poverty programme has stimulated more radical community development initiatives around issues of poverty. Income generation and local economic development have been areas for intervention, which has supported the emergence of credit unions and community cooperatives.

There are few specialist community development workers employed in the statutory social services in Ireland. Local authorities generally have not been major funders of this type of work. Community development is taught as a method on the social work training courses, notably at Maynooth College. The issue of credentials and professionalism has been a dominant one amongst community development workers and has led for example to the emergence of two associations of community development workers in Ireland - the community workers' cooperative (with open membership of paid and unpaid workers) and the Irish Institute of Community Work (membership targeted upon paid community workers only). Ireland's community development workers are not well organised, although the recent national conference does seem to have led to a growing confidence in the 1990s. On the European stage, Ireland hosts the European Community Development Exchange.[15]

## Community Development in the UK

As in the Netherlands community development has been a recognised part of social service provision since the late 1960s. During the 1970s there was a major expansion in the employment of community development workers in social service departments. A parallel development also occurred in the fields of adult education and youth work (Community Education in Scotland). By the early 1980s it was estimated that there were over 5,000 specialist community workers in the UK.[16] In social work training and social work provision, community development had a mixed history during this period being identified both as a specialism and as permeating the concept of community social work.

The 1980s has also been a mixed period for the wider fortunes of community development in the UK. Conservative government policies of cuts in public expenditure and the abolition of the major Local Authorities in the metropolitan cities had a negative effect upon the employment of community development workers. The funding for community development in the UK has been closely related to the Urban Programme, a government scheme set up in 1968 to tackle deprivation. This operates on a short term budget (usually three or four years) jointly funded by local authorities and central government. As a result there has been quite a high turn over of practitioners with little job security.

Community Development has also had a close relationship with the emergence of public participation in planning and more recently decentralisation and consumer participation in the management of local authority services. This has been most developed in Scotland, which has separate social legislation including the Social Work Scotland Act 1968 which specifically refers to the promotion of social welfare. (Associated guidelines were published by the Scottish Office in Circular SW11/1969). Strathclyde Regional Council, the largest local authority in Europe, has identified community development as a central part of its social and economic strategy and currently employs about 280 community workers in its social work department.[17] In Scotland over two thirds of community development workers are employed by local authorities. This is reversed in England and Wales, where such work has no statutory basis and where the voluntary sector is the main employer of community development staff, using short term government funding.

Towards the end of the 1980s there was a renewed interest by local authorities and the voluntary sector in favour of community development, but this time in the context of economic development and urban renewal rather than social service provision. Central government has again begun to adopt much of the rhetoric of citizen action in line with its legislative measures to enhance the role of consumers in public service management, for example in state housing and schools. In Inner City policy, ideas imported from America such as community development trusts and community development corporations have also been introduced.

The polarisation of Britain with an increasing North/South political and economic divide has been reflected in greater support from the largely socialist local authorities in Urban and Inner City areas. In 1989 the Association of Metropolitan Authorities published a set of guidelines for local authorities on implementing community development across all the range of service provision. This report and conferences that went with it have provided a much needed profile of activities as we enter the 1990s.[18]

Community Development practitioners in the UK have also tended to be divided over their relationship to the state and over the desirability of positioning community development methods within the institutions of government and local government. During the 1980s there was a significant and in part divisive debate about whether there should be an institutionalised national centre for community development, but against a background of cuts in expenditure national groupings have emerged. Most significantly the Standing Conference for Community Development was established and in 1990 a national agency for community development was launched - the Community Development Foundation, a central government quango funded through the Home Office.[19]

Thus community development in the UK in the 1990s seems to be on the upturn. Whilst its location within the social services has yet to be clarified during a period of major restructuring in social work provision and training, it has enhanced its influence in other areas of social welfare provision, particularly in housing, community architecture, planning and in economic development. Bodies such as the church and rural development agencies are now using the techniques of community development in their interventions.

Of the five countries briefly reviewed in this paper, community development is better resourced and probably more institutionalised now in the UK than any of the others. Certainly on the European stage, it has been British practitioners who have tended to take a leading role followed closely by the Dutch.

### International Cooperation in Europe

Exchanges between community development practitioners have taken place often on a bilateral basis between countries since the 1970s. In 1979, the European Community Development Exchange was formed specifically to:

- organise seminars every year for field workers from different countries
- support national initiatives in community work, especially those in countries where a support structure for this type of work was weak.

Since then ECDE has given advice and support in the UK, Scandinavia, France, Belgium, Portugal, Spain and Ireland. Its secretariat was initially located in Britain but has now moved to Ireland. There have also been personal relationships built between practitioners and attempts at developing joint training and consultancy work. These include the work of the European Social Development Associates, a group of individual community development academics, who organised joint small scale training and research initiatives and the translation of books and articles on community development into English, Dutch and Spanish.

Towards the end of the decade there was growing recognition of the need for more permanent institutional relationships between community development agencies. The Combined Bureau for Social Development is one example of this, where together several national community development institutes have jointly funded staff to undertake consultancy, training and research work. It is still at an early stage of its development.

Single issue networks of largely non-governmental organisations including community development agencies have begun to emerge on the European stage. Examples are the Poverty Network, the European Social Action Network and the Euro-Citizens Action Service. The European institutions themselves have called for closer links amongst community development organisations. Notably in 1989 the Council of Europe passed a resolution supporting a European community development association, with proposed membership including local and regional authorities and non-governmental organisations.

In the autumn of 1989, a major international conference on community development was held in the UK co-sponsored by the European Commission and the Council of Europe.[20] Practitioners from several member countries attended the conference and during the four days of its deliberations delegates discussed the implications of the single market in 1992 and the move towards political, social and economic integration and harmonisation within the European community. Detailed workshops examined the role of community development on the European stage.

The creation of the single market is going to set in motion or at least accelerate quite an extensive restructuring of the European economy. One aim is to provide a shock to the supply side of the economy which is designed to eliminate over-capacity in quite a large number of sectors. This will have severe effects upon local communities. The significance for people working at the local community level in both urban and rural areas and particularly the peripheral parts of the European Community is that we will be witnessing further take-overs, mergers, plant closures and redundancies. The difference now compared with the restructuring of the 1970s and 1980s is that we do have some early warning of it. Working at the local level, community development workers are well placed to assist community initiatives in partnership with local, regional and national governments and non-governmental organisations. They are beginning to predict and deal collectively with some of the more vulnerable areas and groups during the 1990s.

The European Commission recognises this and a number of its schemes and funds are directly designed to support such localities and regions suffering from this restructuring. We must be doing much more than merely compensating regions, communities, local economies and workers *after* the event. What we must do is to begin to plan ahead and to use these funds for preventive strategies.

Community Development has moved on considerably since the early 1970s when it was often viewed, not least by its practitioners, as a panacea for problem solving. It is clearly not that, but is increasingly playing a functional part in helping to restructure local economies and social systems and to create closer social and community cohesion. In many parts of the European Community it is hardly developed and certainly not well resourced. As we have noted there are different historical traditions and levels of development in the social welfare systems of different member states and in support and funding for community organisation work. Much of this work has not been effectively assessed although there is a growing interest in evaluative research particularly in the Netherlands through NIMO and the UK through the CDF, not least to meet increasing demands by government funders for measurable achievements of this work in action.

The opening of barriers within Europe provides opportunities for an opening for ideas and it would seem to be the case that the more developed experience in Northern Europe is prevailing in terms of policy and practice within the European Community. The 1990s will see a continued debate around issues to do with the training and location of community development workers. It seems likely that a percolation model is likely to prevail whereby community development ideas, techniques and processes permeate the practice of a number of social welfare professions. What is different now is that this can be planned, with community development practitioners and organisations becoming aware of the need to collaborate, to learn from each other, to network and to be more politically sophisticated in influencing the institutions of the European Community.

Community development can enable more assertive, articulate and better organised communities and interest groups to lobby the European Community. Community action is a part of a wider citizens action movement. Both are essential if we are to create a democratic, participatory base and more sensitive and effective institutions of government - local, national and European.

## References

1. Chanan, G. and Vos, K. (1989), *Social change and Local Action, Coping with Disadvantage in Urban Areas*. European Foundation for the Improvement of Living and Working Conditions.

2. ibid. p.58.

3. Twenty Fourth Session, March 7-9 1989, Council of Europe, Strasbourg.

4. Abecasis, N. (1989), *Self Help and Community Development in Towns*. Standing Conference of Local and Regional Authorities in Europe.

5. Santos Boaventura Sousa (1988), 'O Social e o politico na transicao pos-moderna', *Rev Communicacao e Linguagem*. No 6/7.

6. op. cit. Standing Conference of Local and Regional Authorities, 16-17.

7. ibid. 18-19.

8. Martinos, H. and Humphreys, E. (1989), *Urban Regeneration Strategies. European Communities Local Employment Development Programme*. London, South Bank Technopark.

9. Institut de Treball Social I Serveis Socials. Placa Catalunya, 9 4rt Barcelona.

10. Van Rees, W. (1990), 'Towards a Citizens Europe?' In McConnell, C. (Ed.), *Proceedings of the CDF, Council of Europe, European Commission Conference on Community Development in Europe*. London, Community Development Foundation.

11. Bussing, D. (1991), 'Training for Community Development. New Chances for Community Work Training in the Netherlands' *Community Development Journal*.

12. Nederlands Institut voor Maatschappelijke Opbouw, S'Hertogenbosch, Netherlands.

13. Callan, T. et al. (1988), *Poverty and the Social Welfare System in Ireland*. Combat Poverty Agency.

14. Crickley, A. and Devlin, M. (1989), *Community Work in the Eighties*. Unpublished conference paper.

15. European Community Development Exchange, Halston Street, Dublin 7.

16. Francis, D. et al. (1984), *A Survey of Community Workers in the United Kingdom*. National Institute for Social Work, London.

17. Barr, A. (1990), *Beyond Experiment and Rhetoric. Community Development - The Strathclyde Experience*. Community Development Foundation, London.

18. *Community Development, The Local Authority Role* (1989). Association of Metropolitan Authorities.

19. Community Development Foundation, 60 Highbury Grove, London N5 2AG.

20. op. cit. *Towards a Citizens Europe?*

*Chapter 6*

# Community Development in Rural Areas of Greece

## Peter Stathopoulos

### The Context of Community Development Policies and Programmes

First of all some details will be given about some of the key features which influence social policies aimed at the development of rural communities in Greece.

*Demographic characteristics*

Greece is a comparatively small country of approximately 130,000 square kilometers. It contains 3,000 islands in the Aegean and Ionian seas, of which only 150 are inhabited.[1] Three quarters of the country's total area is considered mountainous.

The population of Greece was nearly 9,750,000 according to the last census in 1981.[2] The rate of increase of the population is only about 0.4 per cent per year, but the elderly population is growing rapidly and by the year 2,000 it is expected that just over twenty per cent of the population will be over sixty years of age.[3]

Another trend is that the population in the rural areas is declining while the urban centres are gaining population especially in the Athens and Thessalonica metropolitan areas. The rural population has declined from fifty seven per cent in 1961 to thirty five per cent in 1981 according to the official census. Currently, just over half the population live in towns or cities of more than 10,000 people. The growth of the urban population is mainly due to internal migration from rural areas, rather than natural increase. The movement of people has affected young people disproportionately, so that small rural areas may have a high proportion of elderly economically dependent people, but low numbers of young adults and children. Some primary schools have closed as a result of insufficient pupils.

From the 1950s to the 1970s, the rural parts of Greece also lost population to other countries, particularly North America, Australia and Europe. It is estimated that 450,000 Greeks live in West Germany. Smaller but appreciable numbers went to France, Belgium, Sweden and the UK.[4]

In the 1980s the trend changed and very few Greeks migrate now. On the contrary there is an inflow of Greeks returning home. Very few inhabitants (about three per cent) are not of Greek nationality and the vast majority of the population belong to the Greek Orthodox Church, so that Greece has a very homogeneous population compared with many parts of the EC.

*Administrative structure*

Greece has a centralised government structure. It is divided into fifty two Prefectures (Districts) on the basis of geographical, economic, social and transportation criteria. The Prefector is the representative of the Central Government, responsible for the coordination of central government policies and programmes and for overseeing the operation of the local authorities.

In 1986 the government passed Law 1622 by which it has divided the country into thirteen regions. The population of most of these regions varies from 200,000 to 700,000. Attica has a population of 3,370,000 because it includes the metropolitan Athens area and the region of Thessalonica has a population of 1,600,000. The establishment of this regional tier of government was aimed at the development of structures for more effective planning, delivery of services and citizen involvement. The Regional Director is responsible for planning, budget preparation and development of proposals for the region. The regional council consists of representatives of the local cities and towns, prefectorial councils and central government representatives. Thus at the regional level the central and local government representatives have the opportunity to engage in joint planning and policy formulation.

Greece has a large number of small local government units (communities and municipalities). Over three quarters of the communities have a population below 1,000 and half have fewer than 500 residents. Yet a population of a thousand inhabitants is considered by the government to be the minimum size for a community to develop essential services such as day care, kindergartens, primary schools and health clinics. Thus the vast majority of the communities cannot provide essential services at a reasonable cost. Furthermore most villages are isolated and scattered in mountain districts or on small islands throughout the Aegean sea. During winter, accessibility to these communities is a problem when weather conditions deteriorate.

According to an unpublished Research Report of the Department of Health and Social Welfare[5] each social worker employed at the public welfare department of each prefecture has cases in eight communities in the Athens area while for the mountainous, rural Peloponesse region the ratio is 1:236 communities. In terms of space the ratio for the Athens area is one social worker to fifty six square kilometers, while for the Peloponesse region it is 1:1404 square kilometers. In many rural areas, much of the population lives at a considerable distance from the nearest social service centre. These data clearly indicate the magnitude of the problems in providing services when in many instances the means of transportation used by social workers and health professionals are buses or boats running once a day or twice a week.

Municipalities are usually larger and can support a wider range of services, but even so nearly one third have a population under 5,000 people. About one in ten municipalities have over 50,000 residents.[6]

Health, Education and Social Services are provided by the Central Government. The Health and Social services are mainly financed by the central government and delivered on a decentralised basis, usually at the capital of each prefecture. Recently larger municipalities have also developed health and social services which supplement the state run services, and deal mainly with prevention. During the past five years, six municipalities have established social services departments, providing a range of social, youth and recreational services. There are also private schools, clinics, health and social services run by voluntary organisations, the church and by the commercial sector. The voluntary agencies have pioneered new services, pilot projects and action research programmes. The Greek Orthodox Church runs a range of services including activities for young people and residential institutions for elderly people and those with special needs.

*Social and economic conditions of rural communities*

The size and location of many rural communities causes difficulties in the provision of adequate health, educational and social services. Similarly there is a lack of cultural and recreational opportunities especially for young people. There has been a weakening of traditional social and cultural values especially in areas with a rapid rate of industrialisation. Similarly TV, radio and video programmes have had a considerable impact on traditional values. Young people are exposed to messages from the media about greater affluence and employment opportunities in towns and cities. Greece also receives an estimated seven million tourists per year. Such an influx of foreigners during the summer months has a significant effect on the lifestyle of the younger population.

The economic basis of rural life has been altered by the decreasing numbers of people who are economically active. This has been accompanied by a decline in farming or fishing in many areas. Farm sizes are on average very small compared with other European countries so that farming is often uncompetitive on an international commercial basis. Tourism, forest protection, fruit-picking and public works provide opportunities for seasonal employment and supplementary income.

It is not surprising that recent studies of poverty in Greece indicate that by the most conservative standards ten per cent of the population live in poverty.[7] More liberal estimates increase the percentage to thirty three per cent of the population. One study showed that twenty nine per cent of all households were rural, whereas this was the case for forty six per cent of households in poverty.[8] It was also found that poverty hits hard households where the head is over seventy five years of age. A comparison of the situation in 1974 and 1981 revealed that the position had improved in rural areas, which was probably due in part to government policies aimed at the redistribution of income via tax legislation, subsidies and other measures.

## National Strategies for Social and Economic Development

The principal component of government social and economic policy since World War II has been industrialisation. There have been repeated efforts to attract foreign capital and advanced technology. Yet after forty years of efforts in this direction, Greece currently has had on average a zero rate of economic growth over the last five years. Greece has borrowed extensively during the last fifteen years and its economy is in a serious crisis.

There have been shifts in economic strategy related to external influences. According to Papatheodossiou,[9] Greek policy in the 1950s and 1960s may be characterised as *opportunistic*, with emphasis on technological innovation and specialisation in industries for which the country had particular advantages (e.g. plastics, shipping, tourism). The political dictatorship of 1967-74 and oil crisis of the early 1970s were accompanied by a change to a more *traditional* policy based on handicrafts, services, tourism and banking. Industrialisation slowed down as a result of low investment during this period.

During the subsequent eight years of government by the Socialist Party, efforts were made to promote economic activity by means of cooperatives (e.g. of farmers, craftsmen, consumers). Whatever other benefits they may have had, these largely failed as economic enterprises. They were not able to produce and sell their products and services on a competitive basis with the private sector.

Faced with a small, if not shrinking, private sector the government has become the employer for a large segment of the work force. According to recent Government reports, Greece has five times the number of civil servants that it needs. This has contributed to large budget deficits. Thus the newly elected conservative government is moving towards privatisation of the public sector and reduction of social services. Another round of efforts to recruit foreign investment and tourism has begun.

On a local community level the above mentioned strategies of economic development have not succeeded for a variety of reasons. Some of the obstacles to meeting community needs are related to historical, cultural, social and political factors. Let us examine some of these in more detail.

*Centralised decision making*

For a number of historical reasons central government has the political power, the legal and administrative authority to decide on all major matters affecting the local community. By contrast, the authority and resources of local government are very limited. Thus over the years a strong attitude of dependence on central government has developed in the population. This attitude has two implications. First, local people feel powerless to mobilise and solve local problems. They expect resources and initiatives to come from central government. Second, when the government promises to act on local problems, so many times it fails due to a variety of reasons but mainly to lack of funds and the inefficiency of its bureaucracy. This has fostered attitudes of mistrust about government effectiveness which combines with a lack of confidence about local people tackling problems themselves.

An example of this climate and attitude of dependence is worth sharing with the reader. The author was at the initial phase of a community development project in a village near the city of Patras. The presidents of various organisations and other leaders had assembled at the Community Hall in order to discuss with the community workers the findings of the community needs assessment study which had just been completed. There were twenty five persons present, among them the president of the community - a young progressive and sensitive man, as well as the priest of the village - a tall and energetic elderly man who had served the village for the past thirty five years. When the presentation of the findings was completed the priest said:

'Mr Stathopoulos, have you got financial resources?'

'Father', I said, 'I am afraid I will disappoint you.'

'Have you got political influence and access to government?'

'Again I regret my answer is "No"', I replied.

His face showed his disappointment with my replies. Saddened he continued:

> 'If you don't have money and influence at the Ministry, why did you come to our village? We know our problems.'

Deep silence spread in the room for a moment. Then the community president responded determinedly:

> 'Father you are right. We know our problems, but it is the first time in this village that *we all* are sitting on the same table to discuss them and see what *we can* do.'

I lost no time in reinforcing this observation:

> 'That is true, Mr President. We are all together here, determined to do something about these problems. The community workers - three social work students and two faculty members - are young and determined to offer what they have: enthusiasm, time, commitment and their knowledge.'

The climate had changed. A ray of hope had lighted the room. The group proceeded to set priorities and establish committees to deal with the problems. This has been one of the most successful community development projects I am aware of over the past seven years. For example, an active youth centre, a kindergarten, an amateur choir, counselling services and parents' advice groups have been set up to serve the semi-rural population of 2,000 people. There is also a unit for student social workers with their supervisors who work as community workers.

*Fragmented Administration*

In addition to the bureaucratic structure of the central government, there is the problem of the numerous small and ineffective local authorities. Such units lack the financial resources as well as the trained personnel to undertake major projects for solving their problems. Also centuries of relatively isolated existence of the villagers in the remote mountainous areas of the country have produced an attitude of strong localism.

The government has enacted legislation (N.1416/84) which provides financial and administrative incentives for the merger of small communities into large, viable municipalities, but the results have been disappointing so far.

*Political Parties*

Given the significance of central government in resource allocation, it is only natural that local politics are tied up very much with national party politics. The political parties try to promote their interests and this often leads to attempts to manipulate citizen participation at the local level.

Local government officials and councillors are elected with the support of the national parties, which to a large extent control their commitment and actions. This patronage certainly reduces the autonomy of the local representatives and adversely affects the level, motives and quality of citizen participation in local community development projects.

In general, the structure and strategies of the political parties foster divisions in the population and encourage identification with party policies and programmes rather than with community-wide local issues.

*Cultural Values*

Reference was made earlier to strong feelings of localism among Greeks. In addition Greek culture traditionally stresses individualism. Family ties and obligations to relatives, friends and fellow villagers come before obligations to the state and the community. As Lee[10] says:

> 'Greeks are born into a group and many Greeks, except under foreign influence in the city, never join a group. They are born into the family, into the circle of family friends, into the village community; they do not have to please in order to belong, or to follow regulations.'

These attitudes serve the important function of strengthening family ties and providing support to members of the extended family, but also weaken the ability to work collectively and plan rationally for projects which are of wider significance. Personal relationships and sentimentalism are stronger than rationality and social institutions in Greek society.

*Lack of Trained Personnel*

Community development is a slow and time consuming process. Especially so, when the local population feels let down by government officials, who have failed to make good their promises.

Community development should also be a professional activity, based on knowledge, skills and professional training of the community workers. However traditionally community work has been undertaken by priests, teachers, agriculturists, home economics practitioners, public health visitors and social workers without the necessary specialised training, supervision and administrative support.

Community work undertaken with the support and sanction of professional workers has been mainly within the framework of local self-help projects based on consensus theories and strategies according to Rothman's typology.[11] This is understandable in view of the fact that community workers are paid by the government and the adoption of social action and confrontation strategies could not be tolerated or reconciled with their duties as civil servants. Nonetheless, on numerous occasions citizens' groups have been formed and taken action in order to prevent government policies and/or programmes which they saw as contrary to the local interests. Examples of such projects are the establishment of a petrochemical factory which would pollute the area, the use of a river for waste disposal for the city of Ioannina and the establishment of a shipyard near the town of Pilos in Peloponesse. In all of these and other similar situations indigenous leaders have emerged and organised effectively the affected population. However the action groups tend to survive only as long as the immediate issue is alive, so that there is no continuity nor involvement with other social issues in the area. Useful as these groups may be they are short lived and lack strategies for broader social change.[12]

## Community Development Programmes - Past and Present

We have so far outlined the broader policies of national development, as well as those factors which have a negative impact on local community development projects especially in rural areas. We will now present a historical account of community work in this country.

During the long Turkish occupation up to the early 19th century, local communities maintained a fair degree of autonomy to run their own affairs. Matters of health, welfare, education and public works were considered local affairs. In many parts of Greece well organised cooperatives were established. After the War of Independence in 1821 the central government took over most of these functions, thus fostering a feeling of dependence. Community work prior to the World War II was focused around small irrigation projects, afforestation and building of gravel roads in rural areas.

During the Second World War Greece suffered immense human casualties. Its natural resources, housing stock and roads were depleted and/or destroyed. Efforts for reconstruction began with the aid of International Organisations such as UNWRA, CARE, WCS (World Church Service) and foreign governments, especially British and American. In collaboration with the Greek authorities, these foreign organisations initiated community development projects in many parts of rural Greece and the islands. Most of these projects provided technical support and materials while the villagers contributed the labour, in view of the extensive underemployment.

The philosophical emphasis of community development programmes was on self-help and self-reliance. The aim of the projects was to mobilise the population, instill a sense of hope and optimism for the future and to provide economic resources to meet basic needs of the whole population. In each village and community a community development committee was established by the Ministry of the Interior to initiate and encourage projects undertaken by the local population.[13]

The Royal National Foundation also engaged in extensive community development. It organised a number of conferences and in-service training on the methods and techniques of community development. For example in order to assist rural families economically the Foundation organised tapestry classes for women and consequently undertook to market the products through cooperatives and commercial enterprises. This activity brought appreciable income to families in rural areas.

However the initiation of such projects as well as the development of a state operated network of social services brought into focus the need for professionally trained personnel. It was during the late forties and early fifties that three schools of social work were established. British and American scholars were among the first educators. Prominent among the visitors were Dame Eileen Younghusband, Richard Titmuss and Arthur Dunham who influenced the framework for the curriculum of the schools which provided generic three year training. In-service training in community development methods was also given to some home economics teachers, rural development workers, teachers and others to enable them to work effectively with the population.

During the past decade there have been concerted efforts to strengthen local government. Two laws were enacted (N.1262/82 and N.1622/86) in order to give more authority and independence from the central government. In addition financial resources have been transferred from the state budget to local communities. Both laws also provided for the creation of opportunities and instruments of citizen participation at the neighbourhood, community and regional levels. They also provided for the establishment of Development Associations, which receive government funds and are eligible for financial support from the EC. Each such association covers a number of small communities. The general objectives of these associations are to improve local conditions, engage in local planning and undertake joint action to solve local problems. More specifically they seek to:

a) foster cooperation among the existing small local government units,

b) promote rational utilisation of local resources and the coordination of local development initiatives,

c) encourage the establishment of adequate social services to meet the social ..eeds of the population,

d) make rational use of grants and government funding for local projects,

e) promote citizen participation in local affairs.[14]

Efforts have also been made to stimulate entrepreneurial activities undertaken by local government. These include producers and/or consumer cooperatives, commercial enterprises and the operation of sports, recreational and social services establishments.

Looking back at the outcomes of these legislative initiatives it is not difficult to conclude that their success has been very limited. As Kalliatjidis[15] argues, the lack of initiatives by local government officials is not due to shortage of funds: 'It is rather due to lack of know-how and entrepreneurial spirit on the part of Mayors and Presidents of local communities.' The initial enthusiasm about active and extensive citizen participation has had only limited results. In many instances those citizens involved in participatory processes were members of the national political parties who wanted to control the various councils and other organisations in order to promote their own party's interests at local level. Such manipulative processes have helped to alienate large segments of the local population who chose to abstain from involvement. The growth of Development Associations has been slow too. Between 1984 and 1987 the number increased from only fifteen to thirty.[16]

Similarly the hoped for merger of small communities into large municipalities has been very limited. Strong feelings of localism and party political conflicts have contributed to this. Local authorities have been reluctant to engage in entrepreneurial activities. Amongst the reasons for this are the lack of financial resources, the reluctance of local officials to take risks and the lack of trained personnel. It is worth noting that only ten per cent of the 13,000 employees of local government are graduates of colleges and universities (mainly engineers), whilst twenty per cent did not have a full secondary school education.[17]

According to Tsenes[18] the failure of local government officials to take advantage and make use of the opportunities of the law:

'is related to the lack of administrative structure, the funding mechanisms for local government enterprises, and in many instances the acceptance by local government officials of the socialist philosophy on which some of these initiatives are based.'

In order to overcome some of these problems of technical and organisational nature, the Ministry of the Interior along with the Central Administration for local government established in 1985 the Greek Corporation for Local Government and Development (known as EETAA). This publicly owned non-profit organisation provides technical support to local government units and conducts studies related to social, economic and physical planning. Recently it has moved into staff development activities for local government personnel as well as the training of community development workers who will staff the community development associations. So far approximately 500 graduates of Universities have gone through a 400 hours course on community development. However the economic conditions of the country make it very difficult to recruit new personnel and so it is uncertain how many of those trained will eventually obtain employment. Some of the larger municipalities have also initiated short-term training courses for community development personnel.

It should be noted that formal training for community development workers is offered within the undergraduate generic social work training at the Social Work Department of the Technological Institutes (TEI). There is no university level social work training so far in Greece. A course on rural community development is also offered at the School of Agriculture for graduates who undertake rural development work.

In terms of actual programmes it is impossible to know exactly how many and what programmes exist as there is no research available. Recently EETAA has initiated a study in order to compile a list of community projects by the type of programme (eg housing, recreation, social services) and the sponsoring municipality. It is also expected that once this phase is completed a selection of case studies will be developed for training purposes, as well as a systematic analysis of community development work.

The whole question of the impact of community development policies and programmes on local communities has not been examined in systematic fashion so far. The National Welfare Organisation[19] sponsored a three day seminar on programme evaluation - the first of its kind in 1988. The impetus came from the

European Community funded anti-poverty programmes which require the grantee to conduct evaluation studies for its programmes. Whatever evidence exists comes from informed opinion of the community workers in the field. The significance of community projects can be witnessed in the increased level of citizen participation, the demand for more and better services and the development of some services (chiefly in urban rather than rural areas). Most programmes are focused around specific services rather than questions of social rights and advocacy, as there is no legitimate criterion for such roles by community workers. This domain is claimed by political parties, social movements and labour organisations.

Some of the issues in community work which will gain prominence in the 1990s seem to be related to the protection of environment, conservation of natural resources such as water, pollution control, clean environment, to mention a few. Decentralisation of health and social services (especially as these are related to drug abuse and the prevention of AIDS) will be issues in the new decade. Realising that there is a gap between the urban and rural communities in terms of the availability and quality of services provided, the government has recently declared its intention to develop community Health and Social Services at teleservice centres, as in other European countries.

'Such services which are making use of modern technology aim at reducing isolation of rural villages . . . The computer facilities are for communal use to overcome disadvantages in economic, educational and cultural services'.[20]

Over the next decade, many of the initiatives whether by central government or by the local authorities in urban or rural areas, will depend on European Community policies as well as funding. It is becoming evident as time goes by that EC social policies, directives and legislation have an increasing influence on what happens in the local communities and remote villages of Greece. Moreover, throughout the European Community, organisations representing people living in rural areas are applying pressure for policies to take greater account of their special needs and problems.[21]

## Summary

This chapter has provided an overview of the context and practice of Community Development programmes in rural areas of Greece. Notwithstanding the significance of urban problems in modern Greece, it was deemed important to emphasise the needs of rural communities, their peculiar problems which are related to small population size, their location in remote and often mountainous areas, and their lack of services to meet adequately the social and health needs of the people. The historical, social, political and administrative factors have been described which have impeded the development of effective local government units and hampered the participation of local people in service provision.

Since the War self-help projects have been set up, mostly following a consensus model of community work practice. The entrance of Greece into the European Community and the approaching unification in 1992 has provided an impetus for new kinds of rural community development projects as well as the necessary funding to implement such programmes.

## References

1. *Economic and Social Atlas of Greece* (1964), Social Sciences Centre of Greece, Athens, Table 2.06.

2. *Population Census Report 1981*. National Statistical Service of Greece, Athens, Table I.

3. *National Report on Aging in Greece* (1988), National Center on Social Research, Athens.

4. *GREECE* (1984), HYDRIA Encyclopedia, Athens, volume 4, 1222.

5. *Findings and Conclusions of Research Studies* (1986), Ministry of Health, Welfare and Social Security, Athens, 10-17.

6. *Administrative Divisions of Greece* (1989), Government Printing Office, Athens.

7. 'One in Ten Within the Limits of Poverty' (1990), *ELEFTHEROTIPIA*. Athens, 28.8.1990, 14-15. The article in this newspaper refers to a study conducted by the National Statistical Service on a national sample of 6, 489 households. The methodology used conforms to the one adopted by the EC for similar studies in other European countries.

8. 'The Dimensions of Poverty in Greece' (1990), *PROTI*. 14.8.1990, 22. This article reports on the findings of a recently completed study on poverty in Greece. The study is based on a sample of 6, 035 households.

9. Papatheodossiou, T. (1990), *Changing Needs in Vocational Skills*. Research Report No.6, Ministry of Education, Institute of Technological Education, Athens, 82-85.

10. Lee, D. D. (1951), 'Greece'. In Mead, M. (Ed.), *Cultural Patterns and Technical Change*. Mentor Books, New York, 93.

11. Rothman, J. (1968), 'Three Models of Community Organisation Practice'. In *Social Work Practice*. Columbia University Press, New York.

12. Stathopoulos, P. (1990), *Community Work: Theory and Practice*. ION Publishers, Athens, 248.

13. Makris, D. (1956), *Encyclical to the Prefectors and Eparchs of the State*. Ministry of the Interior, Athens, July.

14. 'Development Associations' (1987), *Local Government Journal*. 2-3, 34.

15. Kalliatzidis, A. (1986), 'Rules and Procedures for the Funding of Municipal-Community Enterprises' *Local Government Journal*. 4, 56.

16. Greek Corporation for Local Development and Self-government, (EETAA), Athens, 8.

17. Macheras, P. (1987), 'Local Development Workers' *Local Government Journal*. 2-3, 55.

18. Tsenes, L. (1986), *Local Government: Theory and Practice*. Phoebus, Athens, 257.

19. National Welfare Organisation (1988), 'Evaluation of Social Welfare Projects.' Proceedings of a Conference on Program Evaluation. *Ekloge*, 79.

20. Overtrup, L. (1989), 'Community Teleservice Centers and the Future of Rural Society.' Paper presented at the Conference on *Community Development in Europe Towards 1992*. Swansea, Sept.

21. Vayias, C. (1988), 'The Social Needs in Rural Areas of Europe' *Ekloge*, 74, 112-123.

# Chapter 7

# Families with Young Children: the Situation in Denmark

### Jacob Vedel-Petersen
*(Translated by Birte Nielsen)*

In this chapter I shall describe the situation in Denmark of families with young children, with particular reference to the principal features of family policy and recent trends in social work with these families. There are many similarities between Denmark and the other Scandinavian countries in this field, so that Danish policy may stand as a representative for the Scandinavian model in the European Community.

Cross-national comparisons of families' living conditions have always caused great difficulties. These depend on a great number of social and economic factors, such as the labour market, housing conditions, the education system and health services. An important influence is family policy, but it varies from country to country which laws and public measures are to be included under family policy and which are not. Acquaintance with the circumstances of families and comparisons between various countries thus presupposes a profound knowledge of the factors and legislation in all fields influencing the living conditions of the population.

It is not possible to make a comprehensive description in a brief article of this kind, nor to make a detailed cross-national comparison. Therefore this chapter will concentrate on drawing attention to some key characteristics of the position in Denmark and will, of necessity, omit much relevant information about the broader context, including the social security system in general.

### Demographic and Political Background in Denmark

Denmark is primarily a country with small families. The birth rate in Denmark is 1.4 live births per 1000 women. The number of families with one child make up about forty five per cent of all families with children. The number of families with two children is growing while families with three or more children are decreasing.

However, the wish to become a mother or father has shown no corresponding decline. Whereas, at the turn of the century, twenty five per cent of women did not become mothers, only nine per cent of women born during 1945-46 had not become mothers by the age of forty.

The number of employed mothers has increased steadily for many years and now eighty to ninety per cent of all mothers are in the labour force. By contrast with other countries, maternal employment does not differ greatly according to either family size or to the ages of the children. Thus we have a very high percentage of employed mothers with three or more dependent children and of employed mothers with very young children. A sizeable number of mothers work part time, but the proportion is decreasing and is now about one-third.

In talking about families with two employed parents or a single employed parent, we are then also talking about the overwhelming majority of families with children in Denmark. Housewives in the traditional sense are a rare phenomenon. This means that policies supporting families with employed parents are concerned not merely with poor families, but rather with the typical Danish family with children. They all share the same problems of finding someone to care for their children and of reconciling a working life with family life.

There is no reason to believe that women's increasing participation in the job market will reverse itself. On the contrary, the trend is continuing. This fact is generally acknowledged and social policy in support of these families will therefore not be aimed at reinstating women in the role of housewives, but will instead assist them in combining job and family responsibilities. However, the official policy in the next few years will probably be targeted at improving parents' opportunities for choosing freely whether and to what extent they want to be employed. There is little dispute about the objective of policy in this area and the main issue is what form policy should take. It is primarily a question of how public money for families from now on will be divided between social services and cash payments.

The past thirty years' improvement in the situation of families with children in Denmark has been backed by a broad political consensus. The political parties in the centre as well as to the right and left of the centre have endorsed a policy of steadily expanding support for families. This applies not only to the laws passed by the Danish parliament, but also to the decisions taken by local government. In this respect it is hard to detect any differences between municipalities controlled by the Conservatives and those controlled by Labour.

It is true that day-care institutions in particular have been the subject of debate, and still are, since they constitute a heavy cost to the public treasury, but this debate was not to any significant extent focused on whether the State, through those institutions, is taking over children's upbringing, thereby undermining parents' role. Nor has there been much debate over whether support for families with working parents is a public responsibility or not. It should be mentioned that demographic implications have also not been prominent in the Danish debate on family policy.

Instead, the debate has concerned the sizeable expenditures and their allocation and also whether the substantial funding, especially of day-care facilities, in a way denied parents their freedom to choose between caring for their children themselves or going to work while placing their children in an institution. What needs to be stressed here is the wide agreement in the population on the policies pursued in this area and hence also among politicians.

This development is linked to powerful social processes that have contributed to the same outcome, first and foremost the increasing need since the early 60s for female workers. Secondly, the equal rights movement encouraged women in large numbers to seek further education and employment. Finally, there was a growing concern about disadvantaged children getting a poor start in school because they come from homes with inadequate economic and cultural resources - in other words, the whole Head-Start concept.

These processes and socio-political ideas have been so powerful that the transformation of the classical family model with a working father and a stay-at-home mother into the family of today with two breadwinners and public money for child-minding and child-rearing has occurred without profound ideological conflicts. In practice, provision has trailed behind the official policy, but this has been due more to the state of economy than to political resistance.

## The Main Elements in Social Support to Families with Children

*Cash benefit*

An amount of well over D.kr. 5,000 is paid yearly per child to all families with children below eighteen years. In addition, single parents receive about D.kr. 4,000 yearly per child. As a rule both amounts are paid to the mother. They are subject to price-index adjustment and are tax-free. (For comparison £1 = 10.5

D.kr. in February 1990 and the annual income of an unskilled worker is about D.kr. 130,000).

*The Various Day-Care Facilities*

The social services authorities are required by law to ensure that day-care needs are met. While that target has yet to be reached, the number of day-care centres have proliferated since the 1960s.

The various day-care facilities comprise:

**1. SOCIAL SERVICES PROVISION**

a. *Nurseries*, which are intended for children aged 0-3. Normally they have as many as 30-40 children divided into groups of 10 children with 2 adults. Nurseries are open daily (except Saturdays, Sundays and holidays) for 10-12 hours.

b. *Nursery schools*, which are intended for children from 2-3 up to school age (which is 6 in Denmark). They enroll from 20 to 80 children, who are usually divided into groups of 20 children with 2 adults. These are all-day institutions whose primary function is to take care of children while their parents work.

c. *Age-integrated centres*, which are intended for children aged 0-14. In practice, however, they include children between the ages of about 1 and 10-12. New day-care centres are now usually organised on an age-integrated basis.

d. *Childminding*, ie care in private homes which is supervised by local authorities. Since 1967, social service authorities have had a programme to recruit and supervise childminders. Initially this was viewed as a short-term measure to provide a cheaper form of care until the requisite number of day care centres had been built. The rising demand has made home care a firmly established alternative, which many parents of small children consider preferable to the institutional facilities.[1]

e. *Recreation centres*, which are intended for children of school age outside school hours. The children are for the most part between the ages of 6 and 10, although the upper limit is 14. Recreation centres are run by local social services departments.

## 2. SCHOOL AUTHORITY PROVISION

f. *Kindergartens*, which are available for children a year before education becomes compulsory. They are voluntary and free of charge like the public schools. Kindergartens form part of the mainstream school system, ie the schools where the children will later enter first grade. They normally attend kindergarten three hours a day, five days a week. Therefore, children attend for shorter hours than in the case of nursery schools (b) and the main function is to prepare children for school.

g. *School-based care facilities*, which are run by the schools and use their premises. Clients and activities are almost the same as those at the recreation centres(e).

Over a period of twenty five years the number of day-care places for children up to the age of seven has increased from 35,000 to 275,000. The need for day-care facilities has increased steadily despite a rapidly falling birth rate. The demand for such facilities has always been greater than the supply. The present shortfall is probably about 30,000 placements.

This development is due first of all to a very high employment rate among mothers with small children. The Danish public day-care system plays an essential part in enabling Danish families with small children to have two incomes and so maintain a high standard of living. At the same time it has been a condition for the growth in the Danish labour force which has taken place during recent years.

Danish day-care centres are expensive to run, especially as a result of staffing costs. Parents with comfortable incomes pay no more than one-third of the actual cost, with the government footing the rest of the bill. Families with low incomes pay smaller fees or none at all. On average, seventy five to eighty per cent of the costs are publicly funded. Even so, day-care may be a big expense for a family with two children.

### 3. MATERNITY AND PATERNITY LEAVE

Female wage earners have a right to be absent from work on account of pregnancy and childbirth from approximately four week before the baby is considered due. After the baby's birth the mother has a right to be away from work for a total of twenty four weeks, of which up to ten weeks may be used by the father from the fourteenth week after the baby's birth. The right to be absent may be used by only one parent at a time.

In addition, the child's father has a right to leave from work for up to two weeks after the baby is born or has come home so that both mother and father are home together during that period.

|  | Birth of child | 14th week |  |
|---|---|---|---|
| Mother: | 4 weeks | 14 weeks | |
| | | | 10 weeks mother or father | Total = 24 weeks |
| Father: | | 2 weeks | |

During their periods of absence the mother and father are entitled to cash payments in compensation for their loss of income (wages and other earnings) amounting to a maximum of D.kr. 2,126 per week or the equivalent of two thirds of an industrial worker's normal wages. Parents with low incomes receive ninety per cent of their normal pay whereas parents with high incomes receive the stipulated weekly maximum of D.kr. 2,126. The figure is adjusted once a year but lags behind the rate of inflation and general wage increases. Parents who are not employed are not eligible for these payments, ie no wages - no cash benefits.

Information is lacking on the number of fathers who take advantage of paternity leave. Apparently quite a lot of fathers use up their own two weeks whereas only a few avail themselves of any part of the second option of ten weeks' leave. This is probably due to the prevalent rigid conception of gender roles plus the fact that cash benefits are considerably lower than most fathers' take-home pay.[2]

## 4. CHILD MAINTENANCE PAYMENTS

When parents are living separately, for instance owing to divorce or unmarried motherhood, the absent father has to pay a maintenance allowance for the child or children. Normally this amounts to well over D.kr. 600 per month per child, and can be more when the father is well off. If the contributor does not pay or is late in paying, then the parent with whom the child is staying can receive an equivalent amount through the social security system. The authorities will then assume the responsibility to collect the money from the contributor. The arrangement solves a great problem for many single parents and the authorities succeed in collecting eighty seven per cent of the amounts due.

## 5. HOUSING POLICY AND HOUSING SUPPORT

Families with children, and especially those with small incomes, receive financial support for housing in two ways. Firstly, the state has for many years subsidised a considerable number of house buildings, mainly aiming at the housing requirements of people with limited means and families with children. The support is made through public subsidy in relation to the building, so that the rent is reduced in comparison with the ordinary housing market. In consequence a good standard of housing is available at reasonable prices for a great number of families with children, amongst others.

Secondly, cash support is given to families living in rented houses or flats, who pay too high a rent in relation to their income. One of the purposes of this is to facilitate access to a suitable dwelling, and to take account of family size in housing assistance. About 50,000 families with children receive such housing benefits, the yearly amount being D.kr. 12-15,000 on average.

## 6. HEALTH SERVICE

Medical attention and hospital care are practically free for both children and adults. Moreover children and young people receive free dental treatment. All homes with newborn children are offered a visit by a health visitor, who visits the home regularly (more often in the beginning), keeps an eye on the child and advises the parents. The frequency of the visits and the point at which to stop the visits are decided according to the need of the family and the health of the child. The arrangement is very popular and only a very small number of parents do not want these visits. The family also has access to medical examinations of the child by their family practitioner or at a clinic a number of times during the first years of life.

*The Social and Financial Situation of Families*

After the above depiction of the main elements of Danish family policy, an evaluation of this will now be briefly presented. The Danish birth rate is low and on a level with most other European countries. Nowadays rather more women have children compared with some decades ago, but the number of children borne to each individual woman is smaller than previously. The number of abortions is high - almost a third of all pregnancies end up with abortion.

In some countries, at certain times family policy has been intended to increase the birth-rate. This has not been a declared policy objective in Denmark and indeed the considerable sums paid to families with young children have apparently had little influence on childbearing patterns.

On the other hand it was an early goal of Danish family policy to tackle poverty in families with children and so ensure the material basis for children to have a good upbringing. This purpose has been broadly achieved, in the sense that the great majority of families with children have an adequate income, whilst poverty and sub-standard housing are rare. Couples with only one parent in paid employment who have several children must often live on a modest scale, as do quite a few single parents. However, dire poverty is an exception and for the great majority their hard work results in a level of income which satisfies the parents and fulfills the conditions under which they wish to bring up their children.

A further aim was to establish day care of good quality for the children while the parents were at work, at the same time giving the children learning and developmental opportunities that life had previously deprived them of in the industrialised urban environments. This has almost been fulfilled too.

Against this background of relative success, the family policy agenda has moved on. One goal on today's agenda concerns reconciling the demands of family life and working life, so that there is time for being together in the family and developing personal relationships. A second point is the wish for more freedom of choice, ie better opportunities for the parents to decide their total participation in working life, taking into consideration the well-being of the children and the family as a whole.

We have seen that the great demand for community child care is explained by women's involvement in the job market, by the need for two incomes in the family, by the few children per family, by people's faith in the quality of community care and by the educational advantages accruing to the children. On the whole parents are quite satisfied with current day care facilities.[3] Nevertheless, some parents - and perhaps mothers in particular - seem to feel torn between, on the one hand, their job and earnings, and, on the other, a concern about their domestic life and their children's rearing.

On several occasions the Danish National Institute of Social Research has therefore asked mothers with small children about which arrangement they consider best suited to families with small children (see Table 1). We gave mothers a choice between different family situations and asked them to indicate their preferences. The clear winner is a family situation where both parents work part-time and the children are in nursery school half the day. The second most popular family type is where the father has a full-time job, the mother works part-time and the children spend half the day in nursery school. The 'traditional family', where the father works full time and mother and children stay home, has rapidly lost support, but just as unpopular is the scenario of both parents working full time and the children in nursery school all day. In other words, the arrangement which is a fact of life for most families is preferred by only a small proportion of them. The actual development has patently been out of tune with what mothers believe to be the soundest solution: the best possible compromise between their different concerns. There is a gap between dreams and reality, and that gap is steadily widening.[4]

**Table 1: Which family types have done best in the opinion of mothers with small children? 1970, 1975, 1985.**

| Man | Woman | Children | Percentages | | |
|-----|-------|----------|------|------|------|
| | | | 1970 | 1975 | 1985 |
| I.   Full-time job | Home | Home | 31 | 25 | 11 |
| II.  Full-time job | Home | Half-day care | 22 | 7 | 6 |
| III. Part-time job | Part-time job | Half-day care | 15 | 27 | 46 |
| IV.  Full-time job | Part-time job | Half-day care | 31 | 38 | 33 |
| V.   Full-time job | Full-time job | All-day care | 1 | 2 | 3 |
| VI.  Home | Full-time job | Home | 0 | 1 | 0 |

The utopian dream of today may well provide themes for the agenda of tomorrow. The evidence is that the family's quality of life and the distribution of such immaterial goods as time for each other, loving concern, a sense of belonging and security will be the main issues.

*Families in Need of Special Support*

In the previous paragraphs I have described in general terms the living conditions of families with small children. In the next section the focus will be on families with special needs for support, in particular families with major internal conflicts and families whose conditions in one way or another are a threat to the welfare and development of the children. Such families are known in all parts of Europe, and amongst the problems to be found are alcohol and drug abuse, family crises, violence towards women and children, frequent changes of partner and an aimless way of life.

It is well known that poverty combined with discordant family relationships are associated with a high risk of poor outcomes for children in terms of life-style and educational achievement. Overwhelmingly, children received into public care come from such backgrounds too. Social workers find that these families are often characterised by hopelessness, lack of self-confidence, isolation and lack of initiative. This group of families requires many resources, including financial assistance as well as the social workers' advisory function and efforts to achieve behavioural change. It can be very difficult for social workers to devote sufficient time to such families in view of their other responsibilities at the public assistance office.

It can also be mentioned that in twenty per cent of all new cases where State cash benefits are started the clients will be supported by the state for a year or more. Families with children make up a considerable proportion of this group. By following a cohort of newly started cases in question and counting the total amount of months these clients are supported by the state, it was found that the twenty per cent of cases lasting more than one year account for sixty seven per cent of the total number of months of support.[5]

## New Trends in Assistance for Families with Special Needs

Social service authorities give advice about questions that in one way or another are a problem to their clients, such as housing, budgeting, education and childrearing. In Denmark, social workers employed by public authorities have the following tasks: assessing financial needs, arranging the payment of benefits and offering personal counselling. The majority of clients are seeking financial support, but some want advice or counselling. Whatever the nature of the referral, it is the social worker's task to become acquainted with the total situation and give financial aid or counselling according to the person or family's circumstances and entitlement. Moreover the social service authorities can arrange for children to go into public care and organise short or long term placements in children's homes or in foster care. They also draw people's attention to clubs, support groups and educational/training facilities. The authorities co-operate with the health services, schools and school psychologists, child guidance clinics, unemployment exchanges and vocational training schools. Financial support can be given to cover living costs for periods in vocational training.

The whole system works reasonably well for a large number of clients, but may have an insufficient effect on a minority who account for a very considerable part of the total cash support. I shall not discuss further 'routine' social work, but describe some new trends in work with the most difficult cases.

For many years criticism has been levelled against the social system from both the right and left wings of the political spectrum. There are many similarities in their comments, but also differences. The Labour Party claims that the system traps in the client role a group of the population who have a marginal relationship to the labour market. They are treated as second class citizens. From right wing parties the criticism is part of a more general criticism of the welfare state. They find that the social aid system is weakening the incentive to make one's own way and take responsibility for one's own life. Furthermore it is suggested that the welfare state dislocates the free and economically sound functioning of the market and wage systems.

From the left wing parties the criticism forms part of a general critique of the combined operations of the state and the market. The exaggerated demands of working life, new technology and the lack of social networks in some housing estates calls for readjustment, education and mobility. Many people are not able to cope with these stresses. The left wing parties point out the difficulties of the weakest in managing their own affairs, the risk of client-making and stigmatisation. All these processes block the road back to a normal self-supporting existence. Moreover, the left wing parties attach importance to the oppressive and disabling nature of these processes, which tend to perpetuate the problems rather than resolve them.

Many people consider unemployment to be a major reason for so many families to be locked into the social services system. There is general agreement that an improved employment situation would solve many social problems, but there is dispute about who should bear the burdens. Employers are inclined to think that the labour market should be responsible for 'able' members of the labour force and for temporary unemployment benefits, but that the social security system should deal with the less able. The left wing view is that employers should also bear part of the burden for those less able to gain work by being more flexible in recruitment.

For some years now the social service authorities have tried to find new ways and methods in social work for families with children in special need of support. Since the beginning of the 1980s, the Government has supported local initiatives and in 1988 the Danish Folketing (Parliament) voted 350 million D.kr. over a period of three and a half years for the development of social work and experiments with new methods. In the Danish context, this is a very considerable amount. The idea is to support local initiatives and to promote new approaches, especially with a view to prevention. The programme is aimed at many different disadvantaged groups, but families with children have a central place. The objective is to stimulate local social services, clubs and groups of citizens to work jointly to strengthen and develop the local community and to enable people to exert more influence. Although the programme is receiving considerable subsidies from the Government, it builds on local ideas and initiatives aiming at transverse co-operation between various public sectors and between the public and the private sector.

In the Danish debate and in many social projects one comes across ideas which are well known in many other developed welfare states. These include notions of prevention, community strategies, decentralisation, de-professionalisation, activating local forces and outreach work. They have roots in the eco-social and community development critiques of existing services as well as in the problems of the welfare state with regard to financing present policies. Many of the ideas point towards dismantling the traditional apparatus.

Thus, in Denmark a great number of projects are going on with a view to helping families with children in new ways. Many of these activities are taking place in certain neighbourhoods with many disadvantaged families. The purpose is to meet them on their home ground, to activate resources in the area and to create a social network to support these families. This is done in co-operation with local organisations and clubs or through the establishment of clubs or groups meeting the special needs of the clients. It is a matter of fusing social work and cultural work. Until now the experiences have been mixed and it is still hard to involve those families with the severest difficulties.[6,7]

Workers are normally aware of the value of early intervention and of the risk of letting a case run too far. Cases of a three months duration are often reviewed in order to estimate whether special efforts should be needed.

Privatisation has been on the Government's programme for many years, but so far it has only been carried out to a limited extent (eg private labour exchanges). However, it is most probable that the Danish social system in the years to come will become more pluralistic and that private organisations and initiatives will play a greater role.

## Conclusions

There is a richness of ideas and initiatives in Denmark. Most local authorities are committed to trying new ways and Central Government has granted resources to support reorganisataion. For example, efforts are being made to provide work or training so that long-term recipients of state benefits may leave the client role. Social workers are also attempting to reduce the isolation and enrich the social experience of the most depressed individuals. The former approach of encouraging people back into 'normal' work roles has broad political support, but many social workers believe that social measures are the only practicable ones in the most difficult cases.

So far so good. However, one must at the same time realise that the development is happening within the framework of the social system. It is a question of adjustments and renewals, but not of radical changes either in the system or in philosophy. It is not a question of transferring all responsibilities to local citizens but of sharing responsibilities so that clients gain independence and self-determination.

I am not suggesting that the new development is only a cosmetic one, as changes in attitudes of far-reaching consequences are taking place. What is happening, however, is only the beginning of a process started by the criticism of the eco-social system. Where it will end cannot be predicted. A radical resettlement of the welfare state is unlikely, because of strong popular approval, but maybe the result will be a far more pluralistic and flexible system than we have today.

## References

1. Christoffersen, M. N. et al. (1987), *Hvem Passer Vore Born?* Socialforskningsinstituttet, Copenhagen.

2. Andersen, B. H. (1990), *Bornefamilier*. Socialforskningsinstituttet, Arbejdsnotat, Copenhagen.

3. Christoffersen, M. N. (1987), op. cit.

4. Christoffersen, M. N. (1987), op. cit.

5. Jorgensen, W. and Thaulow, I. (1984), *Klienternes Levekar og Problemer*. Socialforskningsinstituttet, Copenhagen.

6. Christensen, L. G. (1989), 'Research on Trends in Intervention on behalf of Children and Youth in Aarhus, Denmark'. In Hudson, J. and Galaway, B. (Eds.) *The State as Parent*, Dordrecht, Kluwer, 344-353.

7. Adamsen, L. and Fisker, J. (1986), *Socialt forsogsarbejde i boligomrader*, Amternes og Kommunernes Forskningsinstitut, Copenhagen.

*Chapter 8*

# Responses to Child Abuse in the EC

## Helen Armstrong and Anne Hollows

### Introduction

This chapter considers the range of responses to child abuse within the EC and the extent to which common threads in theory and practice may be discerned. We identify some of the broad, contextual issues before briefly describing the key features of response in most of the EEC states. Finally we develop a model for charting this information in ways which permit some degree of comparison and offer a basis for distinguishing factors likely to lead to further development.

We have obtained information from most EC member states, although in some cases the information is limited. Our coverage of the different countries is varied, reflecting the availability of material, but we have been able to illustrate the range of responses and highlight the dominant influences on their development. For this reason we have included some material from the German Democratic Republic, recognising both the imminence of German reunification and the particular issues thrown up where a society is in the process of major change.

There is no standard statistical data available on child abuse and neglect in Europe and where statistics exist, they are based on local criteria and are therefore difficult to compare. In Holland, a major sector of reported abuse is described as 'emotional' and a significant sector as 'cognitive'; categories which are respectively unusual and unknown in the UK. We have therefore restricted our use of statistical information to the illustration of specific points. We have made detailed use of published papers, many published under the auspices of the International Society for the Prevention of Child Abuse and Neglect (ISPCAN). We have amplified this by referring to practitioners and, in some instances, current affairs publications. Aspects of practice which attract academic attention are therefore set alongside the current dilemmas of practitioners in daily contact with children and families and linked to prevailing attitudes and trends in society.

An EC perspective on child abuse contributes to knowledge and understanding on a number of levels:

1. It offers the potential to examine different approaches to the various component aspects of identifying and working with children who have been abused and their families, and the practical implications of these approaches.

2. It identifies similarities. Throughout Europe the same issues are being raised and answers are being sought to the same sets of dilemmas. In some instances, there may be resolutions, while in others a heightened awareness of the tensions inherent in this work can be offered.

3. Increasing economic mobility of residents in member states means that it will become more likely that social workers will deal with families from other member states or may themselves move to work in other parts of Europe.

4. The differences in practice between member states have their origins in the different historical and sociological contexts of the work. An examination of these differences can stimulate and inform approaches to work at a wider level by posing unfamiliar questions.

However, over and above these factors which apply equally to many international comparisons, the European community currently offers a particular opportunity to review the different patterns of child protection policies and practice in relation to the specific cultural and societal settings prior to the development of the Single Market. With growing economic unity and the greater social interaction which that implies, we can anticipate increased mutual influence on policies of child care between states and eventually community-wide policies to underpin further developments. That stage is still far off. At present we can see, and will examine in this chapter, systems of response which are in different stages of development, all of which embody tensions likely to lead on to further development. It is important that these systems and the factors which have defined them, are detailed in their current variety enabling informed thinking about the implications and parameters of future change and the possibility of a greater unity of approach. For example, it is important to identify how far therapeutic techniques which have an international validity can be brought into play within the administrative structures for responding to child abuse which bear the unique imprint of national history and culture. This tension between those features of response which override national boundaries and those features which are intrinsic to specific cultures will mark all our accounts of national response and underpin the model for comparison which we outline.

We therefore bring together summaries of the major distinctive styles of work in child abuse in the context of differing understandings of the phenomenon of abuse. We have found it essential to set our analysis of the experience of member states in the broader context of their approach to fundamental issues of the relationship of state to individual, and child to family.

### The European Context

The regulations of the EC have their main impact on individuals and families through measures which support the organisation and operation of economic life. The EC's limited concern with child care concentrates on the provision of daytime creche facilities in order that mothers may work. As the single European market brings about greater movements of labour between member states, issues of family life will increasingly be drawn into the arena for EC activity.

All EC members belong to the Council of Europe, a distinct and larger grouping of nations. The Council has monitored the development of family law within Europe and, anxious to avoid increasing disparity between member states, has drawn up legal instruments with a view to European unification and in order to avoid increasing divergencies. With respect to child abuse, the Council recommends a dual strategy of immediate intervention coupled with prevention policy. It further recommends measures concerning four areas: prevention; early detection; management; and training of personnel. The forms of abuse considered by the Council include neglect, deprivation of affection, physical injury, emotional and cognitive abuse. No mention is made of sexual abuse. Furthermore, unlike the EC's regulations regarding economic life, the recommendations of the Council carry no obligations for member states. In preparing this chapter, we cannot avoid the impression that information about child abuse services within member states is sparse, and knowledge about the 'European scene' both among EC staff and among Non Governmental Organisations dealing with children is almost non-existent. An abused child within the EC would have no guarantee of common response, even at a basic level, in the Community. This diversity of services and practices reflects, in part, the practical implications of unresolved dilemmas of socio-legal theory in a subject area where knowledge is developing very fast.

Readers from or within the UK may be familiar with its procedures for responding to child abuse, usually described as child protection. While there are differences (particularly between Scotland and the rest of the UK) in the detail of the legal processes which are necessary to make a child safe from abuse, and further differences in the availability of therapeutic and preventive resources, there is a national system of local authority services in respect of children and their families where abuse has taken place or is perceived to be at risk of taking place. There are detailed duties and guidelines; and regular monitoring and inspection is provided. It is, however, important to recognise that while a comprehensive, nation-wide pattern of response obtains in some EC states this is far from true for all states, and is certainly not the case across Europe as a whole. Even systems with some similarities may have very dissimilar consequences: in the UK the existence of a nationally available service is said to encourage and stimulate local developments and experiments, while in France precisely the same reason is given for the discouragement of local initiatives.

To some extent the absence of a unified approach may be a consequence of different political structures, notably the ways in which the state permits services to be organised at a local level. Some countries have a federal system, or include autonomous regions (Germany, Italy, Spain), so that more power lies at the state/province level than elsewhere. At the same time, devolution to neighbour-hood level has developed furthest in Denmark, while in Holland the traditional role of the state often appears to be permissive rather than regulatory.

In other cases distinctive patterns may derive from particular understandings of the relationship between the state and the family. The Irish constitution elevates the family to a position which is virtually unassailable, resulting in major political tensions around the recognition of intra-familial abuse or indeed any other breakdown in family life. Further variations relate to the position accorded to the child, the perception of children's rights and the priorities which are currently placed on different aspects of children's well being.

An additional issue which occurs throughout Europe in different forms is that of 'communities within communities'. In Germany for example groups of immigrant workers, particularly Turks, tend to establish 'closed' communities within the mainstream culture. Social work within these communities has encountered problems, not least in communication. Child abuse has not yet been identified as a major area of concern though the situation of adolescent children is already an issue. This has parallels with the situation of ethnic minorities throughout Europe. In the UK and Holland, black communities are more likely to have come originally from the Indian sub-continent, the West Indies or the Far East. Issues of race, culture and ethnicity which produce such powerful reactions in all areas of social and political life, are an equally volatile element in working with child abuse and we can anticipate increasing consciousness of this area of work as responses to child abuse become more developed. A related matter is the exploitation of child workers. In southern Europe (notably Portugal, Greece and parts of Italy) there is increasing evidence of an inability by governments to stem this problem, which also occurs in northern Europe among workers who have migrated from the South.

Despite the variety of problems and responses, it is interesting to note that difficulties in implementation may be shared. Reading articles on the state of practice in countries as diverse as Spain,[1] the Netherlands[2] and Denmark[3] the reader is struck by their shared conclusions that for any individual child, poorly co-ordinated systems may result in delays, lack of decisive action, and confusion. Similar findings characterise many of the reports on child abuse inquiries in the UK.

## Services for Abused Children

There are, therefore, significant ways in which political structures and state/family relationships have influenced the development of services in different countries. Running parallel to these influences are the tensions between different models and theories about the nature and prevalence of child abuse itself. All these features contribute to the national understanding and awareness - or sometimes denial - of abuse and that in turn feeds the public response to a child or family in difficulty. With these features in mind, we now turn to the detail of services in some of the EC states.

### The Netherlands

The response to child abuse in the Netherlands is one of the better known models of European practice. The dominant approach is that the goal of all intervention is therapeutic, whether for victim, abuser or other family members. With this concept as the design principle, the protection of children is focused on the 'Confidential Doctor' service. There are now ten Confidential Medical Centres in the Netherlands operating as twenty-four hour reporting agencies taking referrals on a confidential basis from anyone concerned about the welfare of a child.[4] The functions of this service are to co-ordinate the work of child care agencies, to meet the needs of a child and to keep records on long term assistance to the child and family.

Social welfare in the Netherlands is characterised by a large number of small independent agencies, including social work agencies, child and family guidance agencies, psychiatric services and community services such as day nurseries and playgroups.[5] Most cases are dealt with by offering supervision of the child and family. Confidentiality is so central a concept that the issue of criminal prosecution is marginalised[6] with very infrequent recourse to the law. Only five out of 1729 cases reported to the confidential doctors in 1979 were referred for potential prosecution. This contrasts with the reliance in the UK on legal procedures including Place of Safety Orders and Care Orders (Supervision Requirements in Scotland). Since assessment is not strongly influenced by the potential need to meet precise legal requirements in court, action in the Netherlands is based on more open-ended concepts of abuse. Four categories of child abuse are employed: physical abuse; sexual abuse; cognitive abuse and emotional abuse. The category of cognitive abuse includes situations where a child's development is impeded by a parental psychiatric condition or by limiting forms of socialisation. It accounted for seven per cent of all abuse in Amsterdam in 1985-86. In the same year, forty per cent of cases registered in Amsterdam in 1985-86 were for emotional abuse. Findlay[7] contrasts this with one per cent of registrations in the same year in the similar 'failure to thrive' category.

There is currently considerable discussion in the Netherlands on the role of the criminal law with regard to prevention of further abuse. Under civil law the children's court judge may issue 'supervision orders' by which a family supervisor is appointed with powers to enforce co-operation and suggest action to protect the child. Such measures are only undertaken, however, where earlier attempts to achieve voluntary collaboration have failed. The underlying theory is that where abuse occurs, families need help rather than coercion if they are to change damaging modes of behaviour. The system is designed to offer ease of access, confidentiality, and appropriate help. The absence of a strong legal framework for action is striking to those accustomed to the UK model.

The Confidential Doctor system provides a widely-accessible, low-threshold access to facilities, mirroring other aspects of Dutch life such as the emphasis on individual freedom and dislike of bureaucratic control of individual action. It may, however, lead to some anomalies in the field of child abuse when an essentially therapeutic and non-punitive approach to abusers is seen as implying a tolerance of their behaviour. A wider policy example was the proposal by the government in 1985 to reduce the age of consent for sexual activity to twelve, a proposal which was eventually withdrawn in response to public reaction and professional concern. There are parallels with the availability within and from the Netherlands of pornographic videos portraying children. Arguments about the 'liberation' of children to enjoy sexual activity are not purely the preserve of paedophile organisations and derive some strength from a culture which values individual liberty highly. To date, the argument for reducing the age of consent has been unsuccessful in the Netherlands but is currently surfacing in Germany.

*Belgium*

The Dutch model has had an impact in other European member states, notably its neighbour Belgium.[8] Two initiatives have been based on the Confidential Doctor approach, accepting the 'medical' model of the symptomatic nature of abuse with regard to dysfunction of the family. In Belgium the existence of two quite distinct communities - in Flanders and Wallonia - provides a complicating factor, with a stronger sense of progress currently in Wallonia. The issue of the relationship of the therapeutically based services to the judiciary is a central one. Although Juvenile Courts are empowered to take measures for minors whose health and safety are at risk, they are seen to be hampered by inadequate legislation.[9] At the same time, the conflict between the responsibility to report criminal actions (set out in the penal code) and the professional confidentiality of the therapeutic relationship has not been satisfactorily resolved.[10] These conflicts occur throughout Europe where responses to abuse take place within a framework of legislation which predates the recognition of the special circumstances of child abuse.

*The Irish Republic*

The difficulties of child abuse work in a context which is not designed to accommodate the concept of abuse, are illustrated in a more extreme way in the Irish experience. With the 'inalienable and inprescriptable rights' of the family unit set out in article 41.1 of the constitution - rights explicitly described as 'antecedent and superior to all positive law' - those working to protect children from abuse are working against the assumptions which underpin both the law and societal attitudes. Opponents of the Irish Childline argued that its encouragement for children to act autonomously was a threat to family integrity. Although new legislation is currently in progress, professionals in child protection face problems in getting recognition and help for individual cases and broader recognition of the scope and prevalence of child abuse. Where cases are identified, the responding professionals are located in the Health Boards which are medically led and incorporate social work teams.

*France*

Although Girodet[11] reported that there is no structure specifically to deal with child abuse in France, this means that there is no single agency in the field and neither is there any national voluntary agency devoted to child protection. There is, however, a national system where responsibilities for different aspects of the service are shared by different agencies in a formalised way. Centralised regulation of local administration is a well known feature of life in France and French people have a tradition of compliance with bureaucracy. Preventive work in relation to child abuse is rooted within that willingness. Maternity and child benefits are contingent upon regular attendance at clinics and paediatric assessments by the PMI (Protection of mothers and infants). PMI's rigorous screening system up to the age of six years, coupled with its free nursery schools for children from three to six years, offer good opportunities for identifying children at risk.

The French Child Welfare Service, L'aide sociale à l'enfance (ASE), is part of a long tradition of preventive, community based work in France.[12] Its services include preventive and supportive work with families including out-of-home placement on a voluntary basis. It receives referrals of children at risk from other professionals or by anyone else who has knowledge of the child's situation. Failure to pass on information about children who are actually abused is a criminal offence, though midwives and doctors are exempt from this obligation. ASE may deal with a referral themselves on a voluntary basis or pass it on to the children's judge (Juge des enfants).

Juges des enfants can be found in each Département (county). Technically, they can receive referrals wherever a child is perceived to be at risk.[13] Referral is obligatory where actual abuse has occurred to any child under fifteen. The Juge calls for enquiries and reports and then hears the views of parents. He is not, however, obliged to see the child and while the child has the right to be represented and counselled by a lawyer there is no obligation to inform the child of this right. On the basis of the information received, the Juge then develops a plan of action for the case. This is normally implemented by ASE, and may include some form of residential provision or the involvement of 'Éducation surveillée', an autonomous, regional administered system providing community supervision - roughly comparable with the Probation service in England and Wales. In effect, the Juge's intervention enforces the co-operation of the family with the services on offer. The Juge does not, however, have any power to prosecute parents for their actions against their child. He is obliged to refer cases to the Prosecutor but this is a distinct branch of legal services and decisions about prosecution are made in a different setting.

While there has been some controversy in France recently around the obligatory referral to prosecutors, the major tensions have revolved around the assessment and management of risk. The dilemma of leaving children at risk with their birth families or separating them permanently to move to a new family dominates not only the professional scene but also extends into the public arena. In France these issues have been coupled with increasing concern that the child's perspective is often poorly represented or unheard by the Juge. A major public affairs weekly, Le Nouvel Observateur, has launched a campaign to amend the constitution to provide a 'défenseur des enfants' (roughly akin to a Guardian ad Litem) in any case where a child is involved in contentious litigation.[14] The same journal has done much to publicise the problems of denial, particularly in rural communities. Its major feature on abuse in 1989 closely followed by a lengthy television feature resulted in greatly increased awareness among French people. A telephone service for children was set up on the lines of Childline, but the difficulty of training and supporting staff is said to have limited its early response.

*Italy*

Italy too has a phoneline for children, Telefono Azurro. It has faced problems of a different nature: the difficulty of offering a national referral service when in some parts of the country there is nowhere to refer to. In Italy the municipalities have the legal responsibility of guaranteeing services to children in their region. This apparent uniformity is not matched by uniformity of services at local level, where differing ideologies and inequalities of resources may mean that an abused child will receive very different responses in different parts of the country. Telefono Azurro now maintains a database of public and private support services who can assist children and families.[15]

The dominant agency in the Italian response is the juvenile court. In all cases the court initiates action, evaluating the situation of the child within the family, setting in motion appropriate responses and co-ordinating the different agencies. The agents of this response throughout the country are the health and social services units of the municipality. In theory a wide range of resources are available to them to meet their responsibilities. This will be the case in centres such as Milan where there is a longstanding tradition of voluntary and private agencies undertaking therapeutic work with families and children. In other parts of the country, especially in the south, provision is much patchier and an overall lack of resources is a problem. The traditionally high sums spent by municipalities on care of children are mainly used for cash payments and sometimes residential care. This kind of welfare provision is ingrained in local political life and there is some reluctance to develop therapeutic programmes. Further political issues are raised by the apparent ease with which wealthy families adopt children from poor families in difficulty.

Sexual abuse is provided for in a quite distinct way with a legal requirement to report the offence to the criminal court. This provision ensures that sexual abuse receives a different level of response but paradoxically can also lead to reluctance to identify sexual abuse because of the prospect of court action.

Conflicts of ideology and philosophy are apparent in the current climate. As elsewhere this centres on the extent to which therapeutic intervention is affected by voluntary relationships with families as opposed to coercive relationships. In sexual abuse a very different conflict of philosophies is apparent with media calls for strong punitive action while professionals in many areas are working towards a therapeutic and non-punitive response.

*Denmark*

Denmark presents a profile of children's services which differs from other EC countries (see Chapter 7). Almost forty two per cent of children are born to unmarried parents,[16] although they are not necessarily lone parents. Over fifty per cent of mothers of children under three work outside the home. Traditionally well established welfare provision including high unemployment pay, very considerable support to single parents and good nursery provision, has masked the problem of child abuse. Until the late 70s there was still a strong sense that abuse was not a problem in Denmark.[17] Mandatory reporting of abuse was established in 1976.

Welfare provision has a strong emphasis on locally based democratic proce-dures. Social work provision is organised by the local authority in each of the 275 small local communes and the pattern of responsibility is much more community based than is the case for example in the UK. The small, local social services committee develops guidelines and agrees child protection action. The committee can enforce action where voluntary parental cooperation is not obtained by social services. Most action is, however, taken with a strong emphasis on parental cooperation and prevention including access to short term foster and residential care. In some areas family centres have been developed to work with families in protecting children by improving family functioning.

Difficulties of collaboration and a concern that cases are 'slipping through the net' or that children might meet with a confusing multiplicity of concerned professionals were identified in the early 80s,[3] but collaboration has developed over the last ten years in the climate of increasing awareness of child abuse of all kinds. Local review committees of agencies involved in child abuse work operate throughout the country, some having started more than ten years ago.[16] In this context, there has been the opportunity for a wider perspective on abuse to develop. In 1985 the Danish Parliament prohibited physical punishment by parents. The Danish Society for Prevention of Child Abuse and Neglect was a prime mover behind the legislation on parental punishment. It has recently established a national centre with a hotline and plans to work for a national Ombudsman for children.

*Germany*

In West Germany the last fifteen years have been marked by important developments in child protection work, reflecting broad shifts in public attitudes since the mid-seventies. There have been two main kinds of change. The first is a shift in personal and professional attitudes among those working within the state system; and the second is the setting up of new-style centres for child protection work run outside the state system.

Child protection has never been a central focus of state services for youth and child welfare with the result that there has been little formal encouragement towards interagency working. The role of the courts tends to be limited to penal sanctions against the abuser, rather than providing a legal framework for ensuring protection and therapy for the abused child. The development of a system of registration, unwelcome because of historical suspicions of registration of families, is further hindered by a professional culture in which agencies and professionals have little tradition of collaboration. Working within a child care system informed by traditional values can be stressful for professionals who adopt a more therapeutic perspective.

These difficulties have led groups of concerned individuals to set up child protection centres in some areas. The first was set up in 1975 in Berlin by Reinhard Wolff. There are now nine such centres with more initiatives under way. The new centres have introduced a very different philosophy and way of working. They offer a confidential therapeutic model which aims at offering help to child and family rather than punishment of the offender.

The thinking behind this approach has been mirrored by developments in public opinion with a general 'softening' of attitudes and greater awareness of the need for therapeutic input to abuse work. These developments have themselves been recently challenged as the issue of sexual abuse (with its impact on such personal and volatile areas as the family, gender and power issues, and sexuality) has caused a re-appraisal of the need for legal controls on the family.

The national child protection charity, the Kinderschutzbund, sees its remit in broad terms including ecology and work on living conditions. Child abuse work is one issue among many. The Kinderschutzbund is organised in 300 independent local groups, often unable to support the employment of professional staff. It has, however, a management role in some of the new Child Protection Centres.

As the German Democratic Republic moves towards unification with the Federal Republic, it faces changes in both recognising and responding to abuse. In the past, although child abuse was recognised by medical practitioners, there was no attempt to create a public awareness of abuse, this being contrary to the notion of a 'perfect society' promulgated by the communist state. The state did establish a system of developmental screening, closely parallel to the French model, with bonuses paid to mothers on completion of all checks on children. There are also similarities with the French provision of day care with some ninety five per cent of children in day care at the age of three. In spite of the lack of overt publicity about abuse, these twin systems have meant that a steady stream of referrals have been made to doctors and child welfare clinics.

The scale of the problem in the GDR (for experts believe the problem of physical abuse to be substantial) is said to be linked to the stressful living conditions of women. There are high levels of domestic violence and a high proportion of single mothers. Most women have to work and have to spend long hours queuing for shopping in addition to their child care responsibilities. Recent media features on child abuse have generated a high number of letters and phone calls. The professional response to physical abuse tends to follow a medical model, but public opinion on this 'newly recognised' phenomenon is more punitive than in West Germany, seeking harsh sentences for parents who abuse, rather than therapeutic intervention.

Sexual abuse is an altogether different issue. As in Italy, there are legal requirements to report an incident. Proven abuse results in strict court sanctions without any therapeutic intervention. The consequence is the all too familiar 'averting of the eyes' when professionals suspect sexual abuse. There is currently an attempt to increase the low awareness among the public of the fact that most sexual abusers are well known to their victims, often living within the same household.

As the GDR lives through re-unification many aspects of social and economic life are in turmoil. While doctors and social workers try to increase awareness of sexual abuse and treatment of perpetrators, the new voice of public opinion may be working against them. The detailed screening of children and the comprehens- ive day care facilities are increasingly resisted because of their associations with the former communist system. An additional problem is that the reorganisation of the state health service into an independent insurance-based system is jeopardising longstanding professional networks.

*Greece*

The relationship between societal context and child protection practice comes into sharper relief when we focus upon issues which face a rapidly developing country such as Greece, with its emphasis shifting from a mainly rural lifestyle to that of an industrial nation. Child care and child protection policies reflect an older tradition. Culturally, physical punishment of children is not stigmatised[18] and only the most serious cases receive an official response.[19] Investigations by the Institute of Child Health in Athens over a period of years have led to increased levels of awareness and the setting up of the first residential unit for abused and neglected children. A committee under the department of Child Protection was set up to present a national plan for the management of abused children and this report was presented in March 1984.[20] However there are as yet no signs of action being taken upon the basis of that report.

Children who are abused in Greek society rely on the traditional welfare services set up with a remit to work for the overall welfare of children and families, rather than services designed specifically to address abuse. These services may be either state-run or voluntary, although increasingly provision is reliant upon state funding. Help is often in the form of financial assistance to poor families. Many residential institutions set up forty to fifty years ago to accommodate children orphaned in the 1939-49 war and the following civil war are still in current use with practices little altered, in spite of professional concern about the quality of care. Foster care and day care are at an early stage of development. Overall resources for helping the child who is being abused are neither plentiful nor particularly appropriate.

The tensions inherent in a society in rapid change are particularly acute when applied to child abuse. The traditional mode of childrearing has no place for the concept of 'abuse'. Models of childcare are based on narrow interpretations of need developed in a culture with these traditions. This hampers the increasing recognition of child abuse among professionals. New concepts and new ways of working are being put forward by professionals who inhabit a wider community of professional practice and ideas, but these developments are not meeting ready acceptance. Professionals see resources as neither adequate nor appropriate.

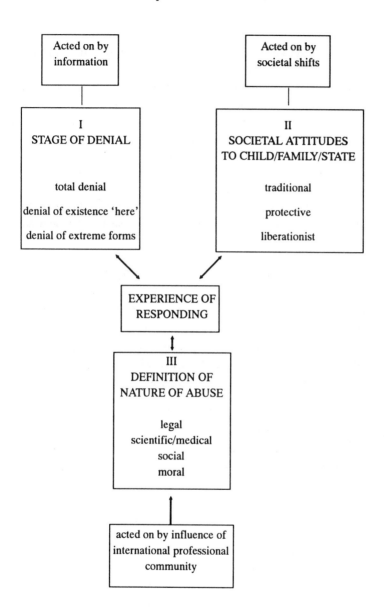

*Figure 1. Changing Responses to Child Abuse*

## A Model of Change

All of the systems we have described are changing in response to developments in knowledge, practice and the societal context in which they are rooted. To clarify some of the complexities and variations we have developed a model of the key elements in the process of responding to child abuse (Figure 1). This should facilitate examination and understanding of local and national responses.

We see the pattern of response to abuse in any country as a product of the interactions between three key contextual 'elements', which are modified, both individually and in relation to each other, by the experience of practice. This produces what may appear to be an erratic and volatile response to child abuse. Responses can be so varied within a single country that it may be helpful to recognise two or more patterns, acknowledging their coexistence and the resulting friction which may emerge in the national process.

*ELEMENT I: DENIAL - and the stages of recognition and acceptance of 'abuse'.*
The concept of 'abuse' has been constructed to identify and understand aspects of behaviour towards children. Denial is the refusal or inability to recognise the concept. Acceptance of abuse as a social problem depends on:

1) acceptance that some behaviours towards children are wrong (including types which were previously permitted such as severe punishment and others formerly not recognised like sexual abuse of young children).

2) admission that the behaviours defined as abusive happen in this society and community, perhaps extensively.

Dealing with abuse requires the overcoming of initial denial of the problem and sometimes encountering a backlash at a later point, following recognition of abuse.

We suggest that there are four stages of dealing with denial. First, acknowledgement of the idea of 'abuse' with recognition that traditional forms of behaviour may be abusive; second, acknowledgement that abuse exists in the particular country/societal group; third, acknowledgement that some particularly unpleasant activities go on and fourth, the backlash.

It is important to recognise additionally that denial in specific cases may be fed by a lack of a clear system of response - lay and professional people will tend to avoid acknowledging a problem where they feel unable to respond. We are currently seeing denial of this kind in the UK over the issue of children who abuse others and in responses to ritual and satanic abuse. Denial may thus persist in pockets or at levels in a society which apparently fully accepts the existence of abuse as an issue.

The force countering denial is primarily information from professional sources and from those who have experienced abuse. Publicity and information sharing through professional and public media at a local, national and international level leads to a broadening of awareness. When the conditions for work in the home country are hostile, international contact and shared research can give peer support to professional groups and offset parochialism. Victims of abuse, on the other hand, commonly continue to feel unique and isolated in their experience, whatever the acknowledgement of abuse in other sectors of society.

*ELEMENT II: SOCIETAL ATTITUDES TO CHILD/FAMILY/THE STATE - rights and responsibilities.*

Rebecca Hegar[21] identifies three major patterns of perceiving the status of children in European culture. These perceptions are fundamental to the development of a national understanding of child abuse. The first is 'traditional' with a focus on the supremacy of the parents over the child. The rights of decision, protection and care are vested in the parents. The second is the 'protective' view in which the state is recognised as having a direct responsibility for protecting children particularly where parental protection is seen to have failed. The third is the 'liberationist' view in which children are seen as best served by a recognition of their independent legal rights. Different countries will respond to the challenge of child abuse with varying senses of the balance of the responsibilities. Each view has implications for the way abuse is seen and for the style of response. Where the traditional view is strongly held, it may fuel denial. It may on the other hand lead to 'child-blaming'. In general the 'liberationist' view is a late development and is currently influencing models which are intrinsically more 'protective' in their style. Pierre Verdier[21] has charted the development of social legislation in France against the dominant attitudes about state/child/family responsibilities. He demonstrates the ways in which a broad children's rights policy operates in practice, modified by a series of legislative changes.

The persistence of the traditional approach will also be influenced by the strength of awareness of gender issues and the liberation of women, and how far patriarchal attitudes inform professional and personal life. It may also be influenced by the existence of variations in racial and cultural patterns among migrant communities. The acceptance of the concept of abuse will inevitably lead to shifts in understanding of the experience of family life, and the rights of the child. Indeed the concept of abuse will make little headway until there has been movement from the 'traditional' view to some degree of acceptance of the autonomous rights of the child.

In order to provide even a rudimentary response to abused children a state must, by definition, acknowledge its protective responsibilities. Countries differ widely in the degree of control which is acceptable by the state over the details of the life of the individual. This context complements that of the ideology of rights over children and will define the limits of acceptable intervention, whatever the rationale of that intervention.

*ELEMENT III: DEFINITION OF ABUSE - what is the nature of child abuse?*

There are a range of models available for 'understanding' child abuse. The particular perspective which has influence in directing response in any society comes to prominence through the interplay of issues incorporated in Element II together with the predominant thinking of influential professionals and professional groupings. Nigel Parton[22] broadly divides responses to child abuse into:

1) the *legal model*, where the abuse is regarded primarily as a crime, presupposing a willful act and therefore deserving legal punishment;

2) the *scientific model*, seeing the act as one determined by forces beyond the individual's control, requiring medical treatment;

3) the *humanistic model*, where a range of social factors are seen as causal, and a range of prevention, counselling and therapeutic approaches may be selected as appropriate.

We suggest adding a fourth category, the 'moral response', where abuse is viewed as a moral problem. This view may be linked to the 'traditional' view of family and child and associated with stigmatisation of the weaker partners in the abuse situation, with images of the seductive child. It is interesting to note that where the form of abuse involves distortions of traditional practices, as in satanic abuse, a moral definition of abuse resurfaces. Thus different forms of abuse may precipitate different definitions.

Each country will incorporate aspects of each of these models into its response, but the dominant model will influence the way in which practice develops and the way in which abuse is defined. For example the dominance of the legal model in the UK leads to a greater emphasis on gathering evidence at the investigation stage and to control based models at the therapeutic stage. Conversely the dominance of the scientific or medical model in Holland leads to a wider definition of abuse and increased emphasis on voluntary therapy, with legal intervention a last resort.

It is worth noting that there is often a discrepancy between how abuse is defined in professional circles and how it is defined in popular consciousness and this tension will be played out in the national response to abuse.

## The Experience of Response

The issues which professionals have to address, and the impact of working across professional disciplines (such as different approaches to confidentiality) will have a major influence on the way in which services develop. Equally important will be the personal impact on workers and the support they are offered. Practice is also affected by public opinion and media coverage. There may be problems of burn-out for the individual professional and of issue fatigue at a societal level which may lead to a backlash. Alternatively increased training and information may extend general awareness of the issues of abuse, more abuse may be identified, and with it an increased sense of urgency in developing effective responses. Confidence in the professional response and the climate of that response, will increase readiness within families to share with the state responsibility for child-rearing; and to increased acceptance that abuse is a problem.

The relationship between responding to abuse and the societal context means that in periods of rapid change the situation of children becomes more precarious while responses are particularly difficult to develop. There will be examples of child care and protection work fighting for priorisation in societies preoccupied with fundamental changes in structure and culture. Where societies are facing major shifts in economic location, changing perceptions of family roles will alter the foundation upon which action can be built. Likewise a loss of confidence in state control (in Eastern Europe for example) may result in a radical reduction of the power of the state to intervene in the lives of individuals which will have important and unforeseeable implications for future developments in child protection and the early detection of risk factors.

## Conclusions

Our analysis of European practice demonstrates that each country has a unique permutation of denial, definition, and response in relation to child abuse; products of the specific interplay between history, culture, stage of development, and experience of responding to abuse. We have noted some examples of attempts to transfer models of response from one society to another, notably the Belgian and

West German introduction of a 'confidential doctor approach'. In each case, however, the different cultural framework results in a different outcome in practice. We have also identified countries where professionals face similar problems: where therapeutic goals may sometimes conflict with public opinion (Italy and the GDR), and where traditional child care theories conflict with developing professional responses to child abuse (West Germany and Greece). In each case, the process of resolving the difficulties and tensions will need to vary according to the local model of response.

The tension between professional models of work nurtured in a professional community working across national boundaries, and the unique model of response in a state or locality puts considerable strain on professionals. Those professionals are aware that it is the children who bear the primary impact of abuse of all kinds, and improving the situation of the abused child is the dominant professional goal. If children are to receive effective help, however, in whatever culture and context, professionals must have appropriate and effective training and support to provide that help. Current training may not equip workers adequately for the particular challenges of child abuse work in their own cultural setting, let alone across boundaries. Training in therapeutic skills in particular is often expensive and may be difficult to find. The structures in which professionals work must be helpful in supporting creative and responsive work with children and families. 'Burn out' is an international phenomenon. Whatever the model of work it will only be effective in the hands of those trained and supported to deliver it.

This in turn requires political will to agree and ensure services to children. As the European Community develops, a new attention and priority to the welfare of children as individuals, and the welfare of the family as the optimal unit for rearing them, is necessary for the complex task of building a 'European' response to child abuse. This has social and political implications in a united Europe. But it has economic implications too. As the increasingly mobile labour force moves around Europe with its share of abused and damaged children, the EC must ask itself if it can afford not to provide some concerted response to its future citizens.

## References

1. Acosta, E. (1989), 'Prevention and Protection in Europe: Spain'. In Davies, M. and Sale, A. (Eds.) *Child Protection in Europe*. NSPCC, London.

2. Wolters, W. H. G. and Dekker-Roelofs, M. A. S. (1983), 'The Battered Child: A Study of the Role of Services in 25 Cases of Child Abuse in the Netherlands' *Child Abuse and Neglect*. 7, 301-307.

3. Gregerson, M. and Vesterby, A. (1984), 'Child Abuse and Neglect in Denmark: Medico-legal Aspects' *Child Abuse and Neglect*. 8, 83-91.

4. Netherlands Ministry of Welfare, Health and Cultural Affairs (1989). 'Fact Sheet on Child Abuse'. Fact Sheet 20 E.

6. Moss, P. (1988), *Childcare and Equality of Opportunity*. Consolidated Report to the European Commission.

   Christopherson, J. (1989), 'European Child-Abuse Management systems'. In Stevenson, O. (Ed.) *Child Abuse - Public Policy and Professional Practice*. Harvester Wheatsheaf, London.

7. Findlay, C. (1987), 'Child Abuse - the Dutch Response' *Practice*. 1, 4, 374-381.

8. Marneffe, C., Boermans, E. and Lampo, A. (1989), 'Prevention and Protection in Europe: Belgium'. In Davies, M. and Sale, A. (Eds.) *Child Protection in Europe*. NSPCC, London.

9. Eliaerts, C. (1989), Panel contribution to Second European Conference on Child Abuse and Neglect, Brussels, (unpublished).

10. Delvoie, G. (1989), 'Interaction Between Therapy and The Law in Child Protection'. Paper presented to the Second European Conference on Child Abuse and Neglect, Brussels.

11. Girodet, D. (1989), 'Prevention and Protection in Europe: France'. In Davies, M. and Sale, A. (Eds.) *Child Protection in Europe*. NSPCC, London.

12. Verdier, P. (1987), *Nouveau Guide de l'Aide Sociale à l'Enfance*. Paidos/Le centurion, Paris.

13. Tonkin, B. (1988), 'A Bench Without Tears' *Community Care*. 14.7.88.

14. *Nouvel Observateur* (1989), 23-29 March.

15. Il Telefono Azurro (1990), *Report*, Bologna, June.

16. Merrick, J. (1989), 'Prevention and Protection in Europe: Denmark'. In Davies, M. and Sale, A. (Eds.) *Child Protection in Europe*. NSPCC, London.

17. Vesterdal, J. (1977), 'Handling of Child Abuse in Denmark' *Child Abuse and Neglect*. I, 193-198.

18. Maroulis, H. (1979), 'Child Abuse: the Greek Scene' *Child Abuse and Neglect*. 3, 185-190.

19. Agathonos, H. (1983), 'Institutional Child Abuse in Greece: Some Preliminary Findings' *Child Abuse and Neglect*. 7.

20. Papatheophilou, E. (1989), 'Prevention and Protection in Europe: Greece'. In Davies, M. and Sale, A. (Eds.) *Child Protection in Europe*. NSPCC, London.

21. Hegar, R. (1989), 'The Rights and Status of Children: International Concerns for Social Work' *International Social Work*.

22. Parton, N. (1985), *The Politics of Child Abuse*. Macmillan, London.

*We would like to acknowledge personal communications from:*
   Dr. Alessandra Vassali, Centro Bambino Maltratto, Milan
   Tom Levold, Bundesarbeitsgemeinschaft, Kinderschutz Zentrum, Cologne
   Claudia Richter, journalist, Berliner Zeitung
   Clodagh Cochrane, Republic of Ireland
   Assistance with translation from Virginia Burton and Michael Procter.

*Chapter 9*

# Astride the Frontiers between Education and Punishment: Youth Services and Juvenile Justice in West Germany

**Hans-Joachim Trapp and Christian von Wolffersdorff**
*(Translated by Monica Koch)*

## Help Instead of Punishment? Ambivalent Progress in the Treatment of Marginalised Youth

There have been striking changes in the treatment of socially maladjusted and delinquent young people in West Germany during the past two decades. Both in youth services and in the area of juvenile justice, new concepts have been developed oriented toward educational aims, which require that repressive sanctions be removed and that conventional residential institutions and prisons for juvenile delinquents be replaced by a network of non-custodial measures as far as possible. It is now possible to speak of a 'non-confinement movement' or 'deinstitutionalisation movement' (ambulante Bewegung) in West Germany, whose focal concerns include prevention and diversion on the one hand, and treatment and therapy on the other.

However, this introduction of pedagogics* into the domain of state punishment has not met with universal approval. What many regard as an admirable success story of modern criminal policy is described disrespectfully by critics as simply the differentiation and refinement of social control, ie 'more of the same' rather than an important change. They suggest to the non-confinement movement that pedagogics has developed into the functional equivalent of punishment as it has been increasingly applied to the administration of justice. Even worse, in order to open up new fields of action for itself it has established itself 'in the basement' of the justice system - tolerated by the latter only to the extent that its

---

\* *Editor's Note: Pedagogics is roughly equivalent to education in its broadest sense (see Chapter 3 for a discussion of this).*

power and competence remain untouched when deciding on sanctions.[1] Criminologists in particular have stated that the alleged successes of the concepts of prevention and diversion are ultimately a kind of optical illusion, like the one described by Hans-Christian Andersen in his fairy tale about the 'Emperor's New Clothes'. Under the guise of helping individuals and respecting offenders' living conditions, both the claims to power of penal law and the professional interests of social pedagogics have been enhanced for their own benefit, as one critic of the concept of diversion commented sarcastically.[2]

In the area of institutional care, the search for appropriate ways of supervising 'difficult' children and young people has also been accompanied by professional and ideological controversies. They relate to the question of how necessary it is to place young people who are aggressive, suicidal, involved in prostitution or runaways in specialised institutions. It has long been debated whether the confinement of children and young people in closed establishments is permissible under the Child Welfare Act and which goals it should pursue.

All these discussions revolve around a theme that has occupied social pedagogics since its very beginnings around the turn of the century - namely, how to draw a line between those who can be reformed and those who are 'incorrigible'.

It is striking that these debates about the 'limits of educability' were already being conducted extremely vehemently in Germany during the 1920s in connection with the pedagogic reform movement of the time.[3] Liberal and progressive pedagogues were convinced of the necessity of classifying the inmates of reformatories in terms of various degrees of educability[4] and of differentiating between the institutions on the basis of certain typologies of young people. The penal law expert F. von Liszt (one of the 'fathers' of the Juvenile Court Act of 1923), in spite of his strong support for an educational law, was of the unequivocal view that confinement in an institution was the only option for a number of incorrigible hard-core offenders.

The discussion of the problem of 'difficult' young people, which was initially conducted quite seriously from a professional point of view, was taken up somewhat later under Nazism within the framework of genetic and eugenic ideas and used to justify 'camps for the protection of young people' (concentration camps for young people).[5] In these camps, the classification of young people into various grades of 'inferiority', 'imbecility' or 'dangerousness' was carried to extremes with 'scientific' meticulousness and had fatal consequences for many of the inmates.

Against this historical background it is understandable that the idea of scientifically guided special treatment for 'problem youths' was discredited for a long time. Even in the 1970s, above all in the discussion about closed institutions, many feared a relapse into the mentality of classification and isolation that had shaped wide areas of youth services in Germany in the first half of the century. Although such fears frequently involved overreactions, they have had considerable influence on the discussion about forms of supervision in the border areas between the administration of justice, psychiatry and residential care.

The treatment of 'problem cases' has often proved to be the Achilles heel of more recent public responses to young people in trouble as well. It was not only those who demanded specialised diagnostic and therapy centres for this category of persons who had trouble with the long-term detention of aggressive young people.[6] More open alternative projects set up in the early 1970s were frequently not in a position to convey helpful perspectives to young people who had grown up in unsatisfactory family and housing conditions.

It is one of the unresolved contradictions in the treatment of vulnerable, socially marginalised young people that, despite all the educational intentions that exist, they are rarely able to experience 'prevention' which is worthy of the name. Instead, they are placed in specialised institutions at an early age, which in turn require for their functioning other specialised institutions to which they can pass on their clients as the need arises. Trust in specialists who will see to such cases 'some time or other' is one of the dubious relief mechanisms which is frequently used to justify the relocation and shelving of young people within the public care system.[7]

There are clear dangers, then, of applying a naive concept of education that involves the development of new measures for 'easy cases' whilst still holding out repression for the rest. In West Germany one can observe that there is an increasing need for care of young people with serious difficulties at the same time as the overall number placed away from home has declined. This dual development reflects important wider social processes. In spite of a long-standing economic boom, the number of poor people living in West Germany according to the newest figures is approximately six million - ten per cent of the total population. A considerable portion of this social stratum are affected on a long-term basis by the economic and socio-psychological consequences of existence 'on the fringes' of society. Housing problems, addictions, violence and family disruptions create or increase the need for placement away from home. It is necessary to prevent a residual category of 'non-divertible' young people from again arising as a result of a lack of reflection about the social causes of poverty and marginalisation.[8] Preventive aid and non-confinement measures should be developed for young petty offenders, and made a component of youth services within a political programme.

In the remainder of the chapter we outline recent developments in youth services and criminal policy in West Germany and assess them in the light of this contention. For this purpose we elucidate the idea of care and protection in West German juvenile justice, discuss the most important alternative concepts in the area of juvenile justice, and describe the tasks of social workers in the proceedings at juvenile courts. Finally we examine the most important activities of the 'non-confinement movement' and of youth services more generally, including reference to our own research work on closed units.[9]

## The Concept of Education in Juvenile Justice

The separation of the treatment of juvenile delinquency from mainstream youth services began with the division of responsibilities set out in the Juvenile Court Act (JGG) of 1923 and the Youth Welfare Act (JWG) of 1924, respectively. The Juvenile Court Act is still valid today, with a few amendments, and is currently being re-enacted once again. It applies to juveniles (aged fourteen to seventeen) and to young adults (aged eighteen to twenty). Children up to the age of thirteen are deemed too young to be criminally responsible. Even if their offences are serious, they are consequently not committed to juvenile prisons, but to residential or psychiatric institutions.

Although the JGG contains some educational elements, it is primarily shaped by penal considerations. This was criticised from the start and even in the 1920s there were demands to unify the two pieces of legislation. Similar demands have been made more recently that the two laws be redesigned and merged, and that youth services institutions be made available for young criminal offenders.[10] However, all these attempts to overcome the dual system of education alongside repression and to reduce custodial sentences for juveniles failed. A decline in reforming zeal as well as growing financial problems gave rise to a political change by the mid 1970s, so that the thrust towards a uniform juvenile law was lost. Since then, efforts have centred around less fundamental amendments to the two laws.[11] The new Child and Youth Welfare Act just passed in the spring of 1990 makes a number of substantial improvements, but still adheres to the traditional dualism between juvenile justice and youth services. The distinction between 'neglected' and 'criminal' youths, which disregards biographical realities and results in arbitrary labelling, will thus continue in future.

Social workers began to demand improvements which formed a 'criminological policy from below', attempting to carry out incremental changes within the
existing legal framework.[12] These approaches were aimed at a reduction in the
number of people charged for offences, the development of alternatives to
custody and improvements in the probation service.

The most important legal regulations of the JGG to which these approaches
relate can only be outlined roughly here. Section 5 lays down that educational
measures can be ordered for juveniles convicted of an offence. Only if such
measures are deemed insufficient is the offence to be punished by quasi-punitive
measures or a prison sentence. A formal order can be dispensed with altogether
if the harmful consequences for the young person are estimated to be greater than
their benefit.

Section 8 of the Act provides for the possibility of ordering educational
measures linked with punitive action, so that there is no clear hierarchy between
educational measures and punishment. Educational measures may consist of
directions; educational supervision; or correctional education.

Section 10 covers rules and prohibitions involving the young person's conduct
(determination of the place of residence in a family or in an institution; the
performance of work; or supervision by a certain person). The young person can
be forced to heed these directions by being taken into custody.

In the area of 'quasi-punitive measures' there are also disposals with partly
educational aims such as reparation for damage done, an apology or an administrative fine paid to a charitable organisation. Quasi-punitive sanctions also include
custody (weekend custody or continuous custody up to four weeks), which has
been particularly subject to criticism. The question of whether a brief deprivation
of liberty ('short sharp shock' therapy) is a means of achieving educational goals
has been answered in the negative by existing studies.[13]

The idea of education can be realised properly if appropriate data and
assessment concerning the young person can also be brought into the court
proceedings. This is done by means of juvenile court assistance, which is a
compulsory task for the municipal youth welfare office. It is performed either by
staff who specialise in this work or by non-specialists employed by the ASD
(General Social Services). The former have the advantage of greater expertise in
relation to court work and sentencing, but have a tendency to conform with the
court and to neglect wider social work considerations. Generic workers may well
have a more intimate knowledge of young people's circumstances, though they
have less experience in dealing with the court. The tasks of juvenile court
assistance can also be delegated to private youth services agencies. Like the

probation service, juvenile court assistance has dual functions of supervision and social assistance.

Cases can be dismissed both by the public prosecutor and by the juvenile court judge (Sections 45, 47), which is the basis for 'diversion'. Sections 71 and 72 permit the judge to avoid remands in custody by ordering a young person to stay in a residential home run by the youth services rather than be sent to a remand prison. This puts pressure on the youth services to make their establishments 'escape proof'.

In order to show how social workers are involved in juvenile court proceedings, a hypothetical example will be followed through in the next section.

## The Tasks of Social Work in Connection with Juvenile Court Proceedings

A young person - let us call him John - steals the cash box from a youth club. The woman in charge finds out that he has committed this criminal offence.

(1) She may attempt to induce John to return the money, find out the causes of the act and offer help in solving any problems he has. She is not obliged to inform the police.

(2) If the act is reported to the police, however, they will pass this information on to the public prosecutor. In some West German Länder the police must also check whether consequences of the offence have occurred for the young person in the meantime which make further prosecution unnecessary.

(3) Depending on the police information, the public prosecutor can dismiss the case. If he or she has doubts,the prosecutor will turn to the juvenile court assistance, who will make a recommendation. At this stage of the procedure, a social worker is thus involved formally for the first time. The public prosecutor may then dismiss the case:

   (a) with no further action, or

   (b) with a formal admonishment, or

   (c) with a compulsory educational measure.

(4) An educational measure is carried out through the juvenile court assistance or else a voluntary organisation. It will generally consist of a work order. The social worker now has the task of advising the public prosecutor and selecting a measure that is suitably related to the act.

(5) If the public prosecutor is in favour of reparation for the damage by means of a victim-offender settlement, he can send John to the youth welfare office or to a private agency (if such a service exists locally). The agency will contact the youth centre and organise the details of compensation. Subsequently, a report is prepared stating whether the compensatory act was performed. If so, the public prosecutor can dismiss the case.

(6) If the public prosecutor thinks that such settlements do not suffice, he or she will request that the juvenile court judge proceeds with a trial. At the same time the juvenile court assistance is requested to prepare a report on John's personal and social situation and possibly make a proposal about which measures should be taken. The juvenile court assistance may simply give an oral report about the facts of the case. Preferably, the worker will try to talk to John personally, not only to collect facts for the report, but also to discuss the offence with the boy.

(7) If the juvenile court assistance arrives at the conclusion that socio-educational help is necessary or useful, it will contact appropriate agencies and encourage John to participate immediately.

(8) The judge is not bound by the recommendation of the juvenile court assistance. It is therefore of great importance for the report to be thorough and competent, with practical suggestions.

(9) The judge can now dismiss the case, impose an educational measure or make another disposal. It is the task of the juvenile court assistance to explain to John the consequences of the disposal.

(10) Should an educational measure be ordered, John must report to a specified project. The judge will then be sent a report indicating whether John has regularly taken part or not. The juvenile court assistance should also receive information about John's progress.

In practice, the educational possibilities of the Juvenile Court Act outlined above have not been fully exploited up to now. This is due partly to the punitive orientation of the legal practitioners involved, but also has to do with the fact that appropriate projects have not been widely available, unlike detention centres and young persons' prisons. From the late 1970s onwards, however, alternatives to detention have been developed, which will now be described.

## Alternative Approaches to Young Offenders

The alternatives enveloped by the 'Non-confinement Movement' have taken very different forms, since some (like work orders) developed from criminal approaches whilst others involved extension of youth services.

*Work orders*

Projects termed 'Die Brücke' (The Bridge) are aimed at the prevention of custody. Initially they mainly organised so-called 'work orders'. Voluntary organisations made job placements available to young offenders. Public prosecutors and judges were increasingly requested to apply this form of sanction. Social workers arranged the placements and supported the young people while they were there. The first 'Bridge' project was founded in Munich in 1978 and soon similar projects developed in other cities. After only one year of operation the Munich project dealt with approximately forty per cent of all youths and young adults involved in juvenile court proceedings.[14] The Cologne project cooperates with about 180 institutions which indicates the importance of these projects.[15] Evaluation studies have indicated that these schemes have been successful, since there has been an accelerated drop in prison sentences in those cities which have Bridge projects compared with those which do not.[16]

*Group work on the basis of Section 10, JGG*

A further approach to supervision in the community is social group work, which developed initially in youth work, but is now offered mainly to young offenders, when it may be called a 'practice and experience course'. The young people are usually subject to a supervision order which assigns them for a definite period to projects in which they are supervised by social workers. Some schemes run workshops (eg a joinery, a bicycle repair shop). Others run groups which take part in outdoor activities like canoe-building, motorcycling, sailing and excursions. In these courses an attempt is made to offer opportunities for social learning oriented toward the young person's abilities. In this way the young people can have fun and at the same time practice independent and responsible behaviour.[17]

Some groups engage in common enterprises like mountain hikes, rapid-river rafting or trips to remote areas in order to develop the relationships between the young people and their supervisors and promote new perspectives on life. Such projects are time-consuming and include not only social group work, but also individual casework (eg to support processes of detachment from the family, help find a place to live). However, such elaborate projects with therapeutic aspects are less common than more limited, task-oriented ones usually lasting about four months.[18] These are concerned to develop group cohesion and norms. This type of group requires fewer resources, but the concentration on 'pedagogic' discussion is off-putting for many youngsters.

*Diversion*

Both projects of the 'Bridge' type and group work in social training courses are frequently described as forms of 'diversion'. This is misleading as this term originally referred to the absence of sanctions without any substitute measures whereas both work orders and participation in regular courses may very well contain elements of coercion for those involved. The ideas behind true diversion have their roots in criminological research showing that juvenile delinquency is largely a transitional phenomenon. It is a common characteristic in certain phases of development and generally disappears in early adulthood without any intervention. Hence it was argued that most young offenders would 'grow out' of law breaking without formal intervention. Inspired by American experiences with programmes to divert young offenders from the justice system, some West German Länder also developed guidelines on diversion in the early 1980s. In the case of petty offences or first offences the public prosecutor (advised by the police or juvenile court assistance) can dismiss the case if the act has had sufficient 'natural' consequences or if the young person makes recognisable efforts to repair the damage caused. Organised 'educational' assistance is to be dispensed with as often as possible in order to prevent it from becoming an automatic addition in cases which would otherwise be dismissed without any legal consequences.[19] Increased usage of such 'diversion to nothing' can be seen as preferable to the proliferation of alternatives to custody supervision projects. The more the latter are relieved from having to deal with petty offenders, the more they can devote themselves to those young people who really need supervision, care and protection.

*Victim-offender schemes*

In various cities of West Germany, pilot schemes for victim-offender mediation have been set up.[20] These, too, are only superficially part of diversion. It is hoped involvement in the scheme will make a trial unnecessary for the offender, but importance is attached to the victim's perspective too. The party who has been harmed is given an opportunity to express feelings towards the offender or to obtain material compensation for the damage.

The development of victim-offender schemes gives social workers the opportunity to evolve individualised forms of settling conflicts with more discretion than usual. Like non-custodial supervision projects, however, such projects will fail in their aims if they are understood merely to be further measures in the catalogue of the JGG. Their innovatory quality lies not in adding to the spectrum of penal sanctions, but rather in offering the new perspective of an informal solution to conflict. This requires an active contribution from the offender instead of regarding him or her as the passive object of a sanction.[21]

The process is initiated by the public prosecutor, who transfers the file to the corresponding project and suggests a form of reparation. First the victim and then the offender are asked whether they want to participate in such a settlement. In separate or joint conversations compensatory acts are agreed upon (eg apology, the repair of destroyed furnishings). The conclusion is reported to the public prosecutor, who then generally dismisses the case.[22]

There have recently been attempts to incorporate victim-offender schemes into the JGG as an educational measure for juvenile delinquents and to adopt it in the Prison Administration Act. For the reasons just stated, these attempts are rejected by social workers as being alien to the nature of voluntary reparation.

## Critiques of the Non-confinement Movement

The 'non-confinement movement' and deinstitutionalisation policies have met with criticism from both directions. Abolitionists have accused the movement of failing to make a contribution to deformalising juvenile court proceedings and instead subtly extending social control by opening up additional forms of sanction. They argue that without the new alternatives to custody more cases would have been simply dismissed.[23] Furthermore, it has been stated that youth services should not devote themselves to the administration of justice but maintain a clear separation between education and punishment. Otherwise, it is said, youth services risk subordination to the judicial ethos rather than orienting their goals toward creating better living conditions for young people.[24]

Critics from the justice viewpoint, on the other hand, have objected that court orders take no account of the gravity of the criminal offence and so conflict with principles of natural justice. They also believe that longer-term pedagogic measures require an element of control in view of the intensity and duration of their intervention in the young person's life.[25]

Further problems result from the fact that funding of projects generally does not permit intensive, continuous work.[26] Hence staff cannot help young people in serious trouble and must seek other clients in the interests of keeping their jobs. The obvious 'market' for expanding their clientele consists of petty offenders, so that the projects have a tendency to 'net-widening' by engaging less troublesome youngsters more heavily in the system than is necessary.

Within the nonconfinement movement itself different assessments of its success have also arisen. In particular, talk-oriented training courses have been criticised. These are said to result more from lack of finance than from pedagogic principles. It has also been claimed that the duration and intensity of courses like those run by Bridge projects mainly reflect the need of juvenile court judges to impose orders of definite length, rather than pedagogic reasons.

Thus there are two contrary interpretations of the recent history of reform in the sphere of juvenile justice. An optimistic version underlines the positive effects that non-custodial measures can have for the young people involved; such as the development of social and cognitive abilities or opportunities to experience success. A pessimistic version stresses, by contrast, that up to now the development of alternatives to custody has not led to a reduction in the traditional institutions of prison and detention for juvenile delinquents, contrary to the ideology on which it is based.[27] The explosive and continuing dispute between these two interpretations is nourished as much by ideology as by evidence, but improved research is needed to clarify their respective claims.

### Current Trends in Youth Services

The last part of this chapter describes recent approaches by the youth services, which deal with the counselling, supervision and treatment of young people in trouble. Some have developed in close association with the above-mentioned forms of practice developed within the juvenile justice system. Others result from an attempt to detach youth services from their traditional role as the safety net for other social institutions and make them a more active instrument of social policy. According to this notion, instead of merely reacting to problems, youth services should address the social causes of marginalisation and criminalisation, and intervene in related spheres of policy (eg employment, housing, community relations). The guiding principle would be to facilitate participation and integration of young people and improve living conditions.[28]

Even in 'rich' West Germany there is a need for youth services to act in this way, since the number of poor people is not decreasing, as many people think, but rising. Families living in poverty are often socially marginalised and have low self-esteem, particularly in the face of lasting unemployment. Other threats have only penetrated into public awareness in recent years - for instance, violence in families and the previously taboo subject of sexual violence against children.

According to expert estimates, approximately 70,000 cases of child sexual abuse take place within one year, about half within the family. The number of young runaways who come in contact with prostitution and drug-related crimes has also risen sharply recently.

These few examples already show the insufficiency of traditional youth services, which are very good at administering cases but not at improving living conditions. The concept of youth services 'oriented toward the social milieu' is much spoken of in West Germany today,[29] but only the future will show whether this can provide a real alternative or is doomed to remain only a declaration of intent like many others. There are some promising signs of such a reorientation - but also obstacles and resistance.

*Crisis Intervention*

In order to participate in the social environment of vulnerable young people, forms of mobile youth work (streetwork) have been developed particularly in urban areas in an attempt to reach those young people who would not normally go to a youth centre, a guidance office or the like of their own accord. This method has been applied particularly in working with groups of aggressive young people (rockers, soccer fans, skinheads;[30] and with young drug-takers.[31] The need for street work has also increased in connection with homelessness: it is estimated that about 40,000 children and young people run away from their families or from institutions in West Germany each year. The young people in question tend to lack training, work or satisfactory accommodation. Many are highly susceptible to the drug and prostitution scenes. Finally, in the context of the women's movement new concepts of crisis intervention have been recently tested for girls and young women which have, in their turn, made an important contribution to removing the taboo from sexual abuse in the family. In West Germany there are at present an estimated 200 women's refuges, while the establishment of refuges for adolescent girls is as yet only in the experimental stage. Considerable resistance to their establishment persists.

The traditional centres for the protection of young people, in which runaways can find temporary accommodation, have in some cases responded to current problems by new ways of working which are more supportive and less controlling. However, there are tensions with the patriarchal and welfare traditions of youth services, so that considerable developmental work remains to be done here.

*The opening of homes and the problem of closed units*
The search for new concepts of open youth services is clearly reflected in the area of institutional care as well. Community homes have undergone great changes in terms of both their organisation and their concepts of work. For the most part, they are far removed today from the repressive welfare institutions that invoked anti-authoritarian demonstrations twenty years ago. In many places they have developed into differentiated institutions in which there is also room for unconventional forms of work. This is apparent not only in the trend to make homes more open, but also in the spread of therapeutic concepts.

The number of children and young people placed in institutions has dropped continuously over the past two decades and is at present below 40,000 in West Germany compared with 100,000 in 1968. During this time the number of children placed with foster families rose and is currently higher than the number of children in homes. Nowadays children's homes are smaller and more open. The average number of places is now forty. At the same time the proportion of staff with professional qualifications has increased. This development is accompanied by a clear trend towards conceptual and organisational differentiation of the homes. Key ideas in these developments are: decentralisation, community work, work with parents, mobile supervision and attendance centres. At present this open form of institutional care can already cater for about 4,000 young people in West Germany.[32]

The question arises of whether the continuing existence of closed institutions is compatible with the requirements of a modern, preventive form of youth services. What appears to some to be a relic of the past appeals to others as a useful 'last resort'. Closed units occupy a marginal position in the spectrum of public facilities in that they have places for just under 400 persons throughout the country, but they are repeatedly at the centre of vehement controversy due to their actual or supposed similarity to prison. Recent research[33] suggests that judgements on this subject should view it as a component of structural contradictions in the treatment of difficult young people. A glance at the biographies of these young people shows that their lives are usually marked by very early experiences of neglect and rejection. School and the 'open' institutions of youth services also contribute in the development of institutional careers.

Only with this wider understanding can we move towards a further reduction and abolition of closed institutions. Several initiatives and model projects have produced positive results. They show that even young people with serious problems and very troubled histories can be taken care of in open institutions under certain basic conditions. It will be an important task in dealing with marginalised young people in the near future to create and further improve these basic conditions.

## Conclusion

This contribution has described a number of current developments which represent attempts to find new ways of dealing with young offenders. What they all share in common is the rejection of traditional concepts of repression and punishment in favour of community-based measures which take account of the environmental contexts of the young people concerned. These new trends need critical analysis. In particular there are dangers of net-widening effects. Probably in some cases non-intervention would be preferable to the creation of alternatives to conventional forms of custody and supervision. Bearing in mind these qualifications, the new schemes deserve to be developed further and scientifically evaluated.

## References

1. Müller, S. and Otto, H. U. (Eds.) (1986), *Damit Erziehung nicht zur Strafe wird - Sozialarbeit als Konfliktschlichtung*. Bielefeld.

2. Ludwig, W. (1989), *Diversion - Strafe im neue Gewand*. Berlin/New York.

3. Peukert, D. (1986), *Grenzen der Sozialdisziplinierung - Aufstieg und Krise der deutschen Jugendfürsorge 1878 bis 1932*. Cologne.

4. Bernfeld, S. (1981), *Sisyphos oder die Grenzen der Erziehung*. Leipzig/Vienna/Zurich, 1925; Frankfurt.

   Bernfeld, S. (1926), 'Psychische Typen von Anstaltszöglingen' *Arbeiterwohlfahrt*, 1.

5. Peukert, D. (Ed.) (1980), *Die Edelweisspiraten. Protestbewegungen jugendlicher Arbeiter im dritten Reich*. Cologne.

6. Thiersch, H. (1978), 'Zum Verständnis von Sozialarbeit und Therapie' *Neue Praxis*, Special Edition, 'Sozialarbeit und Therapie'.

7. Freigang, W. (1986). *Verlegen und Abschieben. Zur Erziehungspraxis im Heim*. Munich.

8. Van den Bogaart, H. (1989), 'Mind the Gap: The Creation of the "Non-Divertable"'. In Hudson, J. and Galaway, B. (Eds.) *The State as Parent*. Kluwer, Dordrecht. 207ff.

9. Von Wolffersdorff, C. and Sprau-Kuhlen, V. (1990), *Geschlossene Unterbringung in Heimen. Kapitulation der Jugendhilfe?* DJI, Munich.

10. Simonsohn, B. (Ed.) (1969), *Jugendkriminalität, Strafjustiz und Sozialpädagogik*. Frankfurt.

    Arbeiterwohlfahrt, Bundesverband (1970), 'Denkschrift der Arbeiterwohlfahrt zur Reform und Vereinheitlichung von Jugendwohlfahrtsgesetz und Jugendstrafgesetz'. *Schriften der Arbeiterwohlfahrt*. 22, Bonn.

Heinz, W. and Hügel, C. (1986), *Erzieherische Massnahmen im deutschen Jugendstrafrecht*. Bonn.

11. Heinz, W. and Hügel, C. (1986), *Erzieherische Massnahmen im deutshen Jugendstrafrecht*. Bonn.

12. Peters, K. (1966), 'Die Grundlagen der Behandlung junger Rechtsbrecher'. *Monatsschrift für Kriminologie und Strafrechtsreform*. 49, 49ff.

13. Eisenhart, T. (1977), *Die Wirkungen der kurzen Haft auf Jugendliche*. Frankfurt.

14. Ludwig, W. (1989), *Diversion - Strafe im neuen Gewand*. Berlin/New York.

15. Mohr, M. (1988), 'Arbeitsschwerpunkte der "Brücke" Köln'. In *Erziehung, Strafe oder Wiedergutmachung - neue Konzepte im Umgang mit Jugendkriminalitat*. Aktion Jugendschutz (Eds.) Cologne, 30ff.

16. Pfeiffer, C. (1983), *Kriminalpolitik im Jugendgerichtsverfahren* Cologne, Brücke e.V., Annual Report, Munich.

    Steinhilper, G. (1985), *Soziale Dienste in der Strafrechtspflege. Praxisberichte und Untersuchungen aus Niedersachsen*. Heidelberg.

17. Busch, M., Hartmann, G and Mehlich, N. (1986), *Soziale Trainings-kurse im Rahmen des Jugendgerichtsgesetzes*. Bonn.

    Hinkel, N. (1979), *Übungs- und Erfahrungskurse - Kurspraxis und Ergebnisse*. Frankfurt.

    Kersten, J. and von Wolffersdorff. C. (1980), '"Unser Kind braucht so was nicht". Übungs- und Erfahrungskurse mit gefährdeten Jugendlichen'. In Böhnisch u.a. (Eds.) *Abhauen oder Bleiben? Berichte und Analysen aus der Jugendarbeit*. Munich. (Materialien Nr. 10 des Institutes für Sozialarbeit und Sozialpädagogik).

18. Cohn, R. (1975), *Von der Psychoanalyse zur themenzentrierten Interaktion*. Stuttgart.

19. Guidelines for Diversion Procedures in Saarland, September1989, *Official Gazette of Saarland*, Oct. 19, 1989, 1451-1453.

20. DVJJ (Deutsche Vereinigung für Jugendgerichte und Jugendgerichtshilfen e.V.). (1983), 'Ambulante Sozialpädagogische Massnahmen für junge Straffällige', *Schriftenreihe der DVJJ*. 14.

    DVJJ (Eds.) (1987), *Und wenn es künftig weniger werden? Die Herausforderung der geburtenschwachen Jahrgänge*. Munich.

    Pieplow, L. (1988), 'Täter-Opfer-Ausgleich - Die Waage e.V. Köln'. In Aktion Jugendschutz (Eds.) *Erziehung, Strafe oder Wiedergutmachung - Neue Konzepte im Umgang mit Jugendkriminilität*, Cologne, 68 ff.

    Messmer, H. (1989), 'Tackling the Conflict: A Framework Analysis of Dispute Settlement'. In Hudson, J. and Galaway, B. (Eds.) *The State as Parent*. Kluwer, Dordrecht.

21. Kuhn, A. (1987), 'Projekt "Handschlag"'. In *Und wenn es künftig weniger werden. - Die Herausforderung der geburtenschwachen Jahrgänge*. Schriftenreihe der Deutschen Vereinigung für Jugendgerichte und Jugendgerichtshilfen, 17, Munich, 312ff.

    Marks, E. and Rössner, D. (1989), *Täter-Opfer-Ausgleich: Vom zwischenmenschlichen Weg zur Wiederherstellung des Rechtsfriedens*. Bonn.

22. Delattre, G. (1989), 'Das Projekt Handschlag Reutlingen', and Kawamura, G. 'Die Waage Köln'. Papers presented to the Conference *'Protection of the Victim and Helping Delinquents - A Contradiction?'*, May 16 to 18, 1989, 'Paritätisches Bildungswerk', Frankfurt.

23. Kerner, H. J. (1983), *Diversion statt Strafe*. Heidelberg.

24. Müller, S. and Otto, H. U. (1986), op. cit.

25. Balbier, R.-W. (1989), 'Judge at the Higher Regional Court, "Brauchen wir eine neues Jugendstrafrecht?"'. *Deutsche Richterzeitung*. November, 404-409.

26. Lower Saxon Higher Labour Court decision concerning non-confinement socio-pedagogic measures under the JGG, 'Betreuen statt Strafen', Hanover 1987.

27. Cohen, S. (1985), *Visions of Social Control*. Cambridge. pp.67ff. Also for a synopsis see Heinz, Wolfgang, (1990), 'Diversion im Jugendstrafverfahren'. *ZRP* 1, 7-11. The crime statistics show that the ratio of non-custodial sanctions to custodial sanctions has shifted only slightly.

28. Bundesminister, für Jugend, Familie, Frauen und Gesundheit (1990), (Ed.) *Achter Jugendbericht - Berichte über Bestrebungen und Leistungen der Jugendhilfe*. Bonn. (Eighth Youth Report).

29. ibid.

30. Specht, W. (1987), *Die gefährliche Strasse*. Bielefeld.

31. Krauss, G. M. and Steffan, W. (1985), (Eds.) *'. . . Nichts mehr reindrücken' - Drogenarbeit, die nicht bevormundet*. Weinheim, Basel.

32. For details of these developments see BMJFFG 1990, 148ff.; Jordan, E. and Sengling, D. (1988), *Jugendschutz*. Weinheim/Basel, 1988.

33. von Wolffersdorff/Sprau-Kuhlen (1990), op. cit.

# Chapter 10

# Elderly People and Social Services in Four EC Countries

## R. A. B. Leaper

The difficulty with comparing systems of care for dependent people in other countries is to know where to begin. Pioneering ventures in one country may be proposed as models for emulation or avoidance in others, but without reference to the cultural, political, financial, or organisational system within which they operate, such comparisons are misleading.[1] The work of professionals such as doctors or engineers is legitimately comparable, but their terms of reference and their administrative constraints will considerably modify their practice. Exchanges of experience between health and social services colleagues in neighbouring countries are useful - but they must be set in their cultural and administrative context. Even specialist vocabulary within a profession presents difficulty in translation or demands an explanatory note on the best linguistic approximation.[2]

In this chapter we compare the situation of elderly people and the social services available to them in Belgium, France, West Germany and the Republic of Ireland. The demographic statistics of these countries compared with those for the United Kingdom are as shown in Table 1.

All the European countries cited have a growing proportion of elderly people, with the Irish Republic well below the rest, and the UK growth lower than the others. The over-75s, who are on average higher consumers of health and social services than the economically active population, show a steady growth, with West Germany ahead of the rest due to a low birth-rate. This will be somewhat altered by German re-unification from 1990, but so many other factors come into play here that demographic influences may be over-shadowed by political and economic change.[4]

**Table 1: Elderly people in Europe (1986, with projections for 2000)**

|  | Aged 65 and over | | Aged 75 and over | |
|---|---|---|---|---|
| *Year* | *1986* | *2000* | *1986* | *2000* |
|  | *%* | *%* | *%* | *%* |
| Belgium | 14.1 | 15 | 6.4 | 5.9 |
| France | 13.2 | 15.2 | 6.4 | 6.5 |
| West Germany | 15.1 | 17 | 7 | 7.1 |
| Ireland | 10.9 | 11.2 | 4 | 5.3 |
| UK | 15.3 | 14.5 | 6.5 | 6.3 |

*Source:* OECD, 1988[3]

Some of the problems inherent in attempting valid comparison even in a fairly homogeneous area like North-Western Europe are dealt with elsewhere in this book. Suffice it to mention here the reference in a recent study of

'another persisting methodological problem in comparative policy studies (which) has to do with finding appropriate indicators'.[5]

Among the indicators of need, the age structure of a country is only one element and even that is a crude one. So many other factors are involved that we must beware of any simple equation between age, dependency and demand for public resources.

**France**

France's demographic balance has altered, despite factors like more widespread contraception, from being the 'oldest' country in the world in 1939 to being seventh in the 'elderly league' of developed countries in 1985. Since 1960 the total number of pensioners has steadily increased and early retirement has been encouraged. There are in 1990 some 3.8 million people in France over the age of 75.[6] In 1986 just over a third of men over 60 were wage earners, though less than a quarter of women in the same age group. Natalist policy had a high priority in French social and economic planning in the aftermath of the first World War which devastated young French manhood. The spectre of an ageing population haunted many French demographic commentators.[7] Pierre Laroque, founding father of French social security programmes, set the general lines of future policy for elderly French people in his seminal report in 1962.[8] In successive national five-year Plans and studies by the Economic and Social Council in 1985, specific references have been made to the needs - and contributions - of elderly people.[9]

There has been concern not to confuse ageing with incapacity. The wide range of social clubs, self-help associations and even 'Universities of the Third Age' are testimony to the energy and initiative of large numbers of officially retired French men and women. There has also been a growing realisation of the economic power of elderly consumers 'who represent thirty seven per cent of air passengers on holiday and dispose of twenty two per cent of the national income'.[10] There has been a concern to distinguish between the Third Age of active retirement and the Fourth Age of comparative dependency.[11] The energy and range of activities under the umbrella of the Office des personnes âgées et retraitées in most large French towns - somewhat akin to British Age Concern groups - have developed into a national union with both promotional and pressure group aspects. The national union recently published a report it had commissioned on housing for elderly people recommending a better co-ordination of the different sources of funding for housing and other services for dependent people.[12]

In 1988 the Théo Braun report set out new guidelines for care for the very elderly, in particular those most dependent.[13] The report covers a wide range of questions concerning elderly dependent French people. Starting with the role ascribed to elderly people by society, the report stresses the wide range of individual differences:

> 'The phenomena of ageing are complex and confound our demands for classification and systematisation. Age groupings and decennial periods are useful for statisticians but do not really relate to the different stages of our lives.'

The report asserts that priority must be given to domiciliary support and explores the care implications of this, concentrating on the need for a better co-ordination of medical and social care and for new methods of financing them.

Théo Braun was subsequently made secretary of state for elderly people within the government department responsible for social services and was thus in a powerful position to influence policy and practice for elderly people in France. However, his Ministry had to work within the parameters of French political organisation at the levels of state, région, département and commune. Théo Braun left the French government in October, 1990, but the post of secretary of state for elderly people remains.

Le Ministère de la Solidarité, de la Santé, et de la Protection Sociale is the present title of the government department responsible for health and social services. There has recently been considerable devolution of functions from central government to the twenty one régions and to the ninety six territorial

Départements. At Département level there has been since the Acts of 1983 an elected general Council responsible for the provision of health and social services led by the Directeur des Affaires Sanitaires et Sociales.[14] The State directorate remains responsible in each Département for inspection, statistical records and advice on policy. The former Préfet remains the State representative in each Département but, with the new title of Commissaire de la République, works in co-operation with the elected Council and its President.[15] In various government guidelines for the operation of the new decentralised system specific mention is made of the need to plan and operate services for elderly people, especially in their own homes. The Braun report strongly recommended that co-ordinating committees in each Département (known as 'CODERPA') should elaborate plans for all aspects of health and social care for elderly people. A working party of the Comité National des Retraités et Personnes âgées published in 1990 a report urging that much more should be done to work out a co-ordinated 'plan géronto-logique' in each Département.[16] At the level of the 36,000 local Communes there are the Centres Communaux d'Action Sociale. Their size and resources vary enormously. The largest have their own extensive social services and residential homes, whilst the smaller communes often form joint unions for these services. The services include domiciliary care for elderly and other dependent people through social workers, home care assistants and home helps, and also 'aide sociale' (needs-tested financial assistance). Applications have to be made to the local CCAS and forwarded to a commission of the Département DAS whose budget finances social assistance.[17] The CCAS is the benefits payment office. Its domiciliary and residential care services are provided either directly or in co-oper-ation with the independent sector. The 1990 Annual Conference of CCAS directors was devoted to 'Ageing and the funding of related services in France'.[18]

Social workers in France are employed by a wide variety of health and social service agencies, both statutory and independent. This differs markedly from the British situation where the large majority of social workers are employed by local authority social services or probation services. The title 'social worker' is reserved for those qualified by a state diploma, and there were about 34,000 of them employed in 1985.[19] Elderly people are served not only by social workers but also by doctors, home helps, family care workers, nursing assistants (auxil-iaries de vie), benefits advisers, and managers of residential establishments.[20]

There has recently been some concern to establish a better co-ordinated network of the many and varied services for elderly people.[21] This may be compared with proposals for identifying 'key-workers' and better co-ordination for social services for elderly people in Britain.[22] Legally families in France are

responsible for the maintenance of their elderly relatives ('l'obligation alimen-
taire') and tax allowances for family dependents reinforce this principle.[23]
However, in practice the strict application of this obligation seems to be modified
by the discretion allowed to Département social services in determining such
questions, particularly in connection with financial aide sociale, and with the
acceptance of insuperable difficulties caused by increased occupational and
geographic mobility.[24] A recent study of the operation of field services and their
interaction with family support in Paris and Lyons affords an interesting comparison with the Kent community care project in England.[25]

Public sector hospitals are under the general supervision of the Département
Commissaire de la République (large regional hospitals are authorised by State
decree only). Independent hospitals require regional consultation and authorisa-
tion. Their running costs and the cost of medical care of all kinds, including GPs'
fees, are covered through social security funds based on occupational groups.[26]
The Funds ('Caisses') are responsible for family allowances, sickness benefit,
and retirement pensions, as well as for meeting the costs of medical care. The
patient is in principle reimbursed for medical expenses on a variable scale
according to the nature of the treatment given, or the prescription dispensed. The
balance is paid by the patient or, if he is unable to, by social assistance. A national
convention between the medical insurance Funds and the two main doctors'
associations sets the annual tariff of charges. Demographic changes have challenged the structures of French health and social services, and recently proposals
for innovation have emerged: joint health and social funding, new forms of
domiciliary care, greater flexibility between the public and independent sectors.[27]
Retired people whose pensions do not reach a national minimum have their
income made up from a government 'solidarity' fund. The total amount paid out
in pensions in 1989 exceeded all other benefits put together. The 'Caisses' are
responsible both for collecting contributions and paying cash benefits. As the
average daily cost of domiciliary care for an elderly person has been estimated
at 400-500 francs, new forms of insurance against the costs of dependency have
recently been explored (so far only for those covered by social insurance funds
for managerial groups).[28]

### Germany

The Federal Republic of (West) Germany had a higher proportion of its population who are elderly than did the former Democratic Republic, which had a
significantly greater percentage of dependent children:

|      |              | Aged over 65<br>% | Aged under 15<br>% |
|------|--------------|-------------------|--------------------|
| 1989 | West Germany | 14.5              | 15.4               |
|      | East Germany | 13.3              | 19.4               |

Any account of social policy and provision in Germany in 1990 must be set in the context of very rapid political and organisational change. What the effects of the differing population structures on contributions to taxes and the use of social services will be after German unification can only be guessed at.

Considerable powers and duties for health and social services in Federal Germany are in the hands of the Länder each of which has an elected assembly. The determination of functions between Federal Government and Land was made on the principle of 'subsidiarity', described by the Constitutional Court as -

'the local community should act first and the State should only intervene when there is no alternative.'

Chancellor Kohl has re-affirmed:

'The principle of subsidiarity is a cornerstone of our social policy. Whatever small organisations are able to handle need not be assigned to larger organisations . . . Subsidiarity also means freedom of choice for the beneficiary as well as diversity of social benefits'.[29]

It follows that prominence is given to the role of independent social agencies, whose Federal Union is the Deutscher Verein für Öffentliche und Private Fürsorge, a powerful and well-staffed body with its headquarters in Frankfurt-on-Main. In 1982 the Federal office of Labour estimated that 182,000 qualified social workers were employed in West Germany working for: local authorities, the Lutheran Church, Caritas of the Roman Catholic Church, the Arbeiterwohlfahrt, the Parity Welfare Group and the German Red Cross.[30]

Germany's early programme introduced by Bismarck from 1883 onwards was a landmark in European social insurance history. With many subsequent reforms, it remains the major item in social expenditure and the basis of social provisions in Germany. The 'social budget' of the Federal Republic was composed as follows in 1989, in percentages:

%

| | |
|---|---|
| Old age, survivors, dependents | 38.8 |
| Health | 33.8 |
| Marriage and family | 12.8 |
| Employment | 8.3 |
| Housing | 1.7 |
| Other social provisions | 4.6 |

*Source:* Manfred Wienand, 1989[31]

Employers and employees contribute equally to the 'Sickness Funds' which meet the costs of health care. As in France, some contribution to costs has to be made by most patients, helped where appropriate by social assistance. The Funds also collect contributions and pay cash benefits in case of certified sickness.[32] Old age pensions are dealt with by the Landesversicherungsanstalt and the Bundes-versicherungsanstalt, the Insurance Institutions whose funds are derived from equal contributions from employers and employees, with a State subsidy. Over ninety per cent of the West German population is covered by the Institutions. A Federal pension reform will be gradually implemented from 1992. Pension ages for both sexes will be raised to 65, but greater flexibility is allowed over arrangements for part-time work and early retirement. Higher contribution rates will have to be paid to cover the new pensions costs. Expenditure from health funds has rocketed upwards between 1970 and 1990 and various attempts have been made to limit it.[33]

The local health authority, financed by local taxes, provides a range of health care including domiciliary services for elderly dependent people. The same authorities are responsible for public health including preventive care.[34]

Following a 1961 Federal Act, social assistance provides a safety net of minimum income for those not adequately catered for by social insurance. Recipients of social assistance doubled to about three million persons (out of a total population of sixty million) between 1970 and 1986, with an increasing proportion of unemployed people as opposed to elderly or disabled people.[35] The local authorities responsible for social assistance have found in some cases their budgets for social assistance are deficient, although overall expenditure on it accounts for only three per cent of the national social budget, compared with sixty per cent for social insurance. Local authorities work in collaboration with independent welfare agencies to whom some social assistance functions are contracted out. Recently attention has turned to the possible provision of a basic minimum income, financed out of local and Federal taxation.[36]

As Wienand makes clear: 'Health services and social care services are two basically separate sectors in the Federal Republic.' Nursing costs fall on the health insurance budget, which cannot meet the increased demand, while the costs of domiciliary and residential care fall upon local authorities. Both are covered in variable ways in each of the Länder. Hans Körber reports that in Munich, for example, the average age of entry into residential care is now as high as 86 years, largely as a result of favouring domiciliary care for as long as possible. Day costs in homes have risen substantially:

> 'subsidies from the Munich city council, for example, have risen from 9 million marks in 1975 to 40.7 million marks in 1988 . . . over the same period day costs per bed have risen from 26 to 91 marks'.[37]

The city of Munich revised its subsidy system in 1989 and has been able to economise on residential care and devote more to domiciliary care as a result. The latter services are generally run by independent agencies or by volunteers. An estimated total of 25,000 paid workers and volunteers are involved in domiciliary care in Federal Germany. As has been noted in studies of other European countries, 'domiciliary care' means in the majority of cases, care by married partners or by other relatives, mainly female. Professional services are generally limited to intermittent nursing care for a minority. The sickness insurance funds pay for about two-fifths of the cost of nursing care in Germany, the remainder coming from user-payments, statutory subsidies and voluntary agency funds. Several writers have recently argued for a revised system of constitution and registration for independent social agencies.[38] They are covered by a general law on voluntary associations which is felt to be inappropriate for major organisations involved in complex and expensive services for a large and increasing sector of the population.

## Ireland

The twenty six counties of the Republic of Ireland have been politically independent since 1923 and the state's present designation dates from 1948. Centuries of association with neighbouring Britain have left their traces on Irish social provisions and the large number of Irish men and women living and working in Britain has brought a familiarity with British models of health and social services. (The six counties of Northern Ireland which form part of the UK have the same services as elsewhere in the UK - except that there are integrated health and social services boards in the province). In the Irish Republic the dominant influence of Roman Catholicism is reflected in matters such as legislation concerning divorce and abortion, and in the partnership of voluntary and statutory services. The country has a pattern of administration and provision of services quite distinct from those of its nearest neighbour.

As has been noted above, the demography of Ireland is unusual. A 1989 National Economic and Social Council study on 'Ireland in the European Community' sums it up thus:

> 'Ireland's population in 1986 was 3.54 million with a low density per km of only 50 . . . it had the highest birth rate in the Community in 1986. Death rates are broadly similar throughout the EC. Consequently Ireland had the highest rate of increase that year . . . but there had been a dramatic fall in the birth rate over the period 1973 to 1986 . . . The in-migration in the 1970s was an exceptional event and the historical pattern of emigration has now re-asserted itself and 1986 emigration undid virtually all the natural increase'.[39]

Ireland has by far the highest percentage of under 15s and the lowest of over 65s in the EC with a high overall dependency rate of 0.66 (the UK is at 0.52 and the EC average at 0.49). Nevertheless, there are 384,000 people aged over 65, about eleven per cent of the population. The Department of Health report in 1986 stated that

> 'life expectancy at 50 compares poorly with the experience in other EC countries and life expectancy for Irish males at ages 65 and 75 has changed only marginally since 1960'.[40]

Ireland has the lowest proportion of over-80s in the whole of Europe, and elderly people are found disproportionately in rural areas.

The Irish social security system appears to the outside observer as a unique mixture of the British state-administered scheme and the Continental system of independently-administered group coverage. With very few exceptions all working people over 16 are covered by 'Pay-related social insurance'. There are a large number of occupational classes and entitlement to retirement pensions varies accordingly, though the majority qualify.[41] Those who do not may be entitled to a means-tested non-contributory old age pension. Social insurance for pensions was extended to the self-employed in 1988 following a report by the National Pensions Board.[42] In addition, occupational pension schemes have grown substantially since 1972 with contributions estimated at £400 million and benefits at £250 million per year.[43] There are many more benefits in kind to elderly people than is the case in other European countries. Every Irish resident aged 66 or over is entitled to free road and rail travel at off-peak hours. Pensioners over 66 are entitled to a free electricity allowance, or a free bottled gas allowance. They also receive a free TV licence (black and white only).[44]

In the Irish health care system certain long-term illnesses are treated without charge to the patient. Otherwise payments for health care are related to income. Just over a third of the population (those with lowest incomes) are medical card holders and so receive health services free. Those in the next income bracket (about half the population) receive free hospital care but pay for other treatment, whilst those earning more than £16,000 a year in 1989 pay for all save in-patient medical care.[45] Voluntary Health Insurance, contributions to which are tax-free, can cover hospital charges, nursing home or private ward charges.[46] About 2,300 Irish general practitioners work in Ireland and 1,400 of them are registered with the Health Boards to provide services to medical card holders. The GP has a key role in the care of elderly or disabled people - particularly in rural areas.[47] The report of the Commission on Health Funding recommended in December 1989 a revision and simplification of the system of health care and its funding but its report has not yet been acted upon.[48] The Health Act of 1970 placed the responsibility for provision of services on the eight regional Health Boards each with three programmes: general hospitals, special hospital services, and community care. The Health Boards therefore employ in their community care teams: public health nurses, home helps, social workers, OTs, and chiropodists. Some services are contracted out to voluntary agencies, for example meals on wheels and laundry services. The National Social Services Board provides a 'Directory of Voluntary Organisations' which includes fifteen national bodies concerned with elderly people.[49] This underlines the important role of the voluntary sector in both domiciliary and institutional care. A drop in religious vocations over the last two decades has placed greater demands on Health Board services, voluntary agencies and - to a smaller extent - private commercial agencies.

The development of 'care in the community' has been the subject of much discussion in Ireland as elsewhere in Europe.[50] A specific section of each Health Board's activities is directed by a 'Programme Manager for Community Care'. There are three parts to the Programmes: health protection, health services, and community welfare - which covers cash payments, grants to voluntary agencies and personal social services. Misgivings have been expressed by the Association of Health Boards about apparent Health Department plans to save money by substituting domiciliary for institutional care. Research studies from the National Council for the Aged have documented such developments, highlighting the special needs of rural areas and advocating a series of detailed local surveys of elderly people's needs.[51] The stereotype of the three-generational Irish family caring for its elderly is no longer general - in 1986 81,000 elderly people lived alone, women outnumbering men by two to one. The continuing migration of young people to urban areas (at home or abroad) undermines the caring network.[52] A 1986 survey for the National Council for the Aged estimated that there were 5,500 elderly people in private and voluntary nursing homes of whom seventy eight per cent were female.[53] This is only one per cent of the Irish Population of 65 years and over. A total of about 15,000 elderly people are recorded by the Irish Department of Health as being in a long-stay unit - provided by the Health Boards' Geriatric Hospitals, Welfare Homes or Voluntary and Private provisions.[54] Only five per cent of old people are in some form of institutional care, with a modest amount of sheltered housing providing for about one per cent of elderly people and a very small number helped by boarding out schemes. The emphasis is still on domiciliary care.[55] Concern about the capacity of carers to cope with dependent elderly people at home led to government agreement in 1990 to introduce a Carer's allowance for 'a person who lives with and provides full-time care and attention to a relevant pensioner'.[56] This came into effect in October, 1990, and replaces the 'relative allowance' scheme.

## Belgium

As even the most casual visitor to Belgium soon becomes aware, the country is divided into two quite distinct linguistic and cultural regions, Vlaanderen (Flanders) in the North and Wallonie in the South. Brussels is the officially bi-lingual capital-region, which has progressively assumed a European identity and where an increasing amount of English is used over and above the French and Flemish indigenous tongues (There is also a small German-speaking area in the East incorporated into the kingdom of Belgium since the end of World War One). The recognition of these distinct cultures has increased over the sixty years that I have known Belgium, until today the country is administered virtually as a Federal state, though maintaining its formal unity under the monarchy. The two main linguistic regions (known in Belgium as 'Communities') have also marked economic and political differences. Wallonie contains a number of the old industrial centres now undergoing renovation, where the Socialist Party is strong and municipal provision takes the lead. Vlaanderen has experienced a rapid economic growth and social transformation coupled with a somewhat greater attachment to the Catholic religion and to voluntary provision for both domiciliary and institutional care. As Table 1 shows (p. 179), Belgium is slightly above the average for the five countries reviewed in terms of the percentage of over 65s in the population. A national survey of the needs and services of people over 65, who formed fourteen per cent of Belgium's population in 1981, emphasised the importance of the linguistic 'communities' in formulating and carrying out social policy for elderly citizens.[57]

Provisions for social security remain a national concern. Basic legislation emanates from the Belgium parliament, but operational responsibility (on the usual continental European model) lies in the hands of a network of public agencies based mainly on occupational identity. These provide benefits for income replacement in the case of sickness, unemployment, invalidity or holidays, and also meet the costs of medical care.[58] Retirement pensions are financed by: contributions from employers and workers, an annual state subsidy, and a special state subsidy to compensate for unemployed workers exempt from contributions. The system is administered by the national office for wage-earners' retirement and survivors' pensions. Self-employed persons have their own pension funds for contributors' retirement and for survivors, financed by compulsory contributions and an annual State subsidy. The National Institute for self-employed workers' insurance is responsible for overall administration. The usual age of retirement is 65 for men and 60 for women, but there is early entitlement to pensions for coal miners (of whom there are now few left) and men who have been in 'arduous employment' and have forty five years insurance contributions. There is a guaranteed minimum pension for those who have spent at least two thirds of their working life in contributory pensionable employment.[59] Belgian pensions are linked to the retail price index and to an annual revaluation factor which takes account of average living standards. This compares with: no automatic adjustment in Ireland but an annual review; a six-monthly review in France linked to the cost of living index; an annual review in Germany based on the previous year's wage trends; an annual review in the UK in line with the general level of prices.[60]

In a critical review of the extent of income redistribution through social security in Belgium, Herman Deleeck and his associates at Antwerp University estimated the comparative situation of retired pensioners and other people dependent on social security benefits over the period 1976-1985.[61] Among the conclusions of this survey were that the real value of pensions rose considerably compared with wages and social security benefits, and the financial situation of elderly people in general improved, except for that of over-75s living alone. Deleeck's study provides rather more detailed information for Vlaanderen than it does for Belgium as a whole and the estimation of adequacy of income is based upon a public opinion survey, but his results seem fairly indicative for Belgium as a whole.

Besides contributory pensions, income-related social assistance is provided for retired people and for others whose income falls below a minimum laid down by Parliament. Twenty four per cent of Belgian GDP was spent on income maintenance in general in 1985. Social assistance is financed out of State taxation funds, but it is administered by a local commune organisation known as the Openbaar Centrum voor Maatschappelijk Welzijn/Centre Public d'Aide Sociale, established by law in 1976 as a reform of public assistance provisions.[62] The centres combine social work and cash benefit functions. This is in marked contrast to the well-established divide in Britain between cash payments and personal social services. Any applicant for income-related cash help in Belgium must be interviewed and assessed by a social worker attached to the OCMW/CPAS. The Centres' other functions include home care, social work with families in need, child care, residential care for the handicapped and the elderly, and local hospitals. The Centres are staffed by professional workers - including qualified social workers - who are accountable to an elected council, composed partly of the local commune councillors. Inter-commune joint councils are established in the case of smaller communes.[63]

The Centres represent a considerable public investment and employ a large staff. In Belgium as a whole there are currently 586 Centres, which employ about 2,000 qualified social workers. A recent study shows that the Belgian public has not yet fully caught on to the multiplicity of functions performed by the Centres but tends to think still of them as cash assistance offices or as providers of local hospital care or of care to needy elderly people.[64] Nevertheless, there has apparently been a growing public acceptance of the Centres as places of general advice and help, open to all without stigma. Nevertheless a recent critical review of the operation of the Centres after twenty five years raises doubts about local democratic control of their activities and the apparent inexorable growth of commune subsidy for them.[65]

The strong centrifugal forces in Belgium tend to favour wide discretion for each Commune Centre whose basic responsibilities are laid down by law, but whose discretion in responding to variable local needs is considerable. For example the Centre at Charleroi, in the heart of an area adapting to the decline of its traditional industries, has a different range of activities responding to the special economic and social problems of this urban agglomeration from those of the Centre at Brugge (Bruges) in Vlaanderen, a comparatively prosperous city with a long tradition of religious philanthropic provision for elderly citizens.[66]

Charleroi's annual report in 1988 did show a range of residential provisions for a rapidly ageing population, mainly provided by the CPAS, but its main preoccupations were with assistance to unemployed people, including those adjusting to severe economic and social change because of the reduction in the steel industry and the virtual closing down of coal mines.[67] Measures designed to help unemployed or single young people were also supported by the European anti-poverty programme.[68] In Brugge there was less involvement with programmes for unemployed people, though a programme for training them in new skills needed to re-enter work will start in 1991. More attention was given to help to elderly people at home or in voluntary residences. Brugge OCMW had also inherited a major hospital from its historic responsibilities, and social services were provided for patients there and on discharge, including elderly people. An analysis of all presenting problems handled by the Brugge OCMW in 1989 shows forty per cent to be concerned with cash, twenty per cent with social legislation, and ten per cent with housing. Elderly people over 65 showed a different distribution of problems: for them the large majority concerned practical services, followed by sickness or handicap problems, with only fifteen per cent concerned with cash.[69]

Residential Homes in Belgium provide for increasing numbers of elderly people. Recent legislation has encouraged the financing through social security funds of the medical care costs of residents in homes which hitherto made only provision for their housing. This development is linked to the familiar policy of progressively closing geriatric wards, with resultant problems of funding care elsewhere. The policy has involved the signing of complex agreements between the social security agencies and the managers of residential homes often leaving unclear the status of some residents who suffer from progressive disability.

However, most elderly Belgians continue to enjoy a home life of their own, helped by a specific category of workers - 'aide seniors/bejaardenhelpster' - or as in other countries, cared for by female members of their own families.[70] As in France, Belgian families are responsible for the maintenance of their elderly relatives. Under the Laws of 1965 and 1976 the OCMW/CPAS is obliged to seek to recover the costs of maintenance of elderly dependent people from those liable for it.[71] The application of this law to the 'débiteurs d'aliments' - legal partner, children or parents of the dependent person - has recently been modified.[72] The system is adversely criticised by, for example, Nicole Delpérée who quotes the case of a Belgian woman working as a secretary with a disabled husband who is obliged to work outside the home in order to meet part of the costs of maintaining her parents-in-law in a residential home.[73] Delpérée has also drawn attention to the need for systematic legal protection for vulnerable dependent elderly people.

Starting with Belgium she has made a comparative survey of the state of the law in this regard in several European countries.[74] The same questions are dealt with in a recent French publication on ethical questions concerning elderly people taking up residence in institutions, including the issue of genuine free-choice.[75] The publication reviews the situation in several European countries, including Britain, during which there are a number of references to the Wagner report and its emphasis upon choice of residence in old age. In France, Adrien Zeller was the moving spirit behind the elaboration of a 'Charter of the Rights and Liberties of Dependent Elderly People'[76] which stresses the obligation of social workers, doctors and nurses to respect the rights to self-determination of dependent elderly people.

As in the other countries covered here, Belgium has had national reviews of services for elderly people, one of the first appearing from the Prime Minister's office in 1981. Its conclusions were the familiar ones of favouring domiciliary care with help from local CPAS (OCMW) services of all kinds, maintenance within the family unit for as long as possible, with residential care as a genuine option for a minority.[77] Within the complex Belgian society, divided into its linguistic-cultural communities, administered through Provinces and Communal bodies, and with a wide range of independent social agencies, elderly people are becoming an increasing percentage of those needing help. The Belgian solution is a classic example of the 'mixed economy of welfare' now becoming more prevalent in European countries.

## Conclusion

If we take the situation of a chronologically defined sector of the population such as that over retirement age in Europe we find a similar pattern of dependency needs and of capacities for autonomy. Variations in forecast demand can to some extent be accounted for by demographic indicators, as illustrated at opposite extremes by West Germany and Ireland. But the very variable institutional responses to demand are the product of historic political, cultural and economic differences, as well as what Heidenhiemer calls 'policy styles'.[78] To account for differences in social policy and provision in the States we have examined in this chapter various attempts at model-building have been made in order to give some kind of apparent order to complexity, but it seems to me that such models are only helpful at a high level of intellectual abstraction. It is clear that we have a very long way to go before the rhetoric about one Europe in 1992 is translated into the daily practice of all those involved in health and social services, whether as paid workers or volunteers. In any case the Commission of the European Communities had until 1990 comparatively little to say about social policy and elderly people. The 1990 EC 'Communication' is a modest document reviewing fairly familiar themes and recalling that 'action for the benefit of the elderly is for the greater part the concern of Member States'.[79]

Some rulings of the European Court of Justice may have effects upon national provisions such as equal rights in occupational pension schemes for men and women, which is consistent with the European Social Charter. Otherwise the interest in, and effect upon, elderly people by the European Commission is marginal. On the other hand it may be that the variety in national provisions is potentially an advantage, encouraging Europeans towards the goal of 'upward harmonisation' which used to be in fashion in the 1960s.[80]

This process will be helped forward by wider dissemination of existing information about the situation of elderly people, of the variety of the services paid for by them in earlier working life and used increasingly in older age, and of the relationships between the generations - economic, social and cultural.[81] We also need studies of the perception of people over retirement age of their own situation and of their own priorities. This goes further than consumer surveys of health and social service clients, important though those are, since only a small percentage of retired people are at any given moment receiving those services. By including in the processes of decision-making the opinions and perceptions of a cross-section of elderly people, we safeguard ourselves against stereotypes of elderly people as dependent and passive recipients of services provided by others. Various initiatives have recently been taken in this direction in individual countries.[82] We need now to undertake comparative studies, using the same methodology, to facilitate reliable European comparisons.

At the heart of our concerns lies an unresolved dilemma - whether to treat chronologically older people as a separate group requiring specific and distinct provision (France seems to have taken this option since the Braun report) or whether to emphasise solidarity, dealing with all citizens according to their individual needs and obligations, treating chronological age as an indication of likely need and capacity but eschewing any separate categorisation of 'the elderly' in society.

# References

1. Jones, C. (1985), *Patterns of Social Policy*. Tavistock, London.

2. Leaper, R. A. B. (1990), 'Notes on Anglo-French Terminology in Social Administration.' École Nationale de la Santé Publique, Rennes.

3. OECD (1988), *Ageing Populations: the Social Policy Implications*. OECD, Paris.

4. Leaper, R. A. B. (1989), Series of articles on care for elderly people in European countries in *This Caring Business*.

5. Heidenheimer, A. J. et al. (1990), *Comparative Public Policy*. Macmillan, London.

6. Armengaud, A. and Fine, A. (1988), *La Population Française au XXe Siècle*. PUF.

7. Bras le, H. (1986), *Les Trois France*. Seuil, Paris.

8. Laroque, P. (1962), *Rapport de la Commission d'Etude des Problèmes de la Vieillesse*. La documentation française.

9. Paillat, P. (1988), *Passage de la vie active à la retraite*. PUF.

10. Grima, M. (1986), 'Le Marché Gris' *Information Sociales*. 5, 3-76.

11. Thévenet, A. (1989), *Le Quatrième Age*. PUF.

12. Comité Nationale des Retraités et Personnes Agées (1990). *Rapport de la Commission sur le Soutien à Domicile et l'Hébergement*. CNRPA.

13. Braun, T. (1988), *Les Personnes Agées Dépendantes*. Rapport au sécrétaire chargé de la securité sociale. La Documentation Française.

14. Gontcharoff, G. and Milano, S. (1983), *La Décentralisation*. Syros.

15. Thévenet, A. (1986), *Les Institutions Sanitaires et Sociales de la France*. PUF.

16. Delaunay, C. (1990), 'Le plan Gérontologique départemental'. In *Documents*. CLEIRPPA, Sept.

17. Thévenet, A. (1987), *L'Aide Sociale Aujourd'hui*. ESF.

18. Association Nationale des cadres des centres communaux d'action sociale (1990). *Le Vieillissement et son financement en France*.

19. Thévenet, A. and Désigaux, J. (1984), *Les Travailleurs Sociaux*. PUF.

20. Direction des Affaires Sociales (DAS), Conseil Général d'Ille-et-Vilaine. Rennes, 1990.

21. UNCCASF (1989). *Bulletin des Centres Communaux d'Action Sociale*. 240.

22. Dant, T. and Gearing, B. (1990), 'Keyworkers for Elderly People in the Community' *Journal of Social Policy*. 19, 3, 331-360.

23. Bertrand, D. (1987), *La Protection Sociale*. PUF.

24. CLEIRPPA. (1989), *Quels financements pour les politiques d'aide aux personnes âgées en perte d'autonomie?* CLEIRPPA, Paris.

25. Frossard, M. (1988), *Travail Familial, Solidarité de Voisinage, et Maintien à Domicile des Personnes Agées*. ENSP, Rennes.

26. Ecole Nationale de la Santé Publique (1990). *Les Institutions Sanitaires et Sociales face au Vieillissement*. ENSP Editeur.

27. Braun, T. (1988), *Les Personnes Agées Dépendantes*. Rapport au sécrétaire chargé de la sécurité sociale. La Documentation Française.
Ecole Nationale de la Santé Publique (1990). *Les Institutions Sanitaires et Sociales face au Vieillissement*. ENSP.

28. Association générale des Institutions de retraite des Cadres (1990). *Assurance-dependance*. AGIRC.

29. Kohl, H. (1988), Address to Berlin Conference on 'Law, Social Welfare and Social Development.' Deutsches Verein.

30. Brauns, H.-J. and Kramer, D. (1986), *Social Work Education in Europe*. Deutsches Verein, Frankfurt.

31. Wienand, M. (1989), *Social System and Social Work in the German Federal Republic*. Deutsches Verein, Frankfurt.

32. Kolb, R. (1988), 'Social Security Statistics and Social Policy'. In *International Social Security Review No.4*. ISSA, Geneva.

33. Körber, H. E. (1989), *The Experience of the Federal Republic of Germany in Financing Care for Elderly Dependent Persons*. CLEIRRPA, Paris.

34. Wienand, M. (1989), *Social System and Social Work in the German Federal Republic*. Deutsches Verein, Frankfurt.

35. Wienand, 1989, op. cit.

36. Körber, 1989, op. cit.

37. Körber, 1989, op. cit.

38. Körber, 1989, op. cit.

39. National Economic and Social Council (1989). *Ireland in the European Community*. NESC, Dublin.

40. Department of Health (1986). *Health - the Wider Dimensions*. Dublin.

41. Department of Social Welfare, Dublin (1989). *Guide to Social Welfare Services*. Dublin.

42. National Pensions Board (1988). *Report on the Extension of Social Insurance to the Self-Employed*. Stationery Office, Dublin.

43. National Pensions Board (1988). *Report on the Tax Treatment of Occupational Pension Schemes*. Stationery Office, Dublin.

44. National Social Service Board (1989). *Entitlements for the Over-Sixties*. NSSB, Dublin.

45. Department of Social Welfare, Dublin (1990). *Rates of Contributions and Payments*. Dublin.

46. Voluntary Health Insurance Board (1990). *Rates and Plans*. VHIB, Dublin.

47. Department of Health (1986), *Health - the Wider Dimensions*. Dublin.

48. Department of Health (1989). *Report on the Commission on Health Funding*. Dublin.

49. Frazer, H. (1990), *Directory of National Voluntary Organisations*. NSSB, Dublin.

50. O'Connor, S. (1987), *Community Care Services: An Overview*. National Economic and social Council, Dublin.

51. Carey, S. and Carroll, B. (1986), *Patch Work*. Glendale Press.

52. O'Connor, J. and Ruddle, H. (1988), *Caring for the Elderly: Part II*. National Council for the Aged, Dublin.

53. O'Connor, J. and Thompstone, K. (1986), *Nursing Homes in the Republic of Ireland*. National Council for the Aged, Dublin.

54. Department of Health (1984). *Statistical Information Relevant to Health Services*. Dublin.

55. O'Connor and Ruddle, 1986, op. cit.

56. *Relate* 17, 8, May 1990. Social Welfare Act 1990. NSSB, Dublin, 1990.

57. A useful symposium on the Belgian constitution and administration appeared in 1990 as a special edition of the review *Pouvoirs* (No.54), published by Presses Universitaires de France, Paris.

58. Ministère de la Prévoyance Sociale. (1989), *Vademecum de la sécurité sociale/Vademecum van de social zekerheid*. Brussels.

59. Ministère de la Prevoyance Sociale, 1989, op. cit.

Beauchesne, M. N. (1989), 'Vieillessement et Population Active: Quelle Problèmatique Sociale?' *Revue Belge de Securité Sociale*. 10 (Year 21), 851-877.

60. Department of Social Security (1989). *Tables of Social Benefit Systems in the European Communities*. DSS, London.

61. Deleeck, H. (1989), 'The Adequacy of the Social Security System in Belgium' *Journal of Social Policy*. 18, Part 1, 91-117. See also Hutsebaut, M. (1989), 'L'avenir de la Sécurité Sociale' *Revue Belge de Securité Sociale*. 11-12, 951-981.

62. De Graeve, A. (1985), *Aide Sociale*. UGA, Courtrai.

Dehaes, V. and Lambrechts, E. (1981), *Van c.o.o. naar OCMW: een nieuwe start?* Ministerie van Volksgezondheid en van het Gezin, Brussel.

63. Bataille, L.-M. and Berger, J.-M. (1989), *Aide-mémoire des CPAS*. Villes et Communes Belges, Brussels.

64. Berger, J.-M. and Jacques, E. (1989), *Droit au Coeur*. Editions Labor.

65. Mouvement Communal (1990), *Dossier Special CPAS*. No.5, UVCB.

66. OCMW Brugge (1989). *Social Dienst. Analyse van de registratie*. Brugge.

67. CPAS, Charleroi (1988). *Rapport annuel*. Charleroi.

68. Jacques, E. (1989), *Resocialisation de jeunes sans emploi: évaluation finale*. CPAS, Charleroi.

69. OCMW Brugge (1989). *Social Dienst. Analyse van de registratie*. Brugge.

70. Mouvement Communal (1990), op. cit.

71. Berger, J.-M. (1982), *La prise en charge et la recupération des frais de l'aide sociale*. UCVB, Bruxelles.

72. Mouvement Communal (1990), op. cit.

73. CLEIRPPA (1987), *Quels financements pour les politiques d'aide aux personnes âgées en perte d'autonomie?* CLEIRPPA, Paris.

74. Delpérée, N. (1988), 'Protection juridique des personnes âgées présentant des troubles de comportement' *Revue Belge de la Securité Social*. 1.

75. Gérontologie et société (1990), *Ethique: l'entrée en institution*. No.53: Cahiers de la fondation Nationale de Gérontologie, Paris.

76. Fondation Nationale de Gérontologie (1987), *Charte des Droits et Libertés de la Personne Agée Dépendante*.

77. Jaumotte, C. (1981), *De diensten voor bejaarden in Wallonie en Brussel*. Diensten van de eerste minister, Brussel.

78. Heidenheimer, A. J. et al. (1990), *Comparative Public Policy*. Macmillan, London.

79. Commission of the European Communities (1990), *Communication on the Elderly*. European Commission, Brussels.

80. Bonnel, M. (1990), *Les personnes âgées dans la Communauté Européenne: présent et avenir*. Comité Permanent des Médicins de la Communauté Européenne, Paris.

81. Centre for Policy on Ageing (1989), *World Directory of Old Age*. Longmans, London.

82. Leaper, R. A. B. (1989), *Age Speaks for Itself*. Exeter Health Authority.

Ecole Nationale de la Santé Publique (1990), *Les Institutions sanitaires et sociales face au vieillissement*. ENSP, Rennes.

*Chapter 11*

# European Cooperation in Social Work: A Scottish View

## Jennifer Speirs

'Oh let us not like snarling tykes*
in wrangling be divided.'

*Robert Burns*

For social workers as much as for other citizens of the member states of the European Community, Europe is a term with a number of definitions, meanings and levels of significance. In political terms, for example, it might refer to the Europe of the Community, the Europe of the Council of Europe, the Europe of western defence, and finally to historic Europe which extended eastwards to the Ural mountains.[1]

I should be surprised if a majority of social workers in the UK were able to name all the member countries of the EC although this may be changing given the recent debates about the UK's membership of the Economic Monetary Union and the forecasts about the effects of the Single European Act. For many of us in Britain, Europe is a cultural, not an economic nor political concept, associated with symbols such as football, Beethoven's Ninth Symphony or driving on the other side of the road. However, as it is the activity of governments which is one of the most significant matters affecting social work, the political decisions of the EC cannot be disregarded. It is the need to contribute to and influence these decisions which make it imperative for social workers to cooperate in a variety of ways with each other and with EC institutions. Successful cooperation may depend on the kind of contacts that we have not just as social workers but also as citizens.

---

* *tyke = dog, cur (Concise Scots Dictionary).*

We cannot exclude the rest of Europe, however defined, when we consider the matter of cooperation. The EC itself will change in character and size in the future and existing structures of cooperation could be extended to social work in new member states. Furthermore, the teaching and practice and development of social work is affected not only by economics and politics, but also by cultural and historical associations, and it is sensible not to put aside existing constructive and longstanding contacts with non-EC countries. This is particularly true for Scotland whose links with Norway and Sweden have involved visits, exchanges and exploration of common problems over many years, and many of whose citizens feel a close affinity with their Nordic neighbours.

## Forms of Cooperation

Although the EC is not the only Europe to which we relate and although the EC itself may strike some practitioners as a remote, confusing and irrelevant institution, social workers do already cooperate together in a great number of ways, both formally and informally, as individual workers or as members of agencies, institutions and associations.

One of the most challenging yet little publicised forms of collaboration occurs at the point of service delivery when the needs or problems of individuals, families or groups require assistance from workers in more than one country for mitigation or resolution. At times this cooperation has to involve a speedy response when the problem arises from the need to safeguard the welfare of those who are vulnerable by virtue of age or infirmity. Cases involving children, for example, include those suspected of being abused, of being abducted by strangers or non-custodial parents, or of being deprived of care through the sudden death, illness or imprisonment of parents or guardians. Families fleeing harassment from neighbours or political enemies are other examples. Work will probably involve liaison with social work agencies in one or more countries and possibly consular officials, police and travellers' aid societies. Access to modern information technology and to interpreters can assist tremendously as can advice and information through existing personal links of the workers concerned.

International cooperation has also been required in social work responses to a number of tragic events such as the Zeebrugge ferry disaster, the Piper Alpha oil platform explosion and the disintegration of Pan Am Flight 103 over Lockerbie. In these situations, immediate assistance has to be followed up by access to practical, psychological and spiritual help on a long term basis in the country of origin of the victims, their relatives and friends, as well as in the vicinity of the disaster itself.

On a somewhat lighter note are the cases recorded indelibly in the folk memory of many an agency, such as teenagers who have managed to cross the English Channel and two state borders without documentation before presenting themselves to Interpol, or of holiday parties of people with mental handicap one of whose members has taken the opportunity to explore beyond the geographical limit of his train ticket. Application of the principles of normalisation means that the greater opportunities for fulfilment for such citizens imply the chance of greater risks as well. Happily, difficulties usually meet with a generous response, in a spirit of common humanity and respect as well as of professionalism.

Although cooperation in service delivery is often ad hoc and spontaneous, other forms both underpin and derive from it. The identification of common problems has led to the development of networks based on issues such as Children's Rights, HIV/AIDS, Community Development and Racism, to international research and evaluation, and to conferences, staff/student exchanges and individual visits by social workers from a wide variety of settings.

At the formal level social workers meet and work together through the European branches of international organisations set up with such cooperation as one of their principal aims. These include the International Association of Schools of Social Work (IASSW) and the International Federation of Social Workers (IFSW), as well as a variety of other bodies like International Social Service, the Red Cross, the Conference Permanente Européene de la Probation (CEP), and the Confederation of Family Organisations of the European Community (COFACE).

## Purpose of Cooperation

In whatever way cooperation is undertaken, it is about working together in a spirit of partnership in order to improve the contribution of social work to society. Many problems are shared by all European countries and many public issues and private troubles spill over national frontiers, particularly as a result of people moving temporarily or permanently between countries.

Participants at the Ninth European Seminar of the International Federation of Social Workers in Switzerland in 1989 discussed methods of cross-border co-operation in work with migrants and refugees. They summed up their conclusions effectively in Resolution 4:

'European integration will create a need for a European Standard of Social Work. In order to develop the standard for European Social Work it is necessary to work together through:

1. International organisations like IFSW and ISS

2. Organising International Seminars.

3. Co-operation of Schools of Social Work.

4. Study visits for Social Workers, Social Work Teachers and Students.'[3]

Such cooperation implies an emphasis on the process involved as much as on the completion of pre-defined tasks. That is not to say that results are unimportant. The value of cooperation in dealing with common issues such as refugees, child abduction, children's rights to knowledge of their genetic origins, and the standards for social work qualifications is very likely to be measured by the extent to which it leads to the formulation of mutually agreed policies and practice. This is certainly the emphasis of the EC Commission:

'From the outset (it) had regarded the initiation of common policies as one of its most important functions'.[4]

On the other hand it has sometimes been questioned how far there should be attempts to harmonise policies on some matters, given that the EC is a

'Community of great cultural, religious and moral diversity'.[5]

and that

'An imposed European policy might hinder the process of forming a consensus within the different countries'.[5]

Ironically these quotations are taken from a report concerned with a subject well suited to a common policy, namely the creation of children by means of assisted reproduction, which often involves the allocation of State resources for the development and use of the technology. Also the conclusions of the report make no reference to the rights and needs of the children. This is a matter about which social workers have acquired considerable expertise, although their views struggle to be heard against those with vested interests.[6] If ever there were an issue where collaboration is required between social workers in different member states of the EC this is one, because the opposition is elusive and deep-rooted. To be fair, however, the report also pointed out that it

'makes more of a contribution when people are encouraged to think more deeply, and possibly to disagree, than when they uncritically accept the conclusions'.[4]

Issues like this touch such raw nerves of our human condition that there are no shortcuts along the road to achieving common policies and practice. The process of the journey makes demands of our personal and professional perspectives and of our readiness to learn from each other in a way that is not only a form of cooperation in itself but is also, I believe, a reason for working together in any case.

Cooperation is important therefore not just as a means to a common goal but also because it enhances the exploration of differences of political and cultural values and how these are expressed in theoretical concepts and in social work practice. One of the workshops at the Ninth IFSW European Seminar was called 'Die Werte der Ungleichheit' (the value of dissimilarity). The presenter, Gyaltag Gyaltsen, pointed out that contact with other cultures can provoke anxiety and insecurity for various reasons and that this hinders frank communication between people. Nevertheless the conflict of values should be taken as an opportunity to learn one from another.[7]

## Resistance and Obstacles

Cooperation across international boundaries has a low priority in many quarters. There are quite enough problems to be sorted out at home, many would say, without having to find time, money and energy for writing to one's MEP (Member of the European Parliament), arranging a seminar, joining a committee, attending a conference.

For social workers in the UK family and personal network contacts and cultural similarities with Commonwealth countries and with the USA may have diverted our attention from putting efforts into collaboration with our European neighbours.

Yet the fact has to be faced that in Britain there is resistance to looking outwards and seeing the benefits that could ensue, although this resistance may weaken as a result of the predicted effects of the Single European Act in 1992. For example, when it was proposed that the Tenth IFSW European Seminar should be held in the UK, the initial feasibility costs had to be largely borne by the British Association of Social Workers and a voluntary social work agency, whilst none of the government agencies responsible for social work training, education, research and service development were willing to contribute.

At the world conference of the IFSW in Sweden in July 1988, out of a total of nearly 2,000 participants there were only thirty eight participants from the UK including just one from Scotland. There are at least two aspects to this apparent reluctance to engage with colleagues from other countries. There is a false modesty prevalent amongst many skilled and experienced workers and a genuine belief that social workers in other countries could not possibly be interested in their work as it is nothing out of the ordinary. Conversely there is a lack of confidence, a lack of practice in describing one's work, perhaps a fear of laying it out for examination, particularly when a number of social workers feel constantly exposed to abuse by their own bosses and by the media. Ultimately this can lead to stagnation:

'Too often, in Scotland, a particular way of seeing our culture, of representing ourselves, has come to dominate our perceptions because it has gone unchallenged - worse, unexamined. The vitality of the culture should be measured by the intensity of the debate which it generates rather than the security of ideas on which it rests'.[8]

Some would suggest that language is the most serious obstacle when trying to work together but my own, albeit limited, experience contradicts this. It is so easy to assume that because people speak the same language, therefore they understand each other and are communicating perfectly. When people speak different languages, it is clear from the outset that no such assumptions can be made and nothing should be taken for granted. Even so care is needed to make sure that misunderstandings do not arise from approximate translations or from the different interpretation of words which appear similar. Discussions and simultaneous translations are more productive in multilingual contexts when people take the trouble to speak slowly and explain fully what they mean. As social workers we should always work hard at our use of language, but where translation is necessary by a third party, there will be costs and extra time required. It is usually the money that is the problem. The time spent in clarifying meaning is time profitably spent.

## What Do We Mean By Cooperation?

I have already referred briefly to a number of ways in which social workers cooperate at both formal and informal levels. Some may be once-off occasions, others may involve individuals or groups working together on a committee or planning a conference, or lobbying the European Commission, over a lengthy period of time. Whatever form cooperation takes, there are a number of principles in common which I believe must be recognised if cooperation is to be productive.

Fundamentally, cooperation means letting go of any assumption that 'we always know best' what the solutions are to problems, or how things should be run. I referred earlier to resistance to sharing knowledge and experience, and I would add that there may be ignorance of, or an inherited wariness about cooperation, because of old enmities between nations. It is important to value the experience and perception that others can contribute.

Cooperation also means being alert to political pressures on colleagues in other countries which may make it difficult for them to be seen to cooperate. Social work ethics may be in head-on conflict with those of society or of the prevailing political climate, and people's livelihoods and personal reputations may be at risk. Maintaining contact with social workers in this situation requires great sensitivity and diplomacy.

In any community (of which there may be many in any one nation), the practice of social work is deeply rooted in the culture of that community. Working together means that we must have an understanding of our own culture, and be prepared to learn about and respect the culture of other communities.

There are also bound to be different values concerning many matters, but putting time aside to explore these, and to describe what problems we have and how we deal with them, stimulates questions in ourselves and others about how and why we have defined the problems as we have and what methods we have been using to deal with them. That can be the start of a process of formulating a common policy or working out a strategy to implement better services. At the very least, such exploration should lead to a deeper understanding of the concepts and values underpinning our own practice.

## Current and Future Trends

It is already apparent that demographic, cultural and economic factors are forcing the pace regarding the need to cooperate. The Single European Act has raised vital issues about social work training standards and about the migration of workers including social workers. We can expect an increase in the difficulties facing migrant family members whether accompanying the breadwinner or whether left behind, and the challenge that they will be to child care, mental health and community development services. There has already been a significant number of elderly people migrating to the warmer southern countries. Citizens with purchasing power will be able to help themselves to private welfare in other countries whether it be a place in an old people's home or a sperm bank baby.

Social workers themselves are showing increasing interest in working outwith their home country. This has been seen as potentially helpful to understaffed social work agencies, provided that suitable adaptation and language courses can be designed, and that past training and experience can be assessed and built upon.

Social workers in some countries now have a higher disposable income than in the past and can afford to travel abroad and to contribute to the costs of attending conferences and meetings, but this is not universal and there will need to be continued use of charitable funds and lobbying for financial support from governments.

One of the most exciting and challenging aspects of cooperation is the importance of using and developing negotiation skills. The philosophy of empowering the users of social work services and, paradoxically, the increasing use of business language in policy planning, have emphasised how vital these skills are for working together, and for minimising conflict. The better we are able to accomplish this in our own communities, the better we shall be able to work together fruitfully at a European level. To paraphrase an old saying, perhaps cooperation, like charity, begins at home.

## Acknowledgements

I should like to thank Hugh Barr, David Jones and Ruth Stark for background information and advice, and Marion Johnston and Beatrice Watt for secretarial assistance.

## References

1. Morgan, R. (1987), 'Questions of Culture' *The European*. 1, 4, 44.

2. Barr, H. (1989), 'Social Work in Europe: the Case for Co-operation' *Social Work Education in its European Context*. Hugh Barr, London.

3. *Sozial Arbeit/Travail Social*. 12 December 1989, 141.

4. Noel, E. (1988) *Working Together - The Institutions of the European Community*. Office for Official Publications of the European Communities, Luxembourg, 20.

5. Glover, R. (1987), 'Ethical and Legal Issues Related to Human Reproduction.' Report to the European Commission, unpublished.

6. British Association of Social Workers. Minutes of the Project Group on Assisted Reproduction, 1990.

7. *Sozial Arbeit/Travail Social*. 12 December 1989, 68-70.

8. Cairns, C. (1989), *A Claim of Right for Scotland*. Polygon, Edinburgh, 1989, Series Preface.

Appendix

# Annotated List of EC Social Legislation and Policies concerning Freedom of Movement, the Social Fund and Poverty

## Franz Hamburger and Astrid Sänger

The consolidation of the economic integration accomplished by the Common Market has certain economic advantages, but is also accompanied by social problems. Some existing problems have been alleviated; others have been intensified; and others have perhaps been brought about by the Common Market. The declared intention of the European Economic Community is to improve people's living conditions and purchasing power and to bring about social equality, but the social policy instruments of the EC are relatively limited. The most significant parts of the Treaty of Rome for social welfare are Article 48 (concerning migration of workers) and Articles 117-128 (about assistance with problems of socio-economic adaption).

## 1. Workers' Freedom of Movement

Article 48:

   a) abolished discrimination based on nationality between workers from the member countries with regard to employment, pay and other conditions; and

   b) gave workers the right to travel freely and dwell in the national territories of the member states (subject to certain considerations of public order, security and health).

Occupations in public administration were excepted from this rule.

   These regulations have been in force since the end of the transitional period (December 31, 1969), with the exception of the provision for residency. The more precise implications have been defined as follows:

   *Guideline 64/221/Common Market from February 2, 1964* Specified limitations of entry and/or residency on grounds of public order, security, or health.

   *Guideline 68/360/Common Market/Council from October 15, 1968* Regulated the termination of workers' entry and residency limitations.

   *Decree, Common Market/1612/68 of the Council from October 15, 1968.* Specified discrimination processes in relation to employment and the living conditions of workers and their families. Eg

   • conferred on migrant workers the same employment benefit entitlements and professional qualification measures as others.

   • included family members in the realm of freedom of movement.

   *Decree, Common Market/1251/70 from June 29, 1970* Regulated the right of a worker from one member country who has worked in another member state to remain there after retirement.

   *Decree, Common Market/1408/71 from June 14, 1971* Dealt with the social security rights of migrant workers.

*Decree, Common Market/574/72 from March 27, 1972* Broadened the concept of freedom of movement.

*Decree, Common Market/1390/81 from May 12, 1981* Introduced freedom of movement for self-employed persons.

## 2. The European Social Fund (ESF)

The foundations of the European Social Fund are laid out in Articles 123-128. It was not particularly effective at the beginning and so has been repeatedly reformed. The ESF is intended to mitigate the hardships and negative consequences for certain regions and groups of persons which have resulted from the creation of a common market. The associated competitive conditions and structural changes affect the location of jobs so that help is needed for workers in terms of retraining, relocation and measures for the creation of new jobs.

In addition, the ESF can assist in the career education of groups of workers whose situation in the labour market is especially vulnerable (youth, women, handicapped persons, and migrant workers). The activities of the ESF have also been directed particularly towards areas with structural economic problems.

The role of the ESF has been developed as follows:

*Resolution of the Council 71/66/Common Market* (2 April, 1971) with regard to the reform of the European Social Fund came into force on May 1, 1972. It extended the ESF and gave priority to underdeveloped regions and continuing career education.

*Resolution Nr. 77/801 Common Market* (27 December 1977) came into force on January 1, 1978. This directed attention to the long term unemployed and to unemployed youth.

*Resolution Nr. 83/516/Common Market/Council* (October 12, 1983) came into force on December 31, 1983. It concentrated on measures for unemployed youth and backward regions (including Spain and Portugal).

*Order Nr. 2052/88/Common Market/Council* (June 24, 1988) and *Order Nr. 4255/88 of the Council* (December 19, 1988) with regard to the Social Fund. These focused on

a. the needs of underdeveloped regions

b. reorientation of regions which find themselves in decline

c. the development of rural regions

d. struggle against long-term unemployment of disadvantaged groups of persons.

Other aspects included a substantial increase in funding by 1993, improved communication and increased efficiency.

## 3. The Politics of Poverty in the Common Market

Issues of poverty came to the fore in the EC during the 1970s as a result of increased unemployment linked to restructuring and increasing technicalisation. In the middle of the 1970s there were estimated to be approximately 30 million poor people in the 9 Common Market states. By 1985 the number in the 12 Common Market countries was about 44 million (approximately 14 per cent of the population), partly as a result of the accession of Greece, Spain and Portugal.

The EC responded as follows:

*Resolution 75/458/Common Market/Council* (July 22, 1975) adopted a common programme for the struggle against poverty. 20 million ECUs were committed for the period 1975-November 1980.

The goal was to trace the dimensions and causes of poverty, with the operational definition 'when the disposable income is smaller than half of average personal income'. The steps in the programme were:

- the compilation of reports concerning the extent of poverty and the effectiveness of national measures against poverty
- the preparation of cross-national studies concerning specific aspects of poverty
- the completion of 50 models plans.

The final report of 1983 recorded the following problems:

- the definition of poverty cannot be determined only in terms of income. Social disadvantages are multi-dimensional and cumulative;
- thresholds of poverty in the different countries diverge considerably from each other;
- perceptions of poverty and the assumption that economic growth alone can eliminate poverty are both problematic.

*Resolution 85/8 Common Market/Council* (December 19, 1984) established a new programme against poverty (1985-88) taking account of the geographical expansion of the EC.

The main elements were to be evaluative projects concerning:

- long-time unemployment
- unemployed youth
- older people
- single people
- migrant workers
- fringe groups
- integrated actions in urban and rural areas.

Also planned were an exchange of information and the transfer of innovative methods. An interim report of November 28, 1988 highlighted the exchange of experience and the application of working models which have been tested in other countries.

*Resolution 89/457/Common Market/Council* (July 18, 1989) set up a medium term programme for the economic and social integration of the most strongly disadvantaged groups (1989-94). The goal was to concentrate on selected programmes of action directed at:

- preventive measures in favour of the disadvantaged
- multidimensional development of innovative models of organisation
- exchange of information and experience
- establishment of the characteristics of poverty.

This programme is different from the first two because of the more direct influence of the Commission as experienced advisor. In addition the ESF is obligated to do its part to promote the reduction of poverty.